Images of Health in Food Advertising

Images of Health in Food Advertising

Misleading Marketing and the Health Belief Model

Debbie Danowski

BLOOMSBURY ACADEMIC
NEW YORK • LONDON • OXFORD • NEW DELHI • SYDNEY

BLOOMSBURY ACADEMIC
Bloomsbury Publishing Inc, 1359 Broadway, New York, NY 10018, USA
Bloomsbury Publishing Plc, 50 Bedford Square, London, WC1B 3DP, UK
Bloomsbury Publishing Ireland, 29 Earlsfort Terrace, Dublin 2, D02 AY28, Ireland

First published in the United States of America 2026

A catalog record for this book is available from the Library of Congress

ISBN: HB: 978-1-6669-6503-2
ePDF: 979-8-216-25594-9
eBook: 978-1-9787-7032-4

Typeset by Newgen KnowledgeWorks Pvt. Ltd., Chennai, India

For product safety related questions contact productsafety@bloomsbury.com.

This book would not have been possible without Peter, who in addition to providing support and love during the writing of this book, fed animals, ran errands, and generally held things together while I wrote. Thank you so much. This book is also dedicated to Anna, Joseph, Melissa, and Tony who give me hope for a better future. You are all amazing.

Contents

Acknowledgments

Publishing a book is a team effort, both professionally and personally. I am blessed to have so many wonderful people on my team. This book would not be possible without my wonderful editor Jesse Tepper who once again believed in my work and supported this project from the very beginning. I am deeply grateful for her suggestions, which helped to shape and organize this book. I am also grateful to everyone else who worked on this book, including Jade Bair and Alyssa Daily.

I am blessed to work at a university that values diversity, inclusion, acceptance, and, most of all, kindness in addition to academic achievement. I have been a faculty member at Sacred Heart University for almost thirty years, and during that time, so many wonderful people have helped to make my time there a professional and personal growth experience, which has resulted in not only deeper academic knowledge but also personal insight. Thank you to everyone at SHU.

On a personal level, I am blessed to have an amazing family that provides a solid foundation of love and strength in my life. My sister Karen and I have been through a lot together. I don't know where I'd be without her continuing support. Likewise, my niece Melissa and nephew Tony along with their children are a great support and inspiration to me. I also gain strength from those no longer with me—my parents, grandparents, and my brother who each played a role in bringing me to this point in my life. I love you all so much!

The animals in my life bring me great joy and love. All my fur babies current and past have touched my heart, and I could not imagine my life without them. My love of horses began at H.O.R.S.E. of Connecticut at a time when my life had changed drastically. I remain grateful to Patty Wahlers and her army of volunteers who work so hard to rescue abused and neglected horses, and sometimes people, too. I am also very grateful to 13 Hands Equine Rescue and Horse Rescue of Virginia for everything they do to save horses including my two current babies. Keep up the good work everyone!

I am deeply grateful to Peter for the time, effort, and love he puts into supporting my writing and teaching as well as the care he provides for the animals that share our lives. Our life together is a true gift. Thank you, Peter, for your love and support.

Finally, I am grateful to God and for the life He has given me. There are no words to express my deep gratitude for the amazing gifts I have been given. My life today is a true miracle. Thank you, God.

Introduction

A partially opened packet of a square grape-flavored Charms candy rests on a carton of Charms Pure Fruit Tablets. The carton is surrounded by fresh fruit including a peach, raspberries, grapes, cherries, a sliced lemon, and a sliced orange. At the bottom of the page in the 1920s print ad, there is an open packet of the lemon-flavored candy. The text promises "luscious goodness" in eleven "famous flavors" that include those of the fruits pictured (Johnseller 2023). Though it would be decades until a definition was created, the tablets, which would eventually morph into lollipops, are considered an ultra-processed food in the current time period, and an unhealthy one at the beginning of the twentieth century.

More than three decades later, a 1959 ad for Life Savers candy features "sad fruit" with an orange, cherries, pineapple, lime, and lemon crying Life Savers "tears" with the text, "Life Savers stole our flavor" (SarahZen Products 2023). Each piece of fruit has a drawn sad face with a tear coming down underneath which appears with the corresponding candy in the same color as the whole fruit. Once again, though the concept of ultra-processed foods had yet to be created, these candies fit that definition today.

Another almost three decades later would bring what some called "The Great Fruit Snack Wars" culminating in an advertising campaign from Fruit Corners Fruit Roll-Ups urging consumers to "Think Twice" before buying competitor Sunkist's Fun Fruits (Robare 2020). In the first of these ads published in 1987, the words "THINK TWICE" appear in green capital letters across a light gray background in the top half of the page (Robare 2020). Underneath this, a box of Fun Fruits is shown on the left and a box of Fruit Roll-Ups on the right. Both are strawberry flavored and contain images of whole strawberries on their boxes. The text underneath the Fun Fruits box says, "Why choose Strawberry Fun Fruits with nearly twice the added sugar?" (Robare 2020). The word *twice* is underlined. The text underneath the Fruit Roll-Ups box reads, "Choose Strawberry Fruit

Roll-Ups with twice the real fruit," with the word *twice* underlined (Robare 2020). Small text underneath both tells consumers that the comparison is between the strawberry flavors of both products only and that Fruit Roll-Ups contain "both strawberries and pear puree concentrate" further noting that "fruit and sugars content of Fruit Corners products vary" (Robare 2020). Both products contain fruit puree concentrate as well as manufactured sweeteners making both ultra-processed foods, and thus, by definition, unhealthy.

Health Halos

All three ads as well as many others during this time period and to follow used a marketing technique known as the "health halo" effect to make their products appear healthier than they actually are. By using images of whole fruit, which consumers know to be healthy, advertisers are counting on the "halo" of the healthy fruit to extend to their products resulting in an increase in sales due to the perceived "healthiness" of the items. Specifically, in this case, the particular halo used is identified as the Natural and Real Health Halo, which is defined as the use of text, colors, or images associated with nature or whole foods in the marketing or labeling of a product that creates a false perception of healthiness. Though at first glance, putting images of fresh fruit near fruit-flavored candy products may seem to fall under the best-practices-in-advertising category, the consequences of this can contribute to serious public health issues. The health halo is almost always used to make unhealthy food appear healthier. The majority of those foods are now classified under the NOVA international nutritional system as "ultra-processed," an "industrial formulation" with five or more ingredients that are among the unhealthiest foods available with little to no nutritional value (Monteiro et al. 2016). Research suggests that "perceptually healthy foods tend to be consumed more . . . suggesting a positive health halo leading to a 'healthy = eat more' consumption pattern" (Bui et al. 2017).

This positive health halo results in overconsumption of unhealthy products through "obfuscation of information, which manipulates people's perceptions of reality to fit the source's purpose" (Andrews, Van Leeuwen, and Van Baaren 2014, 162), by providing a positive appearance to items that have been labeled as "industrially produced edible substances" rather than food (Van Tulleken 2023, 155). In other words, the use of health halos to promote ultra-processed foods provides consumers with a form of permission to eat greater quantities of unhealthy food resulting in an unprecedented level of obesity with projections of over one billion people worldwide living with obesity by 2030 (World Obesity Federation 2022). Despite calls for action, little progress has been made to halt the rise of obesity, which will result in a failure to meet the United Nations goal of halting obesity by 2025 (World Obesity Federation 2022). Even though the introduction of an "Accelerated Plan" at the Seventy-Fifth World Health Assembly to manage obesity included workstream elements to address "regulations on the harmful marketing of food and beverages to protect children," "initiatives to regulate the sales of products high in fats, sugars and salt in proximity of schools," and "public education and awareness campaigns" (World Health Organization 2022), there was no mention of regulations on the techniques used in the promotion of ultra-processed foods to adults pointing to a grave misunderstanding of the effectiveness of the use of health halos in food advertising and on product labels.

Using the theoretical foundation of the Health Belief Model, this study will explore the use of health promotion in ultra-processed food advertisements and on product labels, with a focus on the concept of "health halos" as a means of making unhealthy food appear more nutritious. Though much research exists on both health halos and the Health Belief Model, there is little that focuses on food advertising or product labels as they relate to both concepts. Currently, many different varieties of health halos are grouped together under the one heading offering little insight into the types and themes used in the marketing of ultra-processed foods. Similarly, there is little research examining the use of the Health Belief Model in ultra-processed food advertising as it relates to health halos. The current study is designed to fill this gap in both health communication and advertising research through the thematic classification and exploration of specific health halos used in food advertisements and on product labels for ultra-processed foods by drawing on the theoretical constructs of the Health Belief Model. When appropriate, a brief history of selected products and techniques will be presented as will lists of additional product labels using health halos and Health Belief Model constructs. These lists at the end of each section were created by using a Google image search and then recording each halo/construct use; these are included to serve as indicators of the frequency of use on product labels. While some products in these lists may be regional and thus unfamiliar to all readers, the number of labels and packages contained within serve to create awareness about the regularity and scope with which health halos and constructs are used.

Chapter 1 will outline the history of halos in marketing research and the theoretical framework of the Health Belief Model and then will expand to introduce the concept of health halos and Health Belief Model constructs used in food advertisements and on product labels. Current research into the effectiveness of health halos on product labels and in food advertisements as well as that pertaining to the Health Belief Model will be discussed, and a general overview of food advertising research will be presented. Additionally, various health halos will be classified into three different types, which will be examined in the following chapters.

Chapter 2 will focus on the Natural and Real Health Halo, which includes advertisements using the words "all natural," "real fruit," and "no artificial flavors or preservatives" to create a health halo around the products and to make the food appear healthier than it is. Chapter 3 will explore the Nutrition Health Halo, which is the practice of using words such as "no sugar added," "low fat," "whole wheat," and "gluten free," as well as the concept of advertising vitamin- and mineral-fortified ultra-processed food products as a means of creating a health halo. Chapter 4 will discuss the Identity Health Halo, which draws on consumers' desires to present themselves in a certain way. In this chapter, the focus will be on those ultra-processed product advertisements and labels using the words "diet" and "low calorie" as well as foods marketed as vegan or vegetarian and those that include images of exercise, playing sports, and healthy activities.

The identification and analysis of the Health Belief Model constructs used in conjunction with the different health halos will be woven throughout each chapter, and in many cases, a historical examination of the concepts as well as the current research regarding the practice used in product manufacturing will be presented. Each of the three different health halos discussed previously as well as the appropriate Health Belief Model constructs are defined in the next chapter. In the Conclusion section, an overview of research findings will be presented as well as suggestions for future research.

1

Halos, Health, and the Health Belief Model

In an illustration by famed artist J. C. Leyendecker, a young woman with red hair and a green bow smiles as she holds a spoon up to her mouth. She is dressed in an off white short-sleeve blouse with a thin black tie around her collar. Her cheeks are rose-colored, and she appears to be of normal weight. Underneath her are the words, "A Serving of Kellogg's for Less Than a Cent" (Rose 2024). Below that is an illustration of a box of Kellogg's Toasted Corn Flakes. In the two paragraphs of text below, readers are told that "The most delicious things sometimes cost the least" and the "delicate thin flakes with their appetizing flavor and the wholesome quality of toasted corn" can be eaten for breakfast, snacks, or between meals to be "ready for the call of the healthy, hungry young folks of the family" (Rose 2024). Though this may appear to be a commonplace advertisement, the timing of this ad as well as the promotional technique used exemplify an advertising practice that continues to be used years later to give unhealthy foods the appearance of health. This technique is known as the health halo effect.

In this particular advertisement, readers are encouraged to eat Kellogg's Toasted Corn Flakes, which obviously are made from corn, a vegetable believed to be healthy, as a means of supporting the United States in its war efforts. The same year the advertisement was published, the Food Administration was created by President Woodrow Wilson with a focus on the food needs of both soldiers overseas and those at home. A major part of this initiative was to encourage conservation of food using liberty gardens, later known as victory gardens, to grow food and to find alternatives for white flour, wheat, and sugar products (Johnson 2021). At the time, eating bread was associated "with wealth and refinement long after white flour became affordable and abundant," leading Food Administration officials to encourage Americans to "Save a loaf a week to help win the war" (Johnson 2021). In response, corn was promoted as "the food of the nation," and citizens were advised to use it "some way" at "every meal" to support soldiers fighting in the war (Loukachouk 2024). While corn was promoted to women as "appetizing," "nourishing," and "economical," and as a means of feeding their families "tasty food" with "health benefits" and an "economically wise choice" (Loukachouk 2024), the main reasons consumers were encouraged to use it was to show their support for the First World War. In the Kellogg's Toasted Corn Flakes advertisement, use of the words "ready for the call of the healthy, hungry young folks of the family" is designed to associate the cereal with health as well as remind women about their "call of duty" to conserve certain food products during the war by serving their families what would later be classified as an unhealthy ultra-processed food.

The Halo Effect

The method of encouraging food conservation of certain products and consumption of others as a means of supporting fighting soldiers is a technique known as "the halo effect," which is a way of transferring positive feelings about a product or activity to another product or activity that may not engender positivity on its own. In the Kellogg's Toasted Corn Flakes advertisement, the positive feelings that Americans had about supporting fighting soldiers overseas is used to extend this "halo" onto the cereal in a subtle way by encouraging women to feed their families cereal made from corn and using an image of an attractive, healthy-looking woman to further reinforce this notion. Similarly, an advertising poster produced by the U.S. Food Administration noted, "They Are Giving All. Will You Send Them Wheat?" underneath an image of soldiers fighting (Hester 2016). Once again, the halo technique of supporting fighting soldiers is used to discourage the consumption of wheat products.

The use of wheat conservation to help fighting soldiers was not the only halo employed during the First World War. Many companies promoted their products as both a means of saving money and also as a substitute for wheat without actually mentioning the product. In a 1917 ad for Quaker Oats, consumers are shown a man in a suit and tie eating a bowl of cereal with a headline of "Five-Cent Breakfasts based on Quaker Oats" underneath (Period Paper 2024). Consumers are told that "The average mixed diet costs four times as much as Quaker Oats per unit of nutrition" and told to use the cereal "in bread and muffins, in cookies and pancakes" (Period Paper 2024). They are also reminded that "Oat food is nowadays doubly important because of its economy" (Period

Paper 2024). Though no direct mention of supporting the war effort is found in this advertisement, the idea of economizing and substitutions being "doubly important" exemplifies the sometimes subtleness of the halo technique. In this advertisement, consumers are gently reminded about the economic challenges that Americans are facing because of the First World War thus creating a halo around supporting soldiers without ever mentioning either the war or those fighting overseas.

A similar halo effect can be seen during the Second World War when Americans were encouraged to substitute peanuts for vegetable oils. Peanuts were used not only for snacking but also "as a source of high-quality oil" and "the primary fuel in Rudolf Diesel's first engine" while at the same time "peanut oil was used to produce margarine, used in salad dressings and as a butter and lard substitute in cooking and frying" (Johnson 2023). However, "its most important role was in the production of glycerin and nitroglycerine—a primary component in explosives" (Johnson 2023). A 1942 poster advertisement from the U.S. Department of Agriculture features an image of a soldier with a peanut for a body holding a rifle and wearing a helmet. He has a determined look on his face and is wearing combat boots; there is a tank behind him. The headline says, "Mr. Peanut Goes to War" (Johnson 2023). Though the target audience of this advertisement is farmers, it's important to note that "Mr. Peanut of the USDA was nothing like the monocled, top-hatted suave character Planter's introduced in 1916. This Mr. Peanut was tough, determined to do his part, and aid in the war effort. The USDA expected farmers . . . to do the same" (Johnson 2023).

A more modern version of the halo effect as it relates to national initiatives can be seen in a 2020 commercial for Oreo cookies. The commercial opens with various shots of men, women, and children dancing, riding stationary bicycles, and doing various other indoor activities while having fun. While the images are shown, there is a rap song with lyrics about staying inside as being "the place we're gonna play today" and "not just the little ones but grownups, too" (Luma Research 2020). As the words "grownups, too" are sung, an African American man is shown leaning back in a chair with an Oreo placed on his eye. He moves the Oreo from his eye and into his mouth without using his hands. As the lyrics encourage viewers to check the world "with a different view," that is, as a virtual partying one, an image of a white man throwing an Oreo from behind his back into his glass of milk is shown (Luma Research 2020). The man is laughing and then pulls the cookie from the glass and takes a bite. Following this, there is a shot of family members playing a game with Oreo cookies arranged in rows on a table as the singer tells viewers that they'll "come back together while staying inside" as an image of four video conference squares are shown, one of which contains a mother holding a small baby whose hand she is waving (Luma Research 2020). The commercial ends with an image of an Oreo cookie on a sky blue background above the words, "Stay home" while the singer encourages viewers to "stay playful" (Luma Research 2020).

In this commercial, the obvious halo of having fun during the Covid-19 pandemic, which was arguably one of the most frightening periods in recent American history, is used to encourage consumers to eat Oreo cookies. The not-so-obvious halo used in this commercial is one of American spirit and community. By staying home and making the best of things, albeit with Oreos, viewers can feel good about the actions they are taking to protect others. Additionally, this commercial employs the Identity Health Halo, which draws on consumers' desire to present themselves in a certain way. In this case, the images of dancing and riding a stationary bicycle are associated with health and are designed to create an association between the advertised product, Oreos, and health. As with any halo, the good feelings derived from helping others and images of healthy activities are designed to extend to the product. In this case, the product is an ultra-processed food, which includes such ingredients as sugar, high fructose corn syrup, and soy lecithin, and whose appeal has been compared to the "effects of cocaine" (Levy et al. 2013, 769). The halos used in this commercial during a time when fun was all but nonexistent and activity was replaced by constant monitoring of social media and television while feelings of fear were rampant across the world no doubt served as a welcome respite for many Americans. However, the promotion of unhealthy foods to manage these feelings creates an unhealthy message about using food to soothe distress.

Drawing on the theoretical constructs of the Health Belief Model, this advertisement is designed to address the perceived barriers of weight gain and the consequences of unhealthy eating by providing viewers with images of exercise, health, and normal weight individuals in the advertisement of a product that when eaten in excess results in none of these things. Woven within these images is also the attempt to mitigate the perceived susceptibility and perceived severity to contract certain diseases that result from eating too much of this product as well as a cue to action to change unhealthy associations with this product to healthy ones through the use of the Identity Health Halo. More subtly, the perceived benefits of eating Oreos are portrayed in this commercial as they relate to exercising and normal body size. In short, viewers are given healthy associations to an unhealthy product in an advertisement that subtly addresses health concerns and seemingly portrays benefits to eating the food using the lenses of fun during a fearful time in history.

"Erroneous Judgments" of the Halo Effect

The first known mention of the halo effect was in psychology literature in the second decade of the twentieth century in a study regarding the rating of military officers. In this study, it was noted that "The magnitude of the constant error of the halo, as we have called it, also seems surprisingly large, though we lack objective criteria by which to determine its exact size" (Thorndike 1920, 29). Though the researcher went on to describe "a constant error of suffusing ratings of special features with a halo belonging to the individual as a whole" in rating military officers, the ability of the halo to cause "erroneous judgments," which are "higher than reality," was concluded to be a powerful determinant in inaccurate decision-making (Thorndike 1920, 25). The researcher noted that he was convinced that "even a very capable foreman, employer, teacher or department head is unable to treat an individual as a compound of separate qualities . . . in independence of the others" (Thorndike 1920, 28–9).

Throughout the years, the "erroneous judgments" of the halo effect would be reinforced regarding the evaluation of individuals, notably fifty-seven years later in a study of college students who viewed different instructors. In the study, students were asked to evaluate two instructors, one of whom was warm and friendly, the other, cold. After watching videotaped interviews, students were asked to rate certain attributes of each, some of which included physical appearance and mannerisms (Nisbett and DeCamp Wilson 1977). In addition to reinforcing the findings in the 1920 study, the researchers noted that "the subjects in the present study would surely have been disconcerted to know that they were incapable of rendering an independent evaluation of such characteristics" believing themselves "exempted" from such influence and further noting the power of the halo effect as having a "pronounced impact on evaluations" (Nisbett and DeCamp Wilson 1977, 256). They further note that laymen see "a strong interpretation" of the halo effect in sayings such as "love is blind" and "a face only a mother can love," yet note the power of the halo effect even in evaluations that "are less extreme than love and hate" (Nisbett and DeCamp Wilson 1977, 256).

Over the years, the halo effect has been shown to increase positive feelings about products from companies that are thought to be profitable (Posavac et al. 2010), believed to manufacture higher quality items (Madden, Roth, and Dillon 2012), involved in community sponsorship activities (Vance, Raciti, and Lawley 2016), supported by CEOs and founders in advertising (Agnihotri and Bhattacharya 2019), and those with higher environmental corporate social responsibility (Dong, Chang, and Wang 2017). The halo effect has also been shown to be a positive influence on whether or not consumers trust smartphone advertisements. Research has shown that those who depend heavily on their smartphones trust their devices, "which is transferred to the ad" and "leads to higher purchase intentions" (Stewart and Perren 2023). These studies reinforced the "erroneous nature" of beliefs surrounding the halos used.

Health Halos

Over time, halo effect research has been narrowed to reflect the increase in consumer interest for healthy products even when the products advertised have little to no redeeming positive influence on the consumers' well-being. An obvious example of this is research focused on the Santa Fe Natural Tobacco Company's Natural American Spirit cigarettes. In the study, researchers examined the company's use of health halos in advertising after being officially warned by the Food and Drug Administration regarding misleading claims. The researchers note that even though "Santa Fe was allowed to continue using the word 'natural' in the brand name and the phrase 'tobacco and water,'" they also continued to use "eco-friendly language and plant imagery," which "have also been shown to communicate reduced product harm" (Iles et al. 2021). Researchers showed that "Natural American Spirit cigarette ad tactics mislead consumers" through the use of health halos by making them believe that the products are "healthier and had less potential to cause disease" resulting in "an indirect positive effect on smoking intentions through reduced perceptions of the brand's potential to cause disease and perceived absolute harm" (Iles et al. 2021).

Specific to food advertising and product labeling research, the transition from the halo in psychological and business literature appears to have begun in 1984 when "Kellogg's use of health claims . . . paved the way for a rapid increase in the number and types of diet-disease linkages used in advertising and on food labels," which researchers studied in the late 1990s (Roe, Levy, and Derby

1999, 90). The study involved "1403 primary food shoppers in face-to-face mall-intercept interviews at eight sites: Birmingham, Ala.; Charlotte, N.C.; Dayton, Ohio; Houston, Tex.; Philadelphia, Pa.; Phoenix, Ariz.; San Jose, Calif.; and Waterbury, Conn.," who were shown raisin-bran cereal, lasagna frozen dinner, and strawberry yogurt packages and were then asked a series of questions regarding the products' healthiness and health benefits (Roe, Levy, and Derby 1999, 93–5). Though the researchers list seven outcomes in their findings, two stand out with regard to the concept of health halos. They are "When a product features a health or content claim, respondents view the product as healthier and state they are more likely to purchase it" and "Consumers who view products with a claim are more likely to play back the health benefit mentioned in the claim, both in open- and closed-ended questions" (Roe, Levy, and Derby 1999, 99). These two findings indicate the effectiveness of health halos in product labeling as well as consumers' assimilation of the nutrition claims with the researchers' warning that companies using health claims have "diminished motivation to improve the nutritional content of their products if they are able to use health claims on their products" (Roe, Levy, and Derby 1999, 103).

Similarly, it was shown that "regardless of a food's healthiness, the health halos of benefit-seeking and risk-avoidance appeals worked successfully" to create the appearance of the product as healthy (Choi and Springston 2014, 1058), meaning that, when an unhealthy product highlights health benefits such as low fat or reduced sugar or avoiding risks like lower cholesterol or staying heart healthy, consumers believe the claims even if the food is known to be unhealthy. The researchers also point to the importance of taste claims in food advertisements noting that "respondents significantly showed higher ad-related evaluations for the unhealthy food ads with the taste appeals" rather than higher claims about nutrition (Choi and Springston 2014, 1058).

The effectiveness of health halos was confirmed in a later study of seventy-eight participants over ten focus groups in which individuals were shown product images with health claims, such as "low fat," "a source of vitamin D," "gluten & nut free," or "contains calcium which helps maintain healthy bones," and were then led in discussions by moderators before filling out a questionnaire to gauge their perceptions of "tastiness, healthiness, and satiety" of the products (Benson et al. 2019, 5). After viewing health claims, one participant noted that, "if something has a health claim, like antioxidants, things like that, you do tend to think of them as healthy things or good things (Group 2, female, 36–64 years old)," while another pointed out "I think low calorie, as I was saying, the Weight

Watchers thing, you end up having two or three packets, because you think it's very low calorie (Group 1, male, 36–64 years old)," and still another noted that low-fat labeling meant she could eat more food an hour later (Group 7, female, 18–35 years old) (Benson et al. 2019, 9). The researchers concluded that the health claims "influenced purchasing behavior for some participants" and "captured [the] attention and led . . . to inspect[ion of] a product" for those whose behavior was unchanged (Benson et al. 2019, 11). Similarly, a meta-analysis of thirty-one studies designed to review "the effect of health-related claims, on pre-packaged foods in retail settings, on adult purchasing decisions (real and perceived)" conducted two years earlier concluded that "health-related claims have a substantial effect on dietary choices" (Kaur, Scarborough, and Rayner 2017).

Health Halos and Children

It's important to note that not all health halos involve the use of health claims such as advertising products as "natural," "low fat," "high in fiber," or containing vitamins. Health halos can also take the form of including images or text related to nature or healthy foods, such as fruits and vegetables, as well as healthy lifestyle portrayals, including physical activity, formal exercise, or sports participation. Research has shown an increase of 24 percent in health-related appeals in food advertising on children's televisions channels and an almost 20 percent increase in physical activity (Whalen et al. 2018, 564). "Implicit (physical activity) and explicit (health claims) health messages are increasingly prevalent in UK television food advertising viewed by children and are frequently used to promote unhealthy foods" with the researchers recommending that "policy makers in the UK should consider amendments to the existing statutory approach in order to address this issue" (Whalen et al. 2018, 560).

In the United States, a study of children ages seven to eleven years old, it was noted that health halos for nutrient-poor foods are cause for concern since they can oftentimes be less obvious to children or carefully woven into the narrative of the commercial. The researchers point to the examples of "depicting children engaging in sports and then going out for fast food to celebrate, or an ad for sugary cereals that also shows fruit and milk on the table" as being portrayals that "may cause children to infer that these products are healthy," thus creating dangerous health halos (Harris et al. 2018, 257). Though the researchers found that children understood the healthiness of fruits and vegetables, it was also shown that, "messages about nutrition and physical activity in child-directed commercials for nutrient-poor food/drinks created health halo effects. Viewing these commercials caused children to rate the products as more healthful compared with participants who did not see the commercials" (Harris et al. 2018, 262). Similarly, in twelve- to fourteen-year-olds, it was shown that the body weight of the actors in advertisements affected children's perceptions of the healthiness of food with researchers concluding that "higher BMI adolescents in particular believe a food to be healthier when promoted by a thin character" (Castonguay, Bakir, and Blodgett 2019, 785); yet, in research three years prior, it was shown that children ten to eleven years old were able to recognize the contrasting ideas of "connecting exercise with food high in sugar," and the younger children in the study, ages five to six years old, "who showed recognition [of the contrasting idea] were more likely to select the advertised item" even though the food was not healthy (Castonguay 2015).

Though research into the effects of health halos is relatively new, it's important to note that use of health halos in food advertisements and on product labels is almost as old as the industry itself as examples presented in the following pages indicate. It's also worth noting that classification of the health halos used in food advertising is all but nonexistent. The majority of research focused on health halos in advertisements and on product labels combines various types of health halos into one framework rather than discussing the varying themes of each. Thematic analysis provides researchers with a method of exploring the popularity over time and different uses of various health halos that is not possible without classification. The themes widely used in health halos throughout history and presently are the central focus of this study, which draws on the specific marketing techniques used in food advertisements and on product labels from ultra-processed food through the theoretical framework of the Health Belief Model.

Health Belief Model

Developed in the 1950s by Public Health Service Investigators, the Health Belief Model "grew out of a set of independent, applied research problems" with "the theory and development of the Model" both growing at the same time as a "solution of practical problems" thus making it difficult to trace its exact historical origin (Rosenstock 1974, 328). The model was developed as a means of explaining preventative or protective health behaviors at a time when there was "widespread failure of people to accept disease preventives or screening tests for early detection of asymptomatic disease" (Rosenstock 1974, 328) and "has proven to be one of the most comprehensive conceptual frameworks used in health-based behavior for nearly fifty years (Güner and Çilginoğlu 2023, 375). In the years following, research has expanded globally in many different contexts that include more recently the hesitancy over the Covid-19 vaccine for children (Ellithorpe et al. 2022), green advertising and behavioral intention in South Korea (Kim and Yoon 2017), and the perceptions and barriers regarding seasonal flu vaccines among health-care workers in China (Peng et al. 2024). Specific to food, the Health Belief Model research encompasses eating disorder behavior (Blomquist et al. 2020), the content of YouTube healthy-eating public service health announcements (Zhang et al. 2017), organic food (Yazdanpanah, Forouzani, and Hojjati 2015; Shrish et al. 2025), gluten-free diets (Güner and Çilginoğlu 2023), key factors influencing consumer purchase intentions for free-from gastronomic products (Ocak 2025), and the likelihood of U.S. adults eating nutrient-rich foods (Glick et al. 2024), among many others.

The Health Belief Model posits that behavioral action takes place based on four beliefs, which include the susceptibility, severity, benefit, and barriers regarding making a change (Cross, Davis, and O'Neil 2017, 61). Two additional variables are considered in the Health Belief Model, which are self-efficacy, belief about ability to make the change, and cues to action defined as "stimuli that initiate the decision-making process . . . from noticing symptoms of an illness to being exposed to a health campaign" (Alyafei and Easton-Carr 2024, 2). The first four beliefs are the focus of this study considering that the last two variables are outside the focus of content analysis of food advertisements and are more difficult to illustrate in advertisements. Though arguably the majority of advertisements work to provide self-efficacy and cues to action inherent in their messages, the personal nature of these variables makes pure content analysis impossible since consumer reaction is outside the scope of this study; the focus of this study is to analyze food advertisements using health halos and the Health Belief Model, particularly in ultra-processed food advertisements.

Ultra-Processed Foods

The need to highlight health benefits, both through physical activity depictions and by using health claims, becomes necessary only when the food advertised or sold is classified as unhealthy. Such classification was not formally introduced into scientific literature until a lone researcher began his career in the Ribeira Valley region near São Paulo, Brazil, studying the effect of socioeconomic class on nutrition among plantation workers. Though, at the time, he was focused on researching malnutrition, several years later he saw a "nutritional transformation" of rising obesity in poor communities and a decrease in affluent areas, which would move the focus of his career to understanding the causes of obesity (Van Tulleken 2023, 42–4). The result of this would be the introduction of the NOVA Food Classification System, a mechanism designed to label foods in one of four different categories—Group 1: Unprocessed or minimally processed foods; Group 2: Processed culinary ingredients; Group 3: Processed foods; and Group 4: Ultra-processed food and drink products. As the researcher, Carlos Monteiro, would go on to suggest, foods in Group 4, those that "are industrial formulations typically with five or more and usually many ingredients," were among the unhealthiest and he believed those foods to be a major contributing factor to obesity (Monteiro et al. 2016).

Despite being somewhat controversial in nutritional literature, the concept of ultra-processed foods as a major contributor to obesity would hold up in future research, one in particular that was specifically designed to rigorously study the NOVA Food Classification System (Hall et al. 2019) and, some would say, to prove it wrong (Van Tulleken 2023, 55). Additional research has shown a link between ultra-processed foods and recurrent depression symptoms (Arshad et al. 2024), a greater risk of mental health disorders (Mazloomi et al. 2023), an increase in sarcopenia among chronic kidney disease patients (Shateri et al. 2024), inadequate nutrition in pregnant women and their newborn babies (Ben-Avraham et al. 2023), the development of obesity as well as chronic diseases (Kébé et al. 2024), a decrease in sleep quality (Andreeva, Perez-Jimenez, and St-Onge 2023), "a rise in the incidence of obesity, type 2 diabetes, cardiovascular diseases, colorectal cancer and all-cause mortality" (Laudanno 2023; Pu et al. 2023), nonalcoholic fatty liver disease (Henney et al. 2023), diabetes and hypertension (Nardocci, Polsky, and Moubarac 2021), and an increase in sedentary and unhealthy eating behaviors in children (Oliveira et al. 2024), to name a few. Additionally, ultra-processed food consumption has been linked to adverse environmental effects (Navoda et al. 2023; da Cruz et al. 2024).

Some have criticized the NOVA Classification System as being unclear due to the "overall idea of correlating food processing *per se* with negative health outcomes," which "lacks a fundamental, biologically founded rationale" noting that "the assertion that ultra-processed foods are intrinsically unhealthful is largely unproven, and needs further examination and elaboration" (Visioli et al. 2023). Nutrition literature, however, has consistently supported the concept of ultra-processed foods with one review of thirty-seven studies noting, "There is now a considerable body of evidence supporting the use of UPFs as a scientific concept to assess the 'healthiness' of foods within the context of dietary patterns and to help inform the development of dietary guidelines and nutrition policy actions" (Leonie et al. 2020). It's worth noting that a good portion of the criticism about the NOVA Classification System comes from companies that manufacture ultra-processed foods and fund research calling the system into question in an attempt to discredit the idea of ultra-processed food being "associated with poor health" (Van Tulleken 2023, 66).

Ultra-Processed Food Advertising

Research has repeatedly shown that food advertising affects both children and adults with one classic study noting that the elimination of food advertising "will be central to reducing the prevalence of eating disorders" (Wilson and Blackhurst 1999, 119) and another concluding that exposure to food advertising resulted in study participants eating "snacks with 65 more calories than those exposed to non-food advertising" (Zimmerman and Shimoga 2014). The rise of social media food advertising and online games for children sponsored by food companies has resulted in even greater exposure to ultra-processed food advertisements. The influence of food advertisements to increase consumption of the products advertised and to alter perceptions of the healthiness of the food has been consistently reinforced in current and past literature (Harris, Bargh, and Brownell 2009; Boyland and Halford 2013; Castonguay 2015; Kidd and Loxton 2018; Castonguay, Bakir, and Blodgett 2019; Gearhardt et al. 2020; Smith et al. 2020; Pan, Bhandari, and Meng 2022; Arrona-Cardoza et al. 2023; Scheiber, Karmasin, and Diehl 2023; Bailey et al. 2024).

In a meta-analysis of 19,372 participants from 80 articles and meta-analysis of 96 articles, researchers concluded that "food marketing was associated with increased intake, choice, preference, and purchase requests in children and adolescents" noting that "these findings are largely consistent with, and build on, previous findings" (Boyland et al. 2022). The researchers also pointed out that "WHO [World Health Organization] has previously recommended that member states enact policies to restrict children's exposure to unhealthy food marketing and the review findings support this position" (Boyland et al. 2022). In line with this, it's important to note that the majority of foods advertised to both children and adults are classified as ultra-processed. This is due to the fact that these foods are created concoctions with proprietary recipes and, in many cases, ingredients that allow the manufacturers to produce these products for a low cost and sell them for a higher one (Van Tulleken 2023, 141). In other words, "No one else can really make KitKats, because Nestle owns the recipe and the trademark and everything that creates the KitKat's unique barcode that keeps bringing us back" making it "much trickier to make lots of money from NOVA groups 1–3" (Van Tulleken 2023, 141–2), the result of which is little to no advertising of whole foods, fruits, vegetables, or other minimally processed foods.

Methodology

This study will focus on health halo and Health Belief Model portrayals in ultra-processed food advertisements and product labels. The focus on ultra-processed food takes into consideration both the health dangers of the foods as well as the fact that some experts put the amount of money spent on food, beverage, and restaurant advertising as high as $14 billion with "more than 80% of this . . . [on] fast food, sugary drinks, candy, and unhealthy snacks, dwarfing the entire $1 billion budget for all chronic disease prevention and health promotion at the U.S. Centers for Disease Control and Prevention" (UConn Rudd Center for Food Policy and Health 2017). Advertisements and food product labels will be analyzed using a combination of content analysis and case study methodology, both of which have been applied in a wide variety of media analysis for decades, including health promotion in popular magazines (Friedman et al. 2011), global health organization communication about Covid-19 on social media (Ma, Wang, and Kim 2023), physical activity and cognitive health content in top-circulating magazines (Greer, Corwin, and Friedman 2011), news media representations of nonconsensual, sexual image-sharing (Buiten 2020), the National Basketball Association's digital transformation (Santomier, Dolles, and Kunz 2023), Covid-19 social media data (Shakeri and Far 2020), media coverage of Šumava National Park (Riedl et al. 2018), gender stereotyping lessons in pop music videos (Kelly and Currie 2021), newspaper reports about cults (Zhang, Huang, and Li 2017), and domesticity in women's magazines (Beetham 1996).

Each ultra-processed food advertisement or product label will be collected using online search engines entering the following health halo terms: "all natural," "real fruit," "no sugar added," "low fat," "no artificial flavors or preservatives," "whole wheat (or grain)," "diet" and/or "low calorie," "fortified with vitamins and minerals," "gluten free," "vegetarian" or "vegan," "sports food advertisements," "exercise food advertisements," and "activity in food advertisements." Following this, specific advertisements illustrating the various health halos and Health Belief Model constructs will be studied and discussed in detail within each section. At the end of each section, a list of product labels using the specific health halo and Health Belief Model constructs will be included to indicate the frequency of use of each.

The established NOVA definition of ultra-processed foods will be used to determine appropriateness of food items to study parameters. The definition is as follows:

> Industrial formulations . . . with five or more . . . ingredients . . . such as sugar, oils, fats, salt, antioxidants, stabilisers, and preservatives . . . some [which are] directly extracted from foods, such as casein, lactose, whey, and gluten, and some derived from further processing of food constituents, such as hydrogenated or interesterified oils, hydrolysed proteins, soy protein isolate, maltodextrin, invert sugar and high fructose corn syrup . . . [with] additive[s] [that] include dyes and other colours, colour stabilisers, flavours, flavour enhancers, non-sugar sweeteners, and processing aids such as carbonating, firming, bulking and anti-bulking, de-foaming, anti-caking and glazing agents, emulsifiers, sequestrants and humectants. (Monteiro et al. 2016, 33)

These researchers point out that the main purpose of this processing is to create ready-to-eat foods to replace natural ones, such as nuts, fruits, and vegetables (Monteiro et al. 2016, 33). They further note that one of the main characteristics of ultra-processed foods is superior taste as well as appealing packaging along with relentless marketing, high profits, and claims of health (Monteiro et al. 2016, 33). Among those items classified as ultra-processed are cereal, candy, ice cream, infant formulas, fruit yogurts, pizza, sausages, hot dogs, soups, energy and cereal bars, carbonated and fruit drinks, breads, cakes, and cookies (Monteiro et al. 2016, 33). Consistent with this definition, the term "ultra-processed foods" will be used to identify these foods.

Health Halo Definitions

The health halos identified in this study were chosen based on popularity from previous research conducted by the author and should by no means be considered an exhaustive list. Since many of the health halos discussed have various presentations, each will be identified by a shortened label. Full definitions of each health halo used in food advertisements were created for the purposes of this study. They are defined as follows:

- Natural and Real Health Halo—the use of text, colors, or images associated with nature, or whole, unprocessed, genuine foods free from artificial ingredients in the advertising or labeling of a product that creates a false perception of healthiness about the item. Some examples of the themes used in this health halo include use of the words "all natural," "real fruit," and "no artificial flavors or preservatives."
- Nutrition Health Halo—the use of text, colors, or images associated with food that provides sustenance and nutrients to the human body, is free from unprocessed ingredients, and nutritionally beneficial in the advertising or labeling of a product that creates a false perception of healthiness about the item. Some examples of the themes used in this health halo include use of such words as "no sugar added," "low fat," "whole wheat," and "gluten free" as well as the concept of advertising vitamin- and mineral-fortified food products.
- Identity Health Halo—the use of text, colors, or images associated with consumers' desires to present themselves in a certain way, shape their sense of belonging, or express their values through food choices in the advertising or labeling of a product that creates a false perception of healthiness about the item. Some examples of themes used in this health halo include use of such words as "diet" and "low calorie" as well as foods marketed as vegan or vegetarian and those that include images of exercise, playing sports, and healthy activities.

Health Belief Model Adaptations

The four belief constructs of the Health Belief Model are adapted for the purposes of this study. However, the two constructs affecting behaviors, which are self-efficacy and cues to action, of the Health Belief Model are omitted from this study based on the fact that determining individual beliefs to perform a desired behavior (self-efficacy) and whether an individual's surroundings or experiences influence actions taken (cues to action) are outside the scope of this research and impossible to determine through content analysis of food advertisements. The traditional definition pertaining to health behaviors in the Health Belief Model is outlined below and followed by an illustration of the method of adaptation for the current analysis:

- Perceived susceptibility: "Assessing the probability of acquiring an illness or encountering an undesirable outcome" (Alyafei and Easton-Carr 2024, 2).
  Adaptation: Ultra-processed food advertisements or product labels purporting to reduce the risk of disease or illness prevention in their marketing will be categorized under this construct. Some examples of this include products marketed as "gluten-free," "nut free," or "lactose free."
- Perceived severity: "Understanding the severity of the illness, condition, or unfavorable outcome and what could happen if no additional action is taken" (Alyafei and Easton-Carr 2024, 2).
  Adaptation: Ultra-processed food advertisements or product labels promoting consequences for avoiding their products. Some examples of this include products marketed as "organic," "non-GMO," or "pesticide free" to avoid harmful chemicals, those promising avoidance of unhealthy digestive problems, or those highlighting the natural aspects of the product to avoid harmful food chemicals.
- Perceived benefits: "How the effectiveness of various available actions to reduce the risk of illness are perceived" (Alyafei and Easton-Carr 2024, 2).
  Adaptation: Ultra-processed food advertisements or product labels purporting health or emotional benefits such as managing body size, increasing nutrition, relieving stress, helping the environment, or supporting social causes. Some examples of this include products donating a portion of sales to charitable organizations as well as those advertised as "low calorie," containing probiotics or vitamins, or promising a "break" from daily stress or emotional upset.
- Perceived barriers: "Obstacles to performing a recommended health action that may stop one from doing what is recommended" (Alyafei and Easton-Carr 2024, 2).
  Adaptation: Ultra-processed food advertisements or product labels addressing the practical, psychological, or emotional obstacles to purchasing specific foods. Some examples of this include products generally thought to be

unhealthy but promising guilt-free consumption, those usually suspected to be poor tasting such as vegan or low-fat products emphasizing their good taste, or highlighting the low price of foods that are generally thought to be expensive.

In the next chapter, use of the Natural and Real Health Halo in ultra-processed food advertisements and on product labels is examined. Included in this is a discussion of the regulation around related terms as well as current research into its effectiveness in both advertisements and on product labels. Within the chapter, examples of advertisements and product labels for ultra-processed foods will be discussed with a focus on the use of text, colors, or images associated with nature, or whole, unprocessed, genuine foods free from artificial ingredients that create a false perception of healthiness about the items as well as an analysis of the Health Belief Model constructs used in motivating consumers to purchase these products.

2

Natural and Real Health Halo

The Natural and Real Health Halo is defined as the use of text, colors, or images associated with nature or whole, unprocessed, genuine foods free from artificial ingredients in the advertising or labeling of a product that creates a false perception of healthiness about the item. Some examples of themes used in this health halo include use of the words "all natural," "real fruit," and "no artificial flavors or preservatives." Each of these examples will be discussed in order in this chapter.

All Natural . . . but not Really

"Got the itch to bake from scratch?" asks a 1980 ad for Hershey's baking chocolate in a large headline with the words "Try Hershey's two new all natural baking chocolates" positioned directly below (Savard 2024). These words are above a close-up picture of a pottery mixing bowl with a wooden spoon in it positioned to the left of a darker pottery pitcher filled with milk next to a smaller matching bowl filled with flour. In front of the smaller bowl are two eggs next to a box of Hershey's semi-sweet chocolate, which is next to a box of unsweetened Hershey's chocolate positioned next to what resembles a home-canned jar of cherries. In the front row, there's a box of sweetened chocolate as well as chunks of chocolate, nuts, and butter. In smaller text below the image, readers are told that "nothing beats baking it yourself" and are reminded that Hershey's now has "a whole line of all natural baking chocolates . . . the kind that has made Hershey America's chocolate company for over 75 years" (Savard 2024). Readers are also provided with a 15¢ coupon and reminded at the bottom of the ad that "If you're making it with chocolate, make it with Hershey's" (Savard 2024).

Health Belief Model Constructs Used to Motivate Consumers

The Hershey's advertisement employs the Health Belief Model constructs of perceived severity, perceived benefits, and perceived barriers and is an example of the Natural and Real Health Halo. The use of the perceived severity construct is evidenced by the slogan, "nothing beats baking it yourself" used in conjunction with images of whole foods such as nuts, butter, and the jar of cherries. This construct helps to address consumers' concerns about the consequences that may arise from eating chocolate, a strategy that also touches on the perceived barriers construct regarding consumer knowledge about the processed nature of chocolate mitigated through the use of whole food images. Similarly, the perceived benefits construct is shown in privileging home-baked items and specifically Hershey's chocolate as being superior in taste. Through use of these Health Belief Model constructs, consumers are prompted to buy Hershey's chocolate since it appears to lessen the severity of an unfavorable outcome if they are not able to resist chocolate. By joining images of whole foods with processed chocolate in a private kitchen and using a slogan about home baking, the advertisement addresses perceived barriers of traditional health recommendations to avoid chocolate and other candy products through attempts to persuade consumers that home-baked foods are healthy and higher in nutrition than those that are not made at home.

"All Natural" Regulation

Current regulation on the use of words "all natural" on product labels states that products using the term must demonstrate that "(1) the product does not contain any artificial flavor or flavoring, coloring ingredient, or chemical preservative (as defined in 21 CFR 101.22), or any other artificial or synthetic ingredient; and (2) the product and its ingredients are not more than minimally processed" (United States Department of Agriculture 2024). It is further noted that "minimal processing may include: (a) those traditional processes used to make food edible or to preserve it or to make it safe for human consumption . . . or (b) those physical processes which do not fundamentally alter the raw product and/or which only separate a whole, intact food into component parts" (United States Department of Agriculture 2024). In practice, items using the term "all natural," according to the USDA guidelines, should include an explanation of the term's meaning beneath or beside the claim or by using an asterisk. Examples of these explanations can include the fact that the product includes no artificial ingredients or is minimally processed.

It's important to note that the FDA's (Food and Drug Administration) definition does not take into consideration nutritional or health benefits in its allowance of the use of the "all natural" term and that "regulation of the word 'natural' allows foods to be genetically modified and produced with pesticides, which goes against what many people believe about these products. Additionally, the word 'natural' on a food product does not indicate that the product is healthier than an alternative" (Samson 2021). Despite a recent update and a 2016 call for feedback from the FDA about the meaning of the word "natural," there is no regulation for food using this label, which some consider to be "false advertising" and "hollow and meaningless" (Fera 2014). Research has shown a "natural-is-better bias" in the purchase of many different types of products in addition to food, which researchers believe "may be driven by a natural-is-better default belief as well as the belief that natural items are safer than non-natural items" (Meier, Dillard, and Lappas 2019). Additional research suggests that consumers view the term "natural" as related to or the same as "organic," the latter of which does involve FDA regulation of the manner in which foods are grown (Kuchler et al. 2020).

In a study of 125 adults with a medium age of 48 years and 12 grocery products with 6 product pairs, one of which included an "all natural" label and the other of which did not, participants were asked to place monetary bids on both types of products and were then surveyed to determine what their beliefs were about the meaning of "natural" labels. Products used in the study included a "natural" and a regular version of the following items: "canola cooking oil, kettle-cooked potato chips, creamy peanut butter, frosted bite-size wheat cereal, wheat crackers, and mint-flavored toothpaste" (Butler and Vossler 2018, 550). Researchers found that the "vast majority of respondents stated a belief that 'natural' signals no artificial flavors, colors and/or preservatives" and were "willing to pay 20% more on average for 'natural' products" (Butler and Vossler 2018, 562). These findings coincide with previous research suggesting that "an all-natural front-of-pack label improves consumer perceptions of product quality and nutritional content" (Liu et al. 2017) as well as subsequent research listing "natural ingredients" as the top claim consumers look for and are willing to pay more for when purchasing food, noting that, "seventy-eight percent (78%) of consumers say they would pay more for products listed as all-natural, and . . .

56% would be willing to pay 10–30% more and 33% are willing to spend 20–30% more for all-natural products. Additionally, five of the top six claims are in the clean label, all-natural, no artificial ingredients benefits space" (Ingredion 2023).

"As Nature Intended They Should"

When taking into consideration the lack of governmental regulation around the use of "natural" products as well as the dangers of eating ultra-processed foods, it's not difficult to understand the popularity of this theme in the Natural and Real Health Halo in both food advertisements and on product labels. Though the term "all natural" appears to have gained popularity in the present, historically, the idea was illustrated by using the word "natural" or relating, through text or images, products to nature and/or natural elements. Despite the absence of a food classification system in the early 1900s, many products fell into the ultra-processed foods category due to the ingredients. An example of this is infant formulas, which today are classified as an ultra-processed food, yet in earlier times, these included highly processed ingredients such as milk powder and malted barley. One of the earliest examples of this can be seen in a 1913 ad for Mellin's Baby Food, a product containing malted barley (The Baby Historian 2021). At the top of the black-and-white ad is a banner with the words "Mellin's Food" (Mellin's Food Company 1913). Underneath the banner is a large photo of a bare-chested, healthy, smiling baby sitting with one leg bent. Below that is text that tells the readers that "A radiant face with the flush of joyous, healthy babyhood is the natural result of a Mellin's Food diet. Mellin's Food babies have no cares nor worries. They devote all their time to growing strong and developing properly, as Nature intended they should" (Mellin's Food Company 1913). In smaller print below, readers are encouraged to write for a free trial of the baby food from the Boston, Massachusetts, based company.

The association of "healthy babyhood" as being "the natural result" of using the product thus giving babies time to grow strong and develop properly "as Nature intended" in an advertisement published the year after "more than 40,000 children under two died from diarrhea or enteritis, primarily due to contaminated or infected dairy milk, unsanitary bottles, and unsafe drinking water" is clearly intended to promote the safety of the product (The Baby Historian 2021). The company, which developed a reputation for shady marketing practices "knowingly falsely claimed their product was the 'perfect substitute for mother's milk' and that bottle-fed babies of the time were just as healthy (*even healthier!*) than breastfed babies" even going so far as to create "ads disguised as front-page news during cholera epidemics claiming their product would keep babies safe, yet, their product required mixing with the very water or milk which were transmitting cholera" (The Baby Historian 2021; emphasis in the original).

A decade later, the company would publish an ad that they claimed was "advertised by our loving friends" that included eight photos of "Mellin's Food Babies" from across the United States urging consumers to "use the Mellin's Food Method of Milk Modification for your baby" (Vintage Prints & Collectibles 2024). The following year, another ad would urge "Thinking Mothers" to use Mellin's Food, which was described as "the closest possible equivalent of breast milk" on which "baby naturally thrives" resulting in "strong limbs, firm flesh, a robust constitution, and a happy disposition" (Jeff Morgan 07, 2024). To coincide with these ideas, the company ran a campaign beginning in the early 1900s to reinforce the idea of healthy babies. The "Mellin's Food Babies" ads ran in many women's magazines and newspapers to promote the health benefits of the product and remind consumers that "A radiant face with the flush of joyous, healthy babyhood is the natural result of a Mellin's Food diet" (*The Housewife* 1914, 16).

"Baby's Natural Immune System"

Building on the "all natural" theme, a more recent ad for Aptamil infant formula, features a mother holding a child with the headline, "Your baby's natural immune system. We've done the research, he's doing the development" with text underneath saying that "after 30 years of research into breastmilk," the company's experts have created "a patented milk of special probiotics" designed "to support your baby's natural immune system" (Nymark 2009). Underneath that, in purple text, it says, "inspired by breastmilk, supported by science" (Nymark 2009). "Small print added that the product should only be used as part of a mixed diet and not as a breastmilk substitute before six months" (Nymark 2009). The ad was banned by the Advertising Standards Authority in London based on the fact that the "The National Childbirth Trust felt the ads misleadingly implied that the product could 'boost' the immune system of children or babies" and another claim in the ad about the formula designed to "support your baby's natural immune system" and "whether it could be substantiated" (Nymark 2009). By using a version of the "all natural" wording, the ultra-processed food manufacturer has created a health halo in its advertisement of infant formula through an association of both the "baby's natural immune system" and breast milk.

A current Enfamil Neuro Pro Infant Formula label uses the words "naturally occurring MFGM components" on its label with a note that they are from "whey protein concentrate" next to claims about "brain building," support of "immune health," and inspiration from breast milk. In addition to using the word "natural," the background of the label is bright yellow with rays of light that seem to mimic the sun, thus also providing a health halo with nature itself. Similarly, a Kendamil Organic Infant Formula label, which proclaims to be "made with love in Europe" does not use the word "nature" but instead features a large photo of a mother deer nudging her baby to stand with a background of green grass and mountains, thus creating a nature-inspired health halo.

Health Belief Model and Infant Formula Advertisements

The previous infant formula advertisements make use of all four Health Belief Model constructs including perceived susceptibility, perceived severity, perceived benefits, and perceived barriers. As outlined previously, perceived susceptibility involves determining an individual's likelihood of contracting an illness or adverse health outcomes. Infant formula advertisements pointing to the dangers children may experience, such as diarrhea or enteritis from contaminated dairy milk, are designed to frighten mothers into taking action to protect their children due to the perceived susceptibility of their infants contracting such conditions, which as noted previously were quite common in the early 1900s. Similarly, the perceived severity Health Belief Model construct, which addresses the idea of an unfavorable health outcome without specific action, is illustrated by promises about infant health. Specifically, the idea of "brain building" and "boosting" the immune system of infants through the use of these formulas is highlighted to provide understanding about the consequences of not taking action that would result in infants with unhealthy brains and weakened immune systems.

The perceived benefits of the Health Belief Model construct, which is illustrated by the determination about the effectiveness or reduction of illness taking the action results in, are indicated in both the images of healthy, robust babies and the promises of joy, health, proper and strong development, strength, happiness, immune support, and properly developed brains. This construct can also be seen in the promise that these infant formulas are the equivalent or superior to mother's milk, which is commonly known to contain many healthy nutrients to provide babies with good health. Additionally, the perceived barriers, or obstacles to taking a health action, of using a product that is not truly mother's milk is addressed through the use of images of nature and healthy babies as well as, in one case, the erroneous claim that the formula is healthier than actual mother's milk.

Additional infant and toddler formula products that use the Natural and Real Health Halo and constructs from the Health Belief Model on their labels include but are not limited to the following: By Heart Whole Nutrition Infant Formula, Kabrita Goat-Based Infant Formula, Hipp Dutch Organic Formula, Aussie Bubs Australian Grass Fed Nutritional Milk-Based Toddler Formula, Bubs 365 Day Grass Fed Infant Milk Formula, Bobbie Organic Gentle Infant Formula Milk-Based Powder, Babbie Organic Infant Milk-Based Powder, Similac Pure Bliss Organic Infant Formula, By Heart Whole Nutrition Infant Formula, Holle Stage 1 Organic Infant Formula, Holle Goat Stage Pre Infant Formula, Holle Dutch Milk Goat Formula Stage 1, Holle Stage 1 Cow Milk Infant Formula, Bellamy's Organic Infant Formula, Baby's Only A2 Organic Infant Formula, Baby's Only Organic Toddler Formula, Earth's Best Organic Infant Sensitivity Formula, Little Oak Infant Formula made with Natural Goat's Milk, Serenity Kids Grass Fed Organic A2 Whole Milk Toddler Formula, Fortini Infant Formula, Mt. Capra Whole Goat Milk Powder, Organix Stage 1 Organic Infant Formula, Nannycare Goat Stage 1 First Infant Milk Formula, Pure Goat Stage 1 Organic Complete Infant Formula, Baby's Only Organic Pea Protein Toddler Formula, Jovie Organic Goat Milk Formula Stage 1, Whole Goat Milk by Mt. Capra, Löwenzahn Formula Stage PRE, Bebe M Organic Rice Based Anti-Reflux Stage 2 Infant Formula, Neocate Infant Formula, and Nara Organics Infant Formula.

The Colors of Nature

All natural claims are not limited to infant formulas, however. A fifteen-second, 2019 ad for Adobo Chicken Power Bowls uses the term to describe the meat in its product. The ad, which was posted on social media, opens with a green background filled with a leaf design and upbeat music after which the product fades in to swirling leaves then cuts to an image of the product already prepared with the words "All Natural Chicken" over it in white font ("Healthy Choice Power Bowls TV Spot" 2019). The ad continues to highlight several other ingredients, such as grains, zooming in on them with text "Red Quinoa, Black Barley, Brown Rice" in white font, followed by images of green leafy vegetables on a green background and the words "Chard, Kale, Spinach" over, and then a cut to the prepared product and the words "Wholesome Ingredients," followed by individual shots of each ingredient, which include poblanos, pepitas, guajillo sauce, and then to a shot of the prepared product with some missing and the words "Bold Flavor" over it as more of the prepared product disappears in the background ("Healthy Choice Power Bowls TV Spot" 2019). The final shot is of the product over the green background with the words "26g of Protein, Wholesome Ingredients, All Natural Chicken" ("Healthy Choice Power Bowls TV Spot" 2019).

Through the use of the color green and close-up images of a few ingredients in their natural form as well as the words "all natural" in reference to the chicken, the company has employed a health halo to associate their product with the naturalness of nature. The name of the company, Healthy Choice, is in itself a health halo thus working to remind consumers of the supposed health of the ultra-processed food, which, by definition, is unhealthy. It's also worth noting that the inclusion of images of chard, kale, and spinach may lead consumers to believe that there are more of these vegetables in the product than there actually are. Chard and kale appear on this list of ingredients as the seventeenth and eighteenth, while spinach is the twenty-first ingredient. Considering that food manufacturers are required by the U.S. FDA to list ingredients in descending order, meaning that the first ingredient is the largest by weight, the place of vegetables in the ingredients list does not seem to reflect their importance in the ad in which they fill 1.5 seconds, or almost 7 percent, of the 15-second commercial.

Through the use of green leafy vegetable images, the color green, and the words "Wholesome Ingredients," the advertisement is also employing the perceived severity construct of the Health Belief Model by reminding consumers that "unfavorable" health results may take place without taking action, which in this case means eating healthy foods. The perceived benefits Health Belief Model construct is evidenced by highlighting the ingredients and the protein content while the perceived barriers construct is illustrated with the promise of a strong taste to address the obstacle of consumer association of healthy food with bad taste.

Another example of using the colors of nature is shown in a Nature Valley Crunchy Granola Bars commercial. The advertisement begins with a shot of a package of Nature Valley Oats 'n Honey Granola Bars positioned on top of a stack of uniformly cut sticks, resembling logs yet smaller than the package itself. The package is dark green on the bottom and light green on the top with the Nature Valley logo in bright yellow with oats on one side and honey on the other. The camera pans to a rustic type scale with wooden tag with "1/3" on it to one side and a bowl of oats balanced on the other as the announcer tells viewers that the product "contains one-third of your daily whole grains" before the camera moves on to a ticking clock made from wood that releases an object that triggers the rising of a wood sign with the word "Energy" in yellow letters behind a shot of three packages of granola bars as the announcer says, "So, one-third of this commercial is dedicated to what you can do with all that energy" while the camera continues to pan the table with trees and water in the background (Bits & Bobs 2014). The camera cuts to a shot of a man riding his mountain bicycle through the forest at a swift pace before returning to a shot of the three packages with a photo of the man with peanuts in front of the peanut butter-flavored granola bar and slices of coconut in front of the coconut-flavored one with a pot of honey behind the oats 'n honey one. The background is filled with lush greenery as well as a natural pond while the announcer tells viewers that eating one third of their whole grains means "energy to take the road less traveled" (Bits & Bobs 2014).

Like the Healthy Choice commercial, Nature Valley uses nature not only in the name of the company but also in the advertisement itself, relying on shots of lush greenery and wooded areas to create an "all natural" health halo. In addition to this, on the box, the word "natural" is used twice. On one side, underneath the logo, the words "The Official Natural Energy Bar of the PGA Tour" appear above the organization's logo while on the other side about a third of the way down the package, the words "100% Natural, Excellent Source of Whole Grain" appear in a yellow ribbon that covers a portion of one of the bars pictured on the package. The ribbon covers a bunch of oats while dripping honey is positioned directly below the PGA Tour logo. The background of the package is a mix of light and green stripes resembling a freshly cut lawn forming a hill that connects to a green sky stripped with yellow rays of sun, the center of which is a small rising sun that is positioned between the two bars. Though the use of sun colors is not included in all the company's packaging, the use of the color green appears to remain consistent across different products.

At the same time, the perceived severity Health Belief Model construct is shown by highlighting whole ingredients, fulfilling the suggested daily whole grain requirements and with the promise of having more energy, which also reflects the perceived benefits construct along with the idea of the commercial promising ideas about what to do with the extra energy that consumers are promised by eating the product. The perceived barriers construct is illustrated through images of food known to have good taste such as peanut butter, honey, and coconuts.

The company, which introduced granola cereal in 1973, credits itself with creating the first granola bar designating itself as a "proud partner of the outdoors" based on its support of the National Park Foundation and several other organizations focused on enjoying, protecting, and preserving nature. In line with this, the company launched an advertising campaign to "Take in the Outdoors" through "an immersive microsite (TakeInTheOutdoors.com) where, with just a click, voice command, or scan of a QR code, visitors can explore 360 naturescapes, access a library of 3D audio experiences, and identify their nearest nature escape by entering their zip code," positioning this as an escape for commuters (Mindshare 2024). "Through the creation of an immersive nature-oriented microsite, users decompressed in their nearest nature escape, creating a strong association between nature, relaxation, and Nature Valley" (Mindshare 2024). This extreme focus on nature creates a health halo designed to provide consumers with the idea that this ultra-processed food is healthy when, in fact, many of the company's products include such highly processed ingredients as sugar, canola and/or sunflower oil, rice flour, brown sugar syrup, soy lecithin, corn syrup, cane syrup, dextrose, and corn starch.

Nice & Natural

A product from New Zealand takes the all natural theme even further by including the word natural in its name while using the colors of nature in its promotion and packaging. Nice & Natural Nut Bars are promoted at the manufacturer's website as containing "flavours and ingredients inspired by nature, which means no added artificial colours, flavours and fillers" with ingredients that "do the talking." In a 2015 commercial, a woman identified as Sally Williams, tells viewers that it's difficult to make good snack choices when life is busy but that nuts are a "great solution to snacking dilemmas" pointing out that Nice & Natural Nut Bars are "bursting with nuts" (Buchanan Advertising 2015), which illustrates the perceived barriers Health Belief Model construct by addressing one of consumers' biggest obstacles to healthy eating: lack of time. Sally Williams, who is shown in a grocery store, is dressed in a green blouse, the color of which is reminiscent of grass or leaves. The logo to the side of her includes leaves, whole nuts, and fruit. A display of nine different nut bar flavors a few seconds into the commercial is shown in front of a window with green leaves outside. Following this, a mother in the house with the window in shown tossing her son a nut bar, with the window still visible in the background. Text on the screen says, "no artificial flavours, no artificial colours, bursting with nuts" before Sally Williams encourages viewers to try the product.

The use of the word natural in the name of products containing ultra-processed ingredients, which include sugar, soy lecithin, maltodextrin, and caramelized sugar syrup, to name a few, as well as colors associated with nature, clearly indicate the use of the Natural and Real Health Halo. By using the name Nice & Natural, the company has established a strong association with nature simply through identification and at the same time employed the perceived severity Health Belief Model construct. Adding to this, the information at the company's website tells visitors that "Here at Nice & Natural we like simple. That's why we call the bars we make, what they actually are, Nice & Natural," while telling them that "nice things go into our products." Packaging for many of the company's products also includes natural colors such as green, brown, yellow, and blue with images of nature including leaves, whole fruit, and wheat, thus further establishing the use of the perceived benefits Health Belief Model construct.

All Natural, Outside

The use of outdoor settings is another technique ultra-processed food manufacturers used to reinforce the naturalness of their products. An example of this is an advertisement for Real'Za All-Natural, Frozen Pizza. In the commercial, four adults are sitting outside at a table with pizza on it. They are watching four children playing in a grassy area with trees and bushes. The younger couple who is seated facing the children watches as a young boy puts a sword in his mouth. The woman asks the man if he sees that and the man asks if that's real while the other couple, the parents of the boy, proudly proclaim that the pizza is Real'Za and "all natural and delicious" before realizing that the boy has presumably put the entire sword down his throat as a message on screen tells viewers, "The sword is fake. The pizza is all-natural" (Solve 2018). The parents run to the child while the man asks the woman if she still wants to have kids to which she shakes her head just before a shot of the pizza box with the words "All-Natural Ingredients. All-Natural Delicious" appear as a male announcer speaks the words (Solve 2018). The combined use of the words all natural as well as the lush green setting work to provide a health halo for a product that includes ultra-processed ingredients such as sugar, dry milk, and wheat flour. In addition to this, the words "all-natural" appear directly above "Real'Za Pizza" in the company's logo.

Another pizza company uses the all natural theme in a different way. Freschetta Pizza has a line of "naturally rising crust" frozen pizzas, which in addition to using the word natural in the name, reinforced this in a commercial that introduced Scott the tomato farmer and Tilly May the dairy cow. The 2016 commercial begins with images of Scott on a farm loading tomatoes into a truck as a female announcer offers an introduction of him being a "real farmer" with "real vine ripened tomatoes" before introducing Tilly May as a "real cow" and the company's "go-to for 100% real cheese." The cow moos then and the commercial shows her standing in a beautiful green field with many green trees ("Freschetta TV Spot, 'Real Taste for Real Life'" 2016). Following this, the announcer introduces an oven telling viewers that the heat will make the naturally rising crust rise quickly as a mother is shown frantically slicing up the pizza as kids wait for it. The commercial closes with the announcer telling consumers that they can have "real taste" for their "real lives" ("Freschetta TV Spot, 'Real Taste for Real Life'" 2016).

Included in the ingredients of the four-cheese naturally rising crust pizza are malted barley flour, thiamine mononitrate, sugar, ascorbic acid, guar gum, dextrose, and soy lecithin, to name a few. Though the use of the word "natural" in the name and images of nature in the commercial give consumers the impression that the product is derived from only real cheese and tomatoes, the thirty-plus long list of ingredients does not list tomatoes at all; tomato paste appears about halfway through, while cheese is listed after enriched flour (wheat flour, malted barley flour, niacin, reduced iron, thiamine mononitrate, riboflavin, folic acid) making the focus on the two products not untrue yet surely a marketing strategy designed to closely associate the product with nature and thus take advantage of the Natural and Real Health Halo advertising technique and using the perceived severity, perceived benefits, and perceived barriers Health Belief Model constructs.

All-Natural Pizza

Not only does a 2009 commercial for Pizza Hut exemplify how the Natural and Real Health Halo and several constructs of the Health Belief Model can be used to promote ultra-processed foods, but it also illustrates the importance of using the all natural association in the product name. The commercial opens with two young women carrying cut up pizza on wooden trays in an upbeat, hip restaurant-type setting with brick and red painted walls. Text at the bottom says, "Chef Elizabeth's Pizza Tasting" as a young woman asks two men if they are going to try some of her natural pizza to which they give rave reviews as the camera cuts to several other images of people eating pizza and talking about how great it tastes until finally landing on a young woman who says, "I'm all about the multi-grain" (Comedian Evan Wecksell + Breckett Sage 2009). Following this, "Chef Elizabeth" says she didn't actually make the pizza and that it was delivered by Pizza Hut after which the crowd cheers and the camera cuts to a close up of pizza with the words "The Natural" with two wheat sprigs underneath. A male announcer says this is a "whole new way to eat pizza" and describes the multigrain crust, natural peperoni, and all natural sauces with no high fructose corn syrup made from vine-ripened tomatoes after which consumers are encouraged to "Choose Real Taste" (Comedian Evan Wecksell + Breckett Sage 2009).

Within a year, "The Natural" pizza was unavailable in most restaurants across the country resulting in what some called "a classic case of botched execution and ill-conceived marketing," which "speaks to a strange dichotomy in the food world" in which "people want to buy healthy, wholesome foods at the supermarket, but when they go out to eat, they often really don't care about what may be lurking in that Triple Whopper or those Extreme Nachos" (Warner 2010).

Pizza Hut isn't the only company to use the all natural theme in its products. Some other examples include Pizza Bien described on the product's website as "Handmade from 100% all natural Delicious ingredients" in the company's "Our Food" section. In this 196-word description, there are 7 direct references to the product being natural and another 17 that relate to the natural theme including homemade, no artificial flavors, no hydrogenated oils, no colors or sugars added, and no GMOs, handcrafted, healthy, and traditional, which illustrates the perceived severity and benefits Health Belief Model constructs. Horizon Farms, a Japanese company advertises an "All-Natural Frozen Pizza Margherita From Italy" on its website that contains the ultra-processed ingredient maltodextrin on its website. The Dish Famous Pizza uses the words all natural on the "Our Pizzas" section of its website to describe eleven different pizza combinations. Open Nature Pizza uses the word nature in the title of the company's name in products that include ultra-processed ingredients such as xanthan gum, sugar, and dry milk.

Mystic Pizza uses the words all natural in a ribbon underneath its logo on its frozen pizza boxes. Wise Pies, which proclaims itself "a smarter way to pizza" uses the words all natural on its calzone boxes. The Lunchables line of products includes a "Lunchables Natural Uncured Pepperoni & Cheese Meal Kit with Pizza Crusts & Sauce." The packaging of Totino's Party Pizza pack includes wording that says "Naturally Flavored With Other Natural Flavors" directly next to an image of a square of pizza. Edwardo's also uses natural in the name of the product, identified as Edwardo's Natural Pizza while Connie's uses the words all natural with a green leaf next to the name of its "Chicago's Finest Pizza." Wild Mike's Ultimate Pizza uses the words "100% All Natural/No Artificial Anything" on its packaging. DiGiorno uses the words "Naturally Flavored" on its Garlic Bread Pizza package. Earth's Best Whole Grain Cheese Pizza, which includes a Sesame Street character on the box, labels itself as "all natural" and "70% organic." Naturli uses a take on the word natural in its company name to promote plant-based pizza products. The Pizza Gourmet has a line of Wood Grilled All Natural Pizza Crusts. Combos Pizza Cracker Baked Snacks tells consumers that its product contains "Natural and Artificial Flavored Filling" while Kraft Pizza Mozzarella Cheddar Cheese uses the words "Natural Cheese" at the top of the package underneath the company's logo.

Skinny Pizza

Similarly, another pizza manufacturer includes the Natural and Real Health Halo and perceived severity and perceived benefits Health Belief Model constructs on its website to describe its crust. Skinny Pizza, with locations in New York and Saudi Arabia, which carries frozen pizza in selected stores, includes the following description in the "In Dough We Crust" section on the company's website. "It all starts with a good, healthy crust that is all-natural and made in New York without any potassium bromate and using filtered New York water."

Above that are the words “Real Pizza. Real Thin. Real Fast” with photos of cheese and vegetable topped pizzas, a garlic head, whole tomatoes, sliced peppers, shredded cheese, and sliced onions. Also included on the page is a section titled “We Make Sure You Eat Your Vegetables,” which says, “We are proud to top your pizza with a variety of fresh and flavorful vegetables that are farm-to-table and/ or organic when available.” In addition to the Natural and Real Health Halo, perceived severity and perceived benefits constructs of including photos of fresh vegetables, the use of the words “all natural” to describe what is arguably the most processed part of the pizza provide consumers with the idea that this part of the pizza is natural as well. It’s worth noting that the name of the company employs the Identity Health Halo which will be discussed in Chapter 4.

An examination of the ingredients in the frozen version of the company’s pizza reveals such ultra-processed ingredients as modified rice starch, soy lecithin, xanthan gum, sugar, whey powder, rice and tapioca flour, and cane sugar. The package includes the words “100% Real Cheese” in between the words “Organic Tomato Sauce” and “Rice & Potato Crust” in green font on arched ribbons that spill over into the upper corner of the photo of the pizza. There is a green stripe at the top of the box with the words “Gluten Free” in it, thus also using the perceived susceptibility Health Belief Model construct. As mentioned, green is a color reflecting nature, which conveys a subtle connection to the natural world.

Corncob Crust Pizza

The use of fresh vegetable images to use the Natural and Real Health Halo and perceived severity and perceived benefits constructs can also be seen in a 2023 prank by pizza manufacturer Little Caesars. In one of a series of commercials released in March of that year, a male announcer exuberantly says, “Introducing Corn Cob Crust from Little Caesars. Made with hearty American grown corn, ooey, gooey cheese, and a two-liter bottle of liquified butter” as the camera shows first a pizza with a corn cob crust and corn kernels on it and then a stack of corn cobs and a bottle of liquified butter (Commercial Break 2023). The announcer wraps up by telling viewers that “It’s the crust the world craves. You’re welcome, America” (Commercial Break 2023). In early April, in what some originally thought to be an April Fools’ farce, the company revealed that the corn cob crust pizza commercials were a joke as well as the launch of an advertising campaign designed to highlight the return of the limited-time-only Pretzel Crust Pizza. Though designed as a prank, the campaign "resulted in 42 million views and 1.5 million shares across social media, boosting . . . following by 22%" and earning a "grudging compliment from the CEO of rival Papa Johns" ("Agency Standouts" 2024, 24).

Prank or not, the use of whole corn cobs in the advertising of an ultra-processed pizza, which is actually a commercial for a different product, shows the effectiveness of the Natural and Real Health Halo as well as the perceived benefits Health Belief Model construct. In a series of subsequent advertisements, the company highlighted the social media activity. In one commercial, a male announcer asks, "How do we know you'll love pretzel crust? Cuz this person begged us never to tease them again about their precious pretzel crust" at which point a white square with a social media posting on Twitter (now known as X) by Travis Smith who begs the company that he "can't take another tease" and that he "must have the pretzel crust" is shown over a closeup of a pepperoni topped pizza (Commercial Archiver 2023). After which the announcer happily announces that "Pretzel crust is back" before asking "or is it?" then saying that it is seriously back but "Maybe" then "No, it's back" as the commercial ends (Commercial Archiver 2023).

While this section focused mainly on infant formula, granola bars, and pizza advertisements and product labels, there are many other examples of ultra-processed foods using the Natural and Real Health Halo and perceived severity and perceived benefits Health Belief Model constructs. While it is impossible to list every ultra-processed food company that has used this type of halo in its advertisements, there are a few that stand out. The following is a list of some:

A 2010 Lay's Classic Potato Chip ad describing the oil used in the product as all natural.
A 2012 ad from Frito-Lay telling consumers that they make their products naturally.
The introduction of Natural Tostitos.
Use of the words all natural on Steak Umms packages.
The words all natural on Nathans Uncured Beef Franks packages.
Sabrett Beef Hot Dogs' use of the words all natural on its packaging.
Hebrew National Uncured Beef Franks using the words all natural on the company's packages.
Smithfield using the words all natural on its uncured bacon.
The word natural on Colman uncured bacon.
Jif using all natural on its peanut butter packaging.
Smucker's using the words all natural on its peanut butter and preserves.

Skippy using natural on its peanut butter labels.
Welch's using the word natural on its fruit spread labels.
Trader Joe's using the words all natural on its fruit jellies.
Hunt's using "100% Natural" on its ketchup and tomato sauce labels.
Turkey Hill using all natural on its ice-cream containers.
Breyers using the words all natural on ice-cream containers.
Kashi Go Lean using the words all natural on its instant hot cereal boxes.
Wheatena Toasted Oat cereal using the words all natural on its boxes.
Kellogg's All Bran cereal boxes with the words "Natural Wheat Bran."
Kix Berry Berry cereal boxes including the words "All Natural Corn."
Berry Swirl Lucky Charms boxes containing the words "Flavored with Other Natural Flavors."
Fruit Loops cereal boxes using the words "All Natural Fruit Flavors."
Blueberry Cheerios boxes including the words "Flavored with Other Natural Flavors."
Wellsley Farms using the words all natural on its animal crackers containers.
Ritz Bites including the words "Flavored Filling with Other Natural Flavor."
O.T.C. Oyster & Soup Crackers containing the words all natural on packaging.

This is by no means an exhaustive list, but instead, additional examples to indicate the popularity of the Natural and Real Health Halo as well as the power of using the word "natural" in food advertisements and on food packaging, which illustrates the perceived severity and perceived benefits Health Belief Model constructs. Despite the lack of regulation regarding the use of the word "natural" on product packages and in food advertisements, a 2016 survey found that 37 percent of those surveyed included natural as one of the top three phrases that defined a healthy eating lifestyle (International Food Information Council Foundation 2016, 23). Yet, "there are many toxic chemicals that occur in nature as well—mercury, snake venom, arsenic, and ricin from castor beans. Some chemicals, like iron and oxygen, are necessary for us to live, but at high doses are toxic and can even cause death" (National Center for Complementary and Integrative Health 2024). Though this is not to suggest that ultra-processed foods contain any of these ingredients, it is meant to indicate the nebulousness of the term.

"Real Fruit" but not Really

"Okay, Kids, go for it. Firm 'n Fruity," a male announcer enthusiastically says as images of pre-teens and teens are shown playing football, skateboarding, and playing tennis as the announcer continues telling viewers that it's "The first all-natural kids' yogurt" that's "as good for you as all outdoors" (The Museum of Classic Chicago Television 2023). He continues by saying that the container can be flipped into a sundae that will "flip you out" as images of teens doing gymnastics are shown along with a closeup of the product being flipped with fruit on top of the yogurt. This 1977 commercial uses one of the most popular and oftentimes confusing health halo techniques: the use of text, colors, or images associated with fruit in the marketing or labeling of a product that creates a false perception of healthiness about the item, which also illustrates the perceived severity and perceived benefits Health Belief Model constructs. In this case, the word fruit is in the name of the product creating a clear association between the known-health benefits and prevention of illness provided from eating whole fruit to that of the ultra-processed fruit matter used in fruit-flavored yogurt, which clearly illustrates the real-fruit theme in the Natural and Real Health Halo. Though plain yogurt is not classified as an ultra-processed food, fruit-flavored yogurt is leading some nutrition experts to dub the product as "junk food in disguise" due to the fact that the "strawberry swirl fruit-on-the-bottom or chocolate chip crunch topping can pack a sugary punch" and "contain[s] more sugar in one serving than the daily recommended amount (The American Heart Association recommends no more than 25 grams for women and 36 grams for men)" (Cleveland Clinic 2020). It's worth noting that the majority of fruit-flavored yogurt products use the Natural and Real Health Halo in both advertising and on product labels considering that "the flavored yogurt segment accounts for a significant share of the North America yogurt market" with unflavored yogurt gaining some popularity as a cooking ingredient in recent years but still lagging far behind since "consumers prefer flavored yogurt for its taste and versatility as a snack or dessert option" (Di Market 2024). Additionally, the majority of yogurt sold by companies are produced in several different fruit-flavored yogurt products, some of which are heavily advertised resulting in consumers being exposed to many real fruit health halos on yogurt products.

Fruit-Related Terms and Images

Research has shown how powerful the real-fruit theme can be. In a recent study, the presence of fruit images and terms, including in the name of products, caused children ages four to seven years to believe that the product contained fruit while the absence of both made them more likely to identify what the study authors called "sham fruit foods" (Heller 2015). In addition to this, researchers found that "in both the food label and food advertising conditions, as the informational load increased, children were increasingly misled that sham fruit foods contained real fruit" and that "the presence of fruit images alone had a stronger impact on children's perceptions about a food's fruit content than a fruit name alone," yet "the effect of a fruit image is enhanced by a fruit name" (Heller 2015). In adults, research has historically shown that "consumers use packaging, an extrinsic cue, to infer intrinsic product attributes. In addition, consumers reported a more positive attitude toward the package itself when it included a product picture" (Underwood and Klein 2002) and that marketers using specific "guidelines should benefit from a reduction in the level of package-generated consumer cynicism and an increased potential for enhanced long-term customer relationships" (Underwood and Ozanne 1998).

The targeting of children with both the real-fruit theme and other questionable marketing techniques by the ultra-processed food industry is no accident. Since "food is intertwined with people's history, culture, communities, and families," the ultra-processed food industry works hard to identify consumers' "weaknesses, and leverages their vulnerabilities to convince them that certain products and diets are the best choice" by using "targeted tactics that normalize unhealthy environments, reinforced by promotions, offers, gifts, and discounts" designed to appeal to "senses and feelings, making it all irresistible to the human brain" while promoting freedom and responsibility to generate "positive emotions, enjoyment, freedom, pleasure, self-indulgence, youth, love, etc." designed to begin a relationship "from a very early age" so that "consumers choose brands no matter what, even if they are not the best option for their health" (Global Health Advocacy Incubator 2022).

It's worth noting that in 2007 after fruit and vegetable consumption was increased in the Food Pyramid's daily consumption guidelines, there was a dramatic increase in those foods infused with fruit resulting in "some 240 fruit-infused products — from ice cream to chips — appear[ing] in the first half of 2007, compared with 124 in all of 2000" (Horovitz 2007). Some of these products included "Flat Earth Baked Fruit Crisps—with 1/2 serving of fruit per ounce," "Nabisco Garden Harvest Toasted Chips with fruit pieces . . . baked into the chips," "ready-to-eat Jell-O with fruit pieces in it—dubbed Jell-O Fruit Passions," "T.G.I. Friday's brought back its seasonal Strawberry Fields Salad with balsamic marinated strawberries," and "Baskin-Robbins' Penguin Swirl . . . a kid-friendly mixed-berry blend that turns tongues black" (Horovitz 2007).

A Decade of Fruit Snack Introductions

Some would say the surge in fruit snacks, however, took place decades before the Food Pyramid changes and served as a foundation for today's glut of ultra-processed fruit-flavored snacks (Click Americana 2021). The 1980s would bring the introduction of fruit candy products from General Mills/Betty Crocker, Sunkist, and Del Monte to name a few, which would enjoy high sales, thus firmly proving fruit-flavored candy snacks to be big sellers (Click Americana 2021). A 1980 advertisement introduced one of the most popular of these fruit snacks—Fruit Roll Ups made by General Mills. In the advertisement, the bottom two thirds of the page feature a large basket filled with apples, cherries, strawberries, and apricots in front of boxes of the coordinating flavor of Fruit Roll Ups with individual packages of the product scattered among the fruit. The top of the advertisement lets consumers know that product is new with a tagline below saying, "Get *real fruit* and fun rolled up in one," which is above text that encourages consumers to "unroll" the new product for "an exciting new kind of snack made from real fruit" that is "wholesome and fun to eat" (Click Americana 2021; emphases in the original). The advertisement also showed a smiling girl with red ribbons in her hair and a white-and-red checked shirt eating a red Fruit Roll Up and smiling. At that time, the upper portion of each box featured an image of whole fruit on the top with a yellow corner banner over the right corner reminding consumers that the product was made with real fruit.

Following this, two years later, the company would once again introduce the product in another advertisement that featured a large image of a young girl with rosy cheeks holding a large red Fruit Roll Up ripped in half and looking astonished. The text across the bottom half of the image read, "Introducing the fruit you unroll, peel and chew" above text telling consumers that the product is a new way to eat fruit and that the product is made from real fruit, below which are the four boxes with the coordinating whole fruit and Fruit Roll Ups in front (Click Americana 2021). A 25¢ coupon was included above the tagline "Real Fruit and Fun Rolled Up in One" (Click Americana 2021). It's worth noting that included on the boxes this time was a Fruit Corners logo with drawn images of each whole fruit from the flavors.

A 1984 advertisement for another fruit snack product features a large, bright red strawberry that takes up almost half the page. The strawberry has the middle portion ripped out by a fruit roll with the text "Sunkist Fruit Rolls: A kid's idea of the perfect fruit" running through a portion of the ripped part above smaller text saying, "And a mom's idea of the perfect snack" (Click Americana 2021). Text below informs consumers that the Fruit Rolls are flattened and rolled into a covering that kids can peel anywhere anytime they want. Flavors for this product include cherry, grape, strawberry, and orange. Like the Fruit Roll Ups advertisement, four boxes of Fruit Rolls are shown in the lower portion of the advertisement with the corresponding whole fruit placed directly in front with a coupon for 15¢ included. The packaging also features images of whole fruit on the top.

Also introduced during this decade in a 1985 advertisement was Del Monte Fruit Snacks. The top third of the page proclaims in bold, black letters, "New Energy Sources Discovered," under which the middle two thirds of the page feature images of packages of Yogurt Raisins, Strawberry Yogurt Raisins, dried Fruit Mix, and dried Tropical Fruit with an open package of diced, mixed tropical fruit opened and spilling out in the foreground above the words "A Powerful Good Snack" at the bottom of the page (Click Americana 2021). That same year, an advertisement introduced Fruit Corners Fruit Bars with an illustration of a large strawberry with a smile and a hand holding a fruit bar and text proclaiming that the product "changed the face of fruit forever," reminding consumers that the fruit bars are 100 percent natural as well as 100 percent delicious and come in grape, strawberry, cherry, and pineapple-orange flavors designed to cause "a bite turn[ed] into a smile" (Click Americana 2021). The packaging for this product includes the same Fruit Corners logo used in the Fruit Roll Ups advertisement with images of whole fruit as well as images of the corresponding fruit on the side third of the box. A 1986 advertisement combines both Fruit Roll Ups and Fruit Corners Fruit Bars with a full-page photo of a strawberry and text to the side telling consumers that the fruit wasn't easy to get since they traveled the world to find the best ones to become Fruit Roll Ups and Fruit Corners Fruit Bars, once again highlighting the company's use of real fruit.

Also published during this time were advertisements for Lipton Fruit Nibbles, Fruit Corners Fruit Wrinkles, Sunkist Fun Fruits, Fruit Corners Fruit Swirl Bars, Sunkist Fun Fruits Creme Supreme, Fruit Corners Shark Bites, Sunkist Fun Fruits Dinosaurs, Sunkist Spooky Fruit, Fruit Corners Thunder Jets, and Sunkist Fun Fruits Letters. Each advertisement highlights the fact that the products are made from real fruit and features many images of whole fruit and resulted in what was dubbed "The Great Fruit Snack Wars of 1985" from which both Sunkist and General Mills emerged to continue producing products to this day though some would declare General Mills the victor saying that, "no one has been able to take down General Mills in the fruit snack department" (Robare 2020). A recent TikTok trend evidences this idea. In 2021, videos of a scoop of ice cream wrapped in a Fruit Roll Up began to appear on the social media platform, and it wasn't until

> a few days after TikTok user Golnar Ghavami . . . posted a tutorial of the recipe . . . which has since received nearly 14 million views and 1.6 million likes, spawned *hundreds of others featuring users trying* the Fruit-Roll-Ups-wrapped ice cream for themselves, fueled both by curiosity and nostalgia for the fruity snack they had eaten as kids. (Follett 2023; emphases in the original)

In response to this, the company began posting different ways to eat Fruit Roll Ups on their social media platforms resulting in "over 23 million TikTok views and nearly 2 million combined likes, comments and shares in only a month" with its "best-performing video, [earning] 16.5 million views and nearly 1 million likes" (Follett 2023).

Despite the popularity of Fruit Roll Ups and other fruit snacks introduced during this decade and since, the ultra processing of the fruit included in these products makes them unhealthy and bear little resemblance to whole fruit, the images of which appear on packaging. In order to create fruit leather or dried fruit, the fruit must be boiled in sugar, which strips it of nutrients and results in a sugary fruit-flavored syrup lacking the benefits of whole fruit. Real fruit has natural fruit sugars that are slowly released into the bloodstream while Fruit Roll Ups contain added sugars that raise blood sugar levels quickly and can cause health-related issues if consumed in large quantities (Saleem 2024). Additionally, real fruit is high in fiber, yet Fruit Roll Ups contain little to none, which results in lack of satiety as well as lack of assistance with digestive health (Saleem 2024). Fruit Roll Ups contain artificial ingredients and additives, some of which are color dyes banned in other countries causing some to describe these products as snacks "sometimes chock full of pesticides and sugar" (Evans and Persellin 2022).

Welch's Fruit Snacks is another ultra-processed food that uses the Natural and Real Health Halo and perceived severity and perceived benefits Health Belief Model constructs both on its packaging and in its advertisements. A banner at the top of the pack proclaims, "Fruit is our 1st ingredient" above images of whole fruit. A 2021 commercial opens with a female narrator saying, "When fruit is first in your favorite snack, there's possibility in every pack you might snack delightfully" as images of young men and women are shown happily eating the snack (Welch's Fruit Snacks 2021a). After continuing with other scenarios, the commercial ends with an image of the package surrounded by whole fruit with the words "Snack Fruitfully" at the top and the words "Fruit is our 1st ingredient!" at the bottom (Welch's Fruit Snacks 2021a). It's worth noting that the first ingredient in most of these fruit snacks is fruit puree, which is actually processed fruit made into a thick sweet liquid. Also included in the ingredient list are corn syrup, modified corn starch, inulin, sugar, and several types of acids.

"What Would Pop-Tarts Do?"

Similar processing techniques are used in one of the most popular breakfast items ever created (Rice 2023). Dubbed "a wonderful breakfast treat" that are "always ready for a delicious change-of-pace breakfast" in the 1964 advertisement that introduced them, Pop-Tarts were promoted as "new, tasty, tender pastries already baked-from Kellogg's kitchen . . . each filled with a different and luscious flavor" (Algebramclain 2021). The advertisement features a large image of a toaster with two Pop-Tarts coming out and the words "Kellogg's Pop-Tarts, drop 'em in the toaster or eat 'em just as they are" on it with a plate containing one Pop-Tart split in two and an 8¢ coupon below that (Algebramclain 2021). On the other side of the coupon are four small images of the boxes of each flavor available, which includes strawberry, blueberry, apple-currant, and brown sugar cinnamon. Riding on the popularity in the 1950s and 1960s of "hyper-sweetened food products that could be eaten on the go" coupled with processing innovations used during the Second World War, Pop-Tarts were an instant success so much so that when they were introduced, they almost immediately ran out of stock, even running advertisements apologizing for running out (Wakeman 2024).

In a 1964 advertisement, a large headline below images of four boxes of Pop-Tarts reads, "Oops! We goofed" with smaller text underneath saying, "(Will You Excuse Us, Please)" (CNBC Digital Video 2023). Underneath this and to the left is a large image of a toaster with two Pop-Tarts coming out, with two hands in the foreground breaking a Pop-Tart in two with text underneath saying that they are made with Smucker's preserves. To the right of this are the words, "We ran out of POP-TARTS, the new breakfast treat" with smaller text underneath saying, "You fooled us. We had no idea our Pop-Tarts would become so popular—so soon" (CNBC Digital Video 2023). In the paragraph underneath, the text goes on to say that enough Pop-Tarts weren't made but also that the company had been improving the taste with a better crust and more filling "(more real strawberry and blueberry preserves, more apple-currant jelly, more brown sugar with cinnamon)" (CNBC Digital Video 2023). In the last paragraph, consumers are encouraged to "keep an eye peeled" for the product, which is touted as "the tastiest new idea that's come along to brighten breakfast for a long time" (CNBC Digital Video 2023).

Though some have called Pop-Tarts "the antithesis of a balanced breakfast," which "raises blood glucose to astronomical heights" and which "bottoms you out so you're hungry for another Pop-Tart, which you have, then you get fat, and you get diabetes" (Wakeman 2024), the product has consistently been a success. In 1967, frosting was introduced; 1968 brought about sprinkles; by 1973, there were nineteen different flavors; and today they come in bite-size and extra crunchy (Wakeman 2024). In 2022, about three billion Pop-Tarts were sold (Rice 2023). The battle between Kellogg's and Post to create a toaster pastry was also recently satirized in a comedy film, titled *Unfrosted*, released on Netflix on May 3, 2024.

A recent 2021 commercial illustrates the place the product has garnered in American society. The commercial begins with a male announcer saying, "Asking what would Pop-Tarts do is how you get from toast and jam to that's my jam; from sundae to sun day" with images of first toast and jam, then a Pop-Tart and a sundae, then another Pop-Tart before showing a woman bowling with "What Would Pop-Tarts Do" signs on the alley while the announcer asks, "So, what would Pop-Tarts do here?" as the camera cuts to an image of a homemade rollercoaster with a woman going down a hill to knock over bowling pins as the announcer says, "Yeah, that feels right" ("Pop-Tarts TV Spot" 2021). In another commercial a strawberry Pop-Tart is animated to do an improv session. The commercial begins with a woman eating a Pop-Tart while a male announcer excitedly says, "Rainbow sprinkles, jammy filling and frosting" after which the camera cuts to the animated strawberry Pop-Tart which says, "Friends, Pop-Tarts, pastry mates, lend me your ears" while another Pop-Tart that is holding cue cards next to yet another one holding a phone to video says, "Oh boy, we're going off the crust again" after which one of the Pop-Tarts asks, "Did we get it? I think we got it" standing next to the box (Pop-Tarts 2023). The packaging of the Pop-Tart includes a red banner underneath the word Pop-Tarts, which includes an image of a sliced strawberry with the words “frosted strawberry” in white text.

It’s worth noting that the year before, a lawsuit was filed by Kevin Brown in New York stating that the strawberry Pop-Tarts box was “misleading because the label gives consumers the impression the fruit filling only contains strawberries as its fruit ingredient” (Shivaram 2022). The case was dismissed two years later by a district judge who stated that the strawberry photo needed to be viewed in context saying that “no reasonable consumer would see the entire product label, reading the words ‘Frosted Strawberry Pop-Tarts’ next to a picture of a toaster pastry coated in frosting, and reasonably expect that fresh strawberries would be the sole ingredient in the Product” (Shivaram 2022). However, health experts noted that “in general, food marketing is all about the money. While Kellogg’s may not be claiming that Pop-Tarts are the same as fruits, the company knows that berries are trendy, and people are willing to pay more for them. Over-emphasizing the amount of strawberries in Pop-Tarts is just one of the many examples of manipulative marketing in the food industry” (Brown 2021). Also, researchers found that preservatives used in Pop-Tarts and other snack foods containing TBHQ, or tert-butylhydroquinone, may cause harm to human immune systems noting that they “suppress the immune system and decrease the response to vaccination” which “cannot validate the safety of a chemical for the immune system” (Naidenko 2021).

“True Comfort Can’t Be Faked”

In another commercial for an ultra-processed food using a version of the Natural and Real Health Halo and perceived severity and perceived benefits Health Belief Model constructs, two women comfortably dressed sit on and near a red velvet sofa eating ice cream. A female announcer says, “True comfort can’t be faked. Neither can our strawberries” as the camera focuses on one woman blissfully eating ice cream with a close up on her holding the Häagen-Dazs New York Strawberry Cheesecake container and then cuts to a full-screen shot of very red strawberries dripping juice as the announcer encourages viewers to eat the ice cream (“Häagen-Dazs New York Strawberry Cheesecake TV Spot, ‘True Comfort’ ” 2024). Following this, there is a shot of the two women smiling as they share the ice cream before the camera cuts to a shot of the Häagen-Dazs

New York Strawberry Cheesecake container with several whole strawberries placed near the open container. Though the commercial promotes the fact that the ice cream contains real strawberries that "can't be faked," the ingredients listed include cream, sugar, skim milk, strawberry puree, egg yolks, wheat flour, cream cheese, butter (cream, salt), graham flour, powdered sugar (sugar, corn starch), coconut oil, corn syrup, lemon juice concentrate, pectin, molasses, fruit and vegetable juice color, natural flavor, salt, baking soda. It's worth noting that strawberry puree is fourth on the list, and whole strawberries are not included in the list of ingredients in this ultra-processed food.

Prior to this, a commercial for the company's strawberry-flavored ice cream also uses the real-fruit theme by using images of the whole fruit. The advertisement opens with a close up of a spoon taking a scoop out of a container of strawberry ice cream. Though there is some vanilla ice cream, there are many red chunks in the scoop. Over piano music, a male announcer says, "Through passion and perseverance, Häagen-Dazs transforms the pure and simple into an extraordinary bite" ("Häagen-Dazs Strawberry TV Spot, 'Simple Strawberry'" 2017). As he speaks, the camera first cuts to an image of cream swirling with sliced strawberries being dropped in and then to a swirl of white and red then back to a whole strawberry being cut in half followed by an egg being taken out of a carton followed by sugar being sprinkled and then to another whole strawberry being picked off a bush. The final shot is of the container that features an image of a strawberry sliced in half. For this product, the ingredient list includes cream, skim milk, strawberries, cane sugar, egg yolks, making it unclear whether the strawberries are pureed or not. Even so, by definition, the inclusion of cane sugar denotes an ultra-processed food classification.

In some cases, the Natural and Real Health Halo and perceived severity and perceived benefits Health Belief Model constructs are less obvious but are still quite present. In a 2015 advertisement for Baskin-Robbins, the focus of the commercial is celebrating the company's thirty-one flavors on the thirty-first of the month when consumers receive a scoop for $1.31; a scoop of strawberry ice cream is in the very front of a shot of the various flavors available. In other cases, the use of the real-fruit theme by an ice-cream company is obvious even in the company's name. One of the best examples of this is a 2013 commercial introducing Fruttare ice cream. In the commercial, a female announcer tells consumers, "You've never tased anything like new Fruttare. The taste of delicious strawberries and creamy milk bursting together and perfectly frozen in time" ("Fruttare Strawberry and Milk TV Spot" 2013). Though the commercial is about a camping trip gone bad, which ends with the announcer telling viewers to "look on the bright side" and that "it's all good," there are images of whole strawberries with milk coming up behind them, then being dropped into the milk and formed into the ice-cream bar as well as a version of the word fruit in the company's name ("Fruttare Strawberry and Milk TV Spot" 2013). The company, which is a division of Magnum, the makers of Breyers, Klondike, and Popsicle brands among others, also features banana, peach, mango, lime, orange, and coconut flavors as well with each package featuring its corresponding whole fruit on it thus promising nutrition benefits and prevention of illness while illustrating the use of the perceived benefits and perceived severity Health Belief Model constructs.

Additional ice-cream makers using the real-fruit theme in the Natural and Real Health Halo and perceived severity and perceived benefits Health Belief Model constructs on their packing include, but are not limited to, the following: Yosicle Swirlz Raspberry-Strawberry-Banana, Breyers Natural Strawberry ice cream, Breyers Strawberry Shortcake ice cream, Jolly Rancher Popsicles, Breyer's Mango ice cream, Orange-Cherry-Grape Popsicles, Breyers Frozen Dairy Desert Cherry Vanilla, Firecracker Popsicles (cherry, white lemon, blue raspberry), Good Humor Strawberry Shortcake bars, Breyers Peach ice cream, and Good Humor Creamsicle bars. Other ice cream companies using the fruit health halo on their packaging include, but are not limited to, the following: Ben & Jerry's Strawberry Cheesecake ice cream, Edy's Strawberry ice cream, Perry's Strawberry ice cream, Tillamook Oregon Strawberry ice cream, Creamy Creations Poteet Strawberry ice cream, Turkey Hill Simply Natural Strawberries & Cream ice cream, Little Debbie Strawberry Shortcake Rolls ice cream, Friendly's Strawberry Krunch Strawberry Ice Cream Cake Singles, Turkey Hill Black Cherry ice cream, Ben & Jerry's Cherry Garcia ice cream, Private Selection Amaretto Cherry Cordial ice cream, Tillamook Oregon Dark Cherry ice cream, Häagen-Dazs Cherry Vanilla ice cream, Tillamook Peaches & Cream ice cream, Private Selection Granny Smith Caramel Apple ice cream, Jonny Pops Organic Watermelon pops, Outshine Watermelon Fruit Bars, goodpop Watermelon Agave pops, The Frozen Farmer Orange Cream Frobert, Futero Tangerine ice cream, Sundae Shoppe Orange Cream bar, Häagen-Dazs Pineapple Coconut ice cream, Friendly's Vanilla Pineapple ice cream, Häagen-Dazs Mango ice cream, Valentini Mango ice cream, Blue Bunny Banana Split frozen desert, PET Banana Split ice cream, Futero Coconut ice cream, Tillamook Marionberry Pie ice cream, Häagen-Dazs Blueberry ice cream, Turkey Hill All Natural Blueberry ice cream, and Jeni's Lemon & Blueberries Parfait ice cream.

Amazin' Fruit Gummy Bears

Candy products are another area where fruit themes and Health Belief Model constructs are oftentimes used both in advertisements and on packaging. One product took the idea of using fruit-flavored candies to a different level in the 1990s when it included animated dancing candy bears in its advertisement. A 1993 commercial for Fruit Gummy Bears opens with an animated, red-colored candy bear carrying a whole strawberry chanting, "It's amazing fruit. Yeah," before being joined by a yellow-colored one carrying a pineapple, then a green one carrying an apple, an orange one carrying an orange, and a purple one carrying a bunch of grapes after which an announcer says, "Presenting the one and only fruit bearing Gummy Bears. Made with the goodness of real fruit juice, they're called amazin' fruit," at which point the dancing Gummy Bears carrying the fruit begin to chant "Amazin' fruit" as the camera focuses on a package of the product positioned in a bowl of whole fruit as the announcer says, "Amazin' Fruit is so fruity, you can hardly bear it" (Zyber9 2011). In a less technically advanced advertisement with a similar focus on fruit, a 1997 Starburst Fruit Twists commercial opens with a man at a party holding an orange-colored Starburst Fruit Twist and wiggling it around in front of two women and saying, "See my wiggle . . . my twist . . . my forbidden dance oosh oosh" (Sessions at Studio B 2009). The camera cuts to a pile of whole fruit with a hand holding a package of the product as an announcer introduces the product before a disco ball with the company's logo is shown with whole fruit rotating around it. Both products have been discontinued, though Gummy Bears and Starburst candies are still in stores with both still using images of fruit on their packaging and employing use of the perceived benefits and perceived severity Health Belief Model constructs.

The concept of dancing fruit-flavored gummies, however, is not limited to the 1990s. A 2024 Superbowl commercial for Nerds Gummy Clusters opens with a large, red-colored gummy candy dancing to a song from *Flashdance* with the words, "Oh, what a feeling!" parodying the wet chair scene from the film with Nerds candies poured onto the gummy candy to make a Nerds Gummy Cluster. As the Nerds candies fall onto the gummy candy, a female announcer says, "The union of fruity, sweet gummy and tangy, crunchy Nerds. Nerds Gummy Clusters. Unleash your senses," at which point actress Addison Rae is shown on a couch eating a bag of the product (Best Commercials 2024). Not to be outdone, Haribo Goldbears launched a Super Bowl commercial in the same broadcast, which featured two football players sitting on a bench during what appears to be the game. One is eating the gummy bears and asks the other in a child's voice whether he would like some, telling him that "The longer I chew it, the fruitier and fruitier it gets," to which the other man, also in a child's voice, says, "These are the bestest bears ever" (Wen 2024). This particular commercial will be discussed again in Chapter 4 for its use of the Identity Health Halo as well as the Natural and Real Health Halo described in this chapter.

Use of the fruit themes can also be seen on many other candy packages, including, but not limited to, the following: Hershey's Kisses Strawberry Ice Cream Cone Candy, Colombina Tiger Pops Watermelon & Strawberry Ice Cream Lollipops Pack—Dual-Flavor, Color-Changing Suckers, Lifesavers Hard Candy, Creme Savers, Mike and Ike Original Chewy Assorted Candy, Tootsie Fruit Chews, Jolly Rancher Hard Candy, Chewy Lemonhead Fruit Mix candy, Laffy Taffy Fruit Combos Candy, PUSH POP Gummy Roll candy, Mamba Fruit Chews, Frutati Assorted Hard Candy, Kool-Aid Fruity Chews, Sour Punch Strawberry Bites, Mott's Medley Fruit Flavored Suckers, Fruit-tella Juicy Chews, Tayas Multi Fruit Milky Hard Candy, Lovely Organic Chewy Candies, HI-CHEW Infrusions, Fruit Gushers, Mentos Fruits, Fox's Fruit Flavored Crystal Clear candy, Sakuma Assorted Fruit Drops, Green Apple Chews, Liberty Orchard Delights Fruit Delights, Sweet Tarts Fruit Flavored Soft & Chewy Twisted Ropes, and Starburst Original Fruit Chews.

No Artificial Flavors or Preservatives

It was done quietly. They hoped no one would notice. And, according to the company, they were right. In 2015, Kraft removed artificial flavors, preservatives, and dyes from its Macaroni & Cheese and conducted what the company called "the world's largest blind taste test," which led to a national marketing campaign to inform consumers about their efforts to keep the taste of the product the same (Shannon and Aguayo 2016). Included in the campaign was a 2016 print magazine advertisement with a large headline reading "We would invite you to try it, but you already have" in light blue font on a dark blue background (Fargo's Treasures 2024). Next to the word "have" is a fork filled with Macaroni & Cheese with an image of the product underneath and to the left. Underneath the fork is a paragraph of text which says,

> When we took the artificial flavors, preservatives and dyes out of Kraft Macaroni & Cheese, we wanted to be sure it still tasted like the Kraft Macaroni & Cheese you know and love. So three months ago, we quietly started selling the new recipe in our old boxes to see if you'd notice. And your silence spoke volumes. After all, it's pretty hard to speak with your mouth full. (Fargo's Treasures 2024)

Underneath this at the bottom of the page is one noodle in the shape of a smile with the words, "You know you love it" underneath (Fargo's Treasures 2024). The company "claimed to sell more than 50 million boxes" after the change and before informing customers about it (Shannon and Aguayo 2016).

"It's Changed. But It Hasn't."

Other print advertisements in the campaign featured headlines that included "New and improved and you can't even tell," "We couldn't help but notice that you didn't notice," and "It's changed. But it hasn't" (Salas 2024). In addition to this, a series of television commercials were launched that featured a news-like male announcer dressed in a suit and holding a box of the product telling viewers that three months earlier in the year, they began "selling Kraft Mac and Cheese with no artificial flavors, preservatives, or dyes" and highlighting various people who didn't notice it, such as moms, kids, dogs, a man named Bill, millennials, baristas, a billionaire, and a guy "who says he's working from home" (Salas 2024). At the end of each set of commercials, the announcer reminds people that it "still tastes like Kraft Mac & Cheese" and that "It's changed. But it hasn't" (Salas 2024). As the creative director of the agency originating the campaign writes at her website, "We knew no amount of advertising could convince worried fans that their mac and cheese would taste the same. So we . . . told Kraft the best solution was not to advertise the change at all. Instead, we asked Kraft to package their new recipe in their original boxes, changing only the ingredient label" (Salas 2024).

The no-artificial-ingredients theme as well as the perceived severity, perceived benefits, and perceived barriers Health Belief Model constructs are obvious in these advertisements through the emphasis on natural ingredients that consumers believe have the ability to prevent disease and illness. It's worth noting, however, that the product itself is "not really" any healthier than the older formulation (Shannon and Aguayo 2016). The older version

> contained a significant amount of saturated fat and sugar and an excessive amount of sodium—nearly 40 percent of the Institute of Medicine's recommended daily intake per serving . . . while Kraft's reformulation removed artificial colors and slightly lowered the sugar content (from 7 grams to 6 grams per serving), it did nothing to address the saturated fat or high sodium content. (Shannon & Aguayo 2016)

Included in the marketing campaign was also a checklist on the product box, positioned in the lower right corner on a notebook-like page with checkmarks on it. The headline of the list reads, "The Taste You Love," while the checkmarks are "No Artificial Preservatives, No Artificial Flavors, No Artificial Dyes" with a red checkmark against each and the word "no" bolded. Currently, the product packaging uses the words "no artificial flavors, preservatives or dyes" in white font at the top of its dark blue boxes and near the bottom on its frozen macaroni and cheese packaging. This wording is also used on microwavable four-pack packaging as well as Nickelodeon Paw Patrol and Sponge Bob Square Pants products.

Additional pasta packaging using the Natural and Real Health Halo and perceived severity, perceived benefits, and perceived barriers Health Belief Model constructs include, but are not limited to, the following: Knorr Pasta Sides, which come in various flavors and include text with checkmarks on the right side of the pouch with a headline "Our Promise" and a checkmark beside the words "No Artificial Flavors or Preservatives," and then another checkmark by the words "High Quality, Flavorful Ingredients," Rao's Made for Home PENNE ALLA VODKA, Chef Boyardee Pasta in Tomato and Meat Sauce, Chef Boyardee Spaghetti and Meatballs, Chef Boyardee Lasagna, Chef Boyardee Cheesy Burger Macaroni, Chef Boyardee Pasta in Butter Sauce, Cabot Classic Yellow Cheddar Macaroni & Cheese, Cabot Pepper Jack Macaroni & Cheese, Lean Cuisine Marketplace Chicken with Peanut Sauce Linguini, Woolworth's Italian Style Chicken with Whole Grain Penne Pasta, Annie's Homegrown Quinoa Rice Pasta & White Cheddar, Annie's Homegrown Rice Shell Pasta & Creamy White Cheddar, Annie's Homegrown Macaroni & Cheese Classic Cheddar, Annie's Homegrown Organic Cheesy Ravioli, Simek's Italian Sausage Lasagna, Simek's Italian Sausage Baked Ziti, Marie Callender's Spaghetti & Meatballs Bowl, Birds Eye Martini Marina Veggie Pasta, Birds Eye Penne with Olive Oil Veggie Pasta, Birds Eye Mac & Cheese Shells with White Cheddar Cheese Sause, Manischewitz Mac & Cheese, Simply Nature Organic Deluxe Shells & Cheese, Simply Nature

Organic Deluxe Macaroni & Cheese, Hamburger Helper Four Cheese Lasagna, Hamburger Helper Cheeseburger Macaroni, Milletbank Pasta, and Cook Smith Healthy Wheat Pasta.

FDA Definitions

In its Code of Regulations, Part 101—Food Labeling section, subpart B—Specific Food Labeling Requirements, the U.S. FDA (2023) defines artificial flavor or flavoring as having "the function of which is to impart flavor, which is not derived from a spice, fruit or fruit juice, vegetable or vegetable juice, edible yeast, herb, bark, bud, root, leaf or similar plant material, meat, fish, poultry, eggs, dairy products, or fermentation products thereof." Taken further, this means the use of anything not mentioned above is considered an artificial flavor and would not qualify for use of the Natural and Real Health Halo.

In the same document, chemical preservatives are defined as "any chemical that, when added to food, tends to prevent or retard deterioration thereof, but does not include common salt, sugars, vinegars, spices, or oils extracted from spices, substances added to food by direct exposure thereof to wood smoke, or chemicals applied for their insecticidal or herbicidal properties" (United States Food and Drug Administration 2023). As a result, the use of the exclusions listed above would not qualify for the use of the Natural and Real Health Halo. The FDA's regulations also require that use of artificial flavors, colors, and chemical preservatives be noted on food packages.

"Bester" Hot Dogs and Moldy Whoppers

One of the most popular ultra-processed product types where the no-artificial-ingredients theme is used in advertising and on product labels is packaged meat. An example of a commercial highlighting this type of health halo comes from Hebrew National Hot Dogs in 2012 with a thirteen-second Facebook advertisement. The advertisement begins with the company's logo and then switches to a young girl biting into a hot dog. As her eyes light up, a male announcer says, "Hebrew National Hot Dogs are the best of the best of the best. They don't get any bester than this. OMG. It's Kosher with no fillers, by-products, artificial flavors, artificial colors," as the camera focuses on a graphic with a big

NO on the top and the previous list set below before the announcer ends with "Hebrew National, the better-than-a-hot-dog hot dog" ("Hebrew National TV Commercial for Girl at Carnival" 2012). Five years later, the company would launch a series of commercials reminding consumers about the changes in society such as the way young people contact each other for dates (corded phone versus cell phone) and the hectic life of a mother of four (all four children participating in the same activity versus four different ones), which featured the product package with the words "No artificial flavors, no artificial colors, no fillers, no by-products, no gluten" in the ad along with the reminder that the company remains strict about its standards.

Similarly, a Johnsonville Smoked Sausage commercial uses the product packaging to remind viewers of the naturalness of its product. The 2021, fifteen-second commercial opens with a female announcer saying, "If you're cooking with this" as the camera focuses on a cast iron pan on the stove with sausage as she continues, "and you don't see this," while there is a shot of the product where a red circle is drawn around the words, "Made with 100% Premium Pork," where directly to the side of that are the words in checklist format, "No Fillers, No Artificial Flavors Or Colors, No Msg" (Official Johnsonville 2021). She continues by saying that "then it's not Johnsonville and your family will taste the difference as they dig into this or that" as shots of two dishes containing sausages are shown before the announcer encourages viewers to "cook with Johnsonville Sausage," which she says, "tastes better because it's made better" (Official Johnsonville 2021).

Arguably one of the most controversial advertising campaigns using the Natural and Real Health Halo and perceived severity and perceived benefits Health Belief Model constructs for a meat product was introduced in early 2020. Burger King's "Moldy Whopper" campaign, which featured a large image of the company's signature burger aged for nearly a month and covered in mold and included a tagline of "The beauty of no artificial preservatives," drew comments on social media calling the image "ugly" and "disgusting," yet was viewed for "1.4 million total minutes on Facebook" and earned "8.4 million organic media impressions" making it one of the company's more successful advertising campaigns resulting in "the awareness around Burger King having no artificial ingredients . . . [being] 5× higher among people who saw Moldy Whopper than among those who didn't see Moldy Whopper" (Machado 2020).

A forty-five-second commercial from this campaign begins with several hands putting together a Whopper, which is placed on a stand. The background is black and there is music with Aretha Franklin singing "What a Difference a Day Made." After the Whopper is assembled, there is a cut to black as Franklin sings and words on the screen say, "The Whopper, Day 01" (The One Club for Creativity 2020). The next shot is of the burger as first the lettuce wilts and then the entire burger seems to melt before mold begins to grow on it. The camera shows several closeups of the mold growing and then pulls back to a full shot of the entire burger, which is almost entirely covered in green mold until finally there is a large yellow circle that marks a transition to show the burger with the words "The Whopper, Day 34" over it before a fade to black upon which the words "The Beauty of No Artificial Preservatives" appear as Franklin sings about the difference being you (The One Club for Creativity 2020). The final shot is of the company's logo over the black screen. The commercials in this campaign use strong, repulsive images to drive home the fact that their product does not contain artificial preservatives, thus not only illustrating the no-artificial-ingredients theme in the Natural and Real Health Halo but also the perceived benefits and perceived susceptibility Health Belief Model constructs by reminding viewers that this ultra-processed food does not contain artificial preservatives, which are believed by consumers to cause illness.

Additional packaged meat products using the no-artificial-ingredients theme include, but are not limited to, the following: Nathan's Skinless Beef Hot Dogs, Nathan's Coney Island Beef Frankfurters, Bar S Beef Jumbo Franks, Kayem Old Tyme Beef Frankfurters, Kayem Beef Hot Dogs, Kayem Beef & Pork Hot Dogs, Marketside Jumbo Uncured Angus Beef Franks, Ball Park Smoked Turkey Franks, Ball Park Beef Franks, Stahl-Meyer Hot Dogs, Stahl-Meyer Beef Frankfurters, Stahl-Meyer Chicken Frankfurters, Member's Mark Beef Franks, Berks All Beef Franks, Berks Grill Franks, Hofman Natural Casing German Brand Franks, Organic Prairie Uncured Beef Hot Dogs, Oscar Mayer Classic Uncured Beef Franks, Oscar Mayer Classic Uncured Wieners, McCormick Grill Mates Classic Beef Franks, McCormick Grill Mates Smokey Applewood Beef Franks, Parkview Uncured Angus Beef Franks, Parkview Classic Hot Dogs, Aidells All Natural Chicken & Apple Chicken Sausage, Al Fresco Roasted Garlic Chicken Sausage, Johnsonville Andouille Smoked Sausage, Johnsonville Mild Italian Sausage, Johnsonville Original Recipe Breakfast Sausage, Johnsonville Turkey Breakfast Sausage, Jimmy Dean All Natural Regular Premium Pork Sausage, Jimmy Dean Premium Italian Pork Sausage, Nature's Promise Mango Habanero Chicken Sausage, Nature's Promise Sweet Italian Sausage, Simple Truth Hot & Spicy Sausage Links, Tennessee Pride Mild Sausage Patties, Jack's

Gourmet Beef Merguez Sausage, Jack's Gourmet Mexican Style Chorizo, Burton Apple with Gouda Smoked Chicken Sausage, Vegie Delights Chicken Style Sausages, Vegie Delights Thick BBQ Sausages, Dearborn Hot & Spicy Smoked Sausages, Dearborn Jalapeno Smoked Sausages, Meat Crafters Cumerland Banger English Breakfast Sausage, Jennie-O Turkey Chorizo, Coleman Polish Kielbasa Uncured Sausage, Parkview Turkey Polska Kielbasa, Johnsonville Polish Turkey Kielbasa, Pelleh Poultry Duck Kielbasa, and Kayem Small Batch Polska Kielbasa.

"Love Cereal Again"

Over the past decade or two, cereal manufacturers have focused on using the Natural and Real Health Halo and all four of the Health Belief Model constructs in their advertisements. In early 2016, General Mills began an advertising campaign to remind people to "Love Cereal Again" and to highlight the reformulation of seven of its cereals to remove artificial flavors and colors (Ramstad 2016). One of the first advertisements in this campaign begins with various shots of children having fun, including a little girl running around inside a revolving door yelling "again," a group of kids at a party yelling "again" as one swings a stick at a piñata, others yelling "again" when they are flying a remote-controlled airplane, a child "swung in circles while wearing a cape and [another] swinging between two adults as they walk over a bridge" before there is a shot of a young girl eating a bowl of Trix cereal while her father reaches for the box and a female announcer says, "General Mills is removing artificial flavors and colors from our cereals" as the camera switches to a shot of five boxes of cereal including Cocoa Puffs, Cinnamon Toast Crunch, Honey Nut Cheerios, Reese's Puffs and Rice Chex as the female announcer continues, "so you can love cereal" as the camera focuses on the father throwing cereal in his mouth while the young girl yells, "again" before the words "love cereal again" appear over the image ("General Mills TV Spot, 'Again'" 2016). In addition to using the Real and Natural Health Halo, this advertisement employs the perceived severity and perceived benefits constructs of the Health Belief Model by promising avoidance of illness and the benefit of "loving" an ultra-processed food product. The perceived barriers construct is also evident in the overcoming of the obstacle of cereal's reputation as an unhealthy food while doing little to improve on the nutrition of the product.

Another advertisement in this campaign featured three Honey Nut Cheerios rolling over the top of the cereal box with a string attached to all of them as they roll of the edge and dangle next to the side of the box with the words "No Artificial Colors, No Artificial Flavors, No High Fructose Corn Syrup" above the sign the Cheerios were holding which says, "Gluten Free" and the three Cheerios each in place of the "o" in the word "No" before a final shot is shown of four boxes of different Cheerios flavors ("Cheerios TV Spot, 'Rappel'" 2016). Amongst a backlash due to the muted "natural" colors of Trix cereal, the company re-released what they called Classic Trix, which described the product on its box as "naturally and artificially fruit flavored sweetened corn puffs" and advertised "They're back! 6 Fruity Colors" beside a large photo of a bowl of the colorful cereal. The association of bright, fruity colors, albeit chemically created, is firmly entrenched in the cereal's history. "When Trix cereal was first released in 1954, advertisements trumpeted its 'bright fruit-colors!' and personified its colorful puffs as though they were eager to be eaten: 'Gay little sugared corn puffs in a happy mixture of colors—red, yellow, orange. Fun to see! A joy to eat!' Color itself promised to communicate pleasure," creating a powerful draw for many that can override health concerns in which "nostalgia for childhood Trix colors emphasizes the pleasures of the product's bright colors over its chemical dangers in what might be hedonistic amnesia" (Keyser 2017). Some would say that "perhaps instead of abjuring these dyes . . . we would do better to recognize our kinship with a 'silly rabbit' who articulates our still-unsatisfied hunger" (Keyser 2017).

At the Cheerios website homepage and in recent commercials, the heart-healthy benefits of the cereal are advertised. There is no mention of artificial flavors or preservatives in the majority of the company's advertising. A recent example of this is a commercial for a limited edition of heart-shaped Honey Nut Cheerios in which the company's mascot "Buzz" says, "Great news, America. Back for a limited time, we've changed the shape of Honey Nut Cheerios because we want people to know that they're delicious and can help lower cholesterol," as he is shown sitting on a doctor's desk holding a heart-shaped Cheerio before he continues, "Heart healthy. Get it? A heart. Ha, ha" before a shot of him in heart costume is shown in front of five boxes of different flavored Cheerios (Cheerios 2021). This advertisement illustrates the use of all four Health Belief Model constructs by first promising avoidance (perceived severity) of heart health problems (perceived susceptibility) with a delicious taste (perceived benefits) resulting in good health (perceived barriers).

Natural Images

Cereal bars are another product area where the no-artificial-ingredients theme is used quite often yet sometimes with the addition of further clarification. An example of this comes from a 2017 Nature Valley cereal bar commercial. The commercial begins with a long shot of grass-covered hills and a valley with the company's logo at the forefront. A male announcer says, "At Nature Valley, we believe in carefully selected, delicious ingredients" as the camera cuts to a shot of oats growing in a field then to shots of nuts on a baking sheet and honey in a jar as the announcer continues, "so we use no artificial flavors, no colors and no preservatives in any of our cereal bars," during which time there are different shots of the cereal bars being created in a kitchen setting with the words "Nature Valley Recipe Development Kitchen" in the bottom right corner (Nature Valley UK 2017). The announcer says "Nature Valley" while a final shot of three boxes of the product on a table with the company's logo above and the words "No Artificial Flavours, Colours, or Preservatives" in between the two (Nature Valley UK 2017). It's also worth noting that the company's logo background is sunshine yellow with grass green letters.

In addition to touting the absence of artificial colors and preservatives, the company has taken the Natural and Real Health Halo a step further by adding beautiful images of nature as well as those of natural products including nuts and oats growing in a field. While it's not uncommon for ultra-processed food manufacturers to combine more than one type of theme or construct, the sprawling images of nature combined with the reminder about no artificial colors or preservatives results in the addition of strong visual cues that reinforce the Natural and Real Health Halo as well as the perceived severity, perceived benefits, and perceived barriers Health Belief Model constructs. The company has a long history of including striking images of nature in its commercials. Though the actual reminder about no artificial colors and preservatives is not always included in the commercial, the images of nature are designed to serve as a visual reminder. A good example of this is the company's partnership with the National Park Foundation, which is highlighted in a recent commercial with images of nature to remind consumers of the absence of artificial colors and preservatives. The commercial opens with a close up of an individual package of Nature Valley Crunch Oats 'N Honey granola bar. As the wrapper opens in the middle, a female announcer says, "On average we spend 93% of our lives indoors" as the camera shows a woman and a young girl sitting on a log looking at a lake ("Nature Valley Oats 'N Honey Crunchy Granola Bars TV Spot, 'You Could Miss It'" 2024). The camera pans around to show the young girl with an open mouth in a surprised state of emotion as the camera pans around again to show a rainbow over the lake and the female announcer continues, "but can you image missing a moment like this?" as the woman opens a package of Nature Valley granola bars and gives one to the young girl ("Nature Valley Oats 'N Honey Crunchy Granola Bars TV Spot, 'You Could Miss It'" 2024). They are shown eating together and then hugging as the announcer says, "Life happens out there" with the words above the two looking at the lake with the rainbow above before a final shot mimicking the opening one with the addition of the words, "proud partner of National Park Foundation" below ("Nature Valley Oats 'N Honey Crunchy Granola Bars TV Spot, 'You Could Miss It'" 2024). In this case, the beautiful lake with a rainbow above serves as a reminder that there are no artificial ingredients and preservatives added to the product.

Additional cereal products using the no-artificial-ingredients theme include, but are not limited to, the following: Good & Gather Organic Frosty Flakes, Annie's Homegrown Organic Berry Bunnies Oat, Corn, and Rice Cereal, Annie's Homegrown Organic Coca Bunnies Oat, Corn, and Rice Cereal, Annie's Homegrown Organic Cinna Bunnies Cinnamon Cereal, Mom's Best Cereals Honey Nut Toasty O's, Mom's Best Cereals Toasted Wheatfuls Whole Grain Wheat Cereal, Cookie Crips cereal, Nature Valley Raisin Oat Clusters cereal, Nature Valley Chocolate Oat Clusters cereal, Nature Valley Honey Oat Clusters cereal, Kroger Honey Nut Toasted Oats cereal, Total 100% Whole Grain Flakes, Essential Everyday Honey Nut Toasted Oats cereal, Essential Everyday Toast Oats cereal, Berry Berry Kix cereal, Kix cereal, Nature's Path Cinnamon Bun Rhino Rolls organic cereal, Nature's Path Peanut Butter & Chocolate Leapin' Lemurs organic cereal, Barbara's Bakery Organic Wild Puffs, Apple Cinnamon Chex cereal, Vanilla Chex cereal, Chocolate Chex Gluten Free cereal, Quaker Instant Maple Brown Sugar Oatmeal, Quaker Instant Apples & Cinnamon Oatmeal, Quaker Simply Granola Nuts, Honey & Almonds, Quaker Chewy Oatmeal Raisin Granola Bars, Quaker Chewy Chocolate Chip Granola Bars, Quaker Chewy Peanut Butter Chocolate Chip Granola Bars, Trix Cereal Bar, Nutri Grain Strawberry Breakfast Bars, Nutri Grain Apple Cinnamon Breakfast Bars, Nutri Grain Cherry Breakfast Bars, Quaker Chewy Dipps Chocolate Chip Chocolate Covered Granola Bars, Quaker Chewy Dipps Peanut Butter Chocolate Covered Granola Bars, Nestle Fitness Chocolate Breakfast Cereal Bar, Happy

Belly Almond Granola Bars, Happy Belly Peanut Granola Bars, and Our Family Sweet & Salty Peanut Granola Bars.

"We Believe in Real Food"

While there are many other ultra-processed food product categories that use the no-artificial-ingredients theme in the Natural and Real Health Halo and perceived severity and perceived benefits Health Belief Model constructs, space does not permit an overview of all of them; however, there are two worth mentioning. The first comes from Subway restaurants with a 2017 commercial featuring a man in a restaurant waiting while a Subway worker makes his sandwich and highlighting the fact that it is a Footlong Steak & Cheese sandwich, which "is the master of the menu," offered for a limited time for $6, "made with lean steak and now triumphantly free of artificial preservatives flavors" (Commercials Funny 2017). The other is an advertisement for Whole Foods Market that opens with images of parents feeding young children as a female announcer says, "At Whole Foods Market, we believe in food that's naturally beautiful and fresh, delicious and powerful, and full of nutrients. Food that makes us nourished and mighty" as images of a couple cooking salmon are shown before images of feet running in water and then finally resting on a woman holding a surfboard while eating an apple as the announcer says, "and connects us to the natural world so there are no artificial colors, no artificial flavors, no artificial preservatives in any of the food we sell" (Whole Foods Market 2017). The final shot is of people eating dinner as the announcer says, "We believe in real food" as a woman smiles and eats a forkful of food (Whole Foods Market 2017).

While the Natural and Real Health Halo is used frequently in both ultra-processed food advertisements and on product labels, use of the words "no sugar added," "low fat," and "whole wheat," "fortified," and "gluten free" are also used quite frequently. The Nutrition Health Halo will be examined in the next chapter as it is used in ultra-processed advertisements and on product labels.

3

Nutrition Health Halo

The Nutrition Health Halo is defined as the use of text, colors, or images associated with food that provides sustenance and nutrients to the human body, is free from unprocessed ingredients, and nutritionally beneficial in the advertising or labeling of a product that creates a false perception of healthiness about the item. Some examples of this health halo include the use of such words as "no sugar added," "low fat," "whole wheat," and "gluten free" as well as the concept of advertising vitamin- and mineral-fortified ultra-processed food products.

No Sugar Added . . . Well, Almost

It was a war of words, fought in the pages of medical and nutrition literature fueled by an onslaught of cardiovascular-related deaths in the late 1950s and President Eisenhower's 1955 heart attack. On one side stood American nutritionist Ancel Keys touting fat as the main dietary cause of these deaths, while on the other, British nutritionist John Yudkin targeted refined carbohydrates, mainly sugar, as the culprit. After beginning his major Seven Countries Study, Keys concluded that fat was the main cause of heart-related diseases while Yudkin was also conducting a study in which he named sugar as the main cause. Both published the results in peer-reviewed journals culminating in a nutritional war that involved Yudkin discrediting Keys's facts as awkward and convenient to his personal beliefs. It would, however, be decades later that Yudkin's ideas were given the same attention as Keys's due to "the dominance of 'low-fat' dietary recommendations that followed" resulting in "Keys and his critique of fat [winning] the debate and Yudkin's warnings about sugar [staying] dormant until recent years" (Meach 2018).

It wasn't until the publication of his bestselling book, *Pure, White, and Deadly: How Sugar Is Killing Us and What We Can Do to Stop It*, in 1972 after years of writing weight loss books promoting sugar as the cause of obesity that Yudkin's ideas would gain wider appeal. In his book, Yudkin included "two key statements that no one can refute," the first of which is that "there is no physiological requirement for sugar" noting that "all human nutritional requirements can be met in full without having to take a single spoon of white or brown or raw sugar, on its own or in any food or drink," and the second one being that "if only a small fraction of what is already known about the effects of sugar were to be revealed in relation to any other material used as a food additive, that material would be banned" (Yudkin 1998, 2–3). He would go on to name sugar as the cause of many diseases, including obesity, heart disease, cancer, diabetes, hyperactivity, eczema, and arthritis. Despite the initial reluctance to accept Yudkin's ideas, many others have now joined his war against sugar including author and Dr. Robert Lustig and Chef Jamie Oliver (Meach 2018). Yudkin's book was reprinted in 2012 and "hailed a 'prophecy' which foretold the consequences of our increasing consumption of sugar long before the scientific evidence was available" (Meach 2018).

The result of this is the creation of the Nutrition Health Halo with a zero-sugar theme, which is especially popular in cereal product advertisements and labels today. In the 1950s, however, drawing on the perceived benefits construct of the Health Belief Model, the inclusion of sugar was advertised as a benefit in cereal products, with some companies even using the word in the name of the product such as Post's Sugar Crips, Post's Sugar Rice Krinkles, Kellogg's Sugar Smacks, Kellogg's Sugar Frosted Flakes, General Mills' Sugar Smiles, General Mills' Sugar Jets, and Nabisco Sugar Sweet Rice Honeys. Three decades later, the absence of sugar became a major selling point for cereal manufacturers. An example of this is a 1984 commercial featuring a young Wayne Gretzky. The commercial begins with an image of the hockey legend in action as a male announcer introduces a new star—Pro Stars cereal. The camera cuts to Gretzky sitting at a breakfast table saying,

> My mother taught me that a good nutritious breakfast is important. That's why new Pro Stars cereal is part of my breakfast now. First, an ounce of Pro Stars cereal with four ounces of milk is a good source of protein. Second, Pro Stars have a great toasted oats taste, lightly sweetened without added sugar. See, no sugar added that's good (Retro Rabbit Ears 2018),

at which point the camera cuts to a close up of the box where the words "No Sugar Added" are in yellow at the top of the box (Retro Rabbit Ears 2018). Gretzky then tells viewers that his mom likes his picture too just before the final shot of the box of cereal with the words "A Touch of Sweetness Without Added Sugar" next to it are shown (Retro Rabbit Ears 2018). The Health Belief Model constructs of perceived severity, perceived benefits, and perceived barriers are employed in this commercial with Gretzky telling viewers about the lack of added sugar and the higher protein content (perceived severity), the light sweetness without added sugar (perceived benefits), and the good taste (perceived barriers).

The 1980s would bring an even greater focus on healthy eating resulting in increased use of the no-sugar-added theme in cereal advertisements. Following are several examples. A 1980 commercial for Shredded Wheat featured a family sitting at a picnic table in a wheat field singing about how they never eat the cereal whole but instead mash them up after which a male announcer tells viewers that the product is made of 100 percent whole wheat with no added sugar or salt. The final shot in the commercial is of two boxes of the cereal with the words "100% Whole Wheat No Added Sugar" in red font underneath (Dave's Archives 2020). A 1982 Grape-Nuts commercial opens with a close up of a squirrel eating a nut and a child telling his grandfather that the squirrel is eating the nuts they picked. The grandfather replies saying, "That's because they've got a natural goodness and good taste he just loves" to which the grandson replies that he gets a treat for breakfast as the grandfather reminds him that they do, too, with Grape-Nuts whose "goodness starts with nature's wheat and barley" with "crunchy nuggets baked up and toasted for a good nutty taste. No sugar added" as the camera cuts to a close up of the box (Dave's Archives 2020). A 1984 Kellogg's Corn Flakes commercial begins with an African American man jogging as an announcer asks viewers whether they want to "build a super day," and if so, then they need to start with the cereal that is delicious and low in sugar and their most nutritious corn flakes ever (Dave's Archives 2020).

Similarly, a 1987 commercial for Kix cereal begins with a sleepover and a group of young boys looking for something to eat. They find the Kix and begin to eat as they try to read the box. One of them pointing to the words "Low in sugar, no added colors, no added flavors" asks what it says while another one responds saying that he doesn't know before an even younger girl comes in and says that she knows but she won't tell before an announcer says, "Kix, still low in sugar. Great new taste. Ask your kids" (Dave's Archives 2020). Another commercial that same year would feature country music singer John Denver camping by a lake while advertising Post Raisin Bran. In the commercial, he would tell viewers that Post Raisin Bran is superior to other raisin bran cereals as the camera shows a close up of him holding a handful of sugar-coated raisins and a handful of larger, uncoated Post raisins, which he tells viewers are not hidden by sugar and are naturally sweet.

Like the information in the previous chapter, the use of nature and natural images and lack of sugar in products illustrate the use of the perceived severity Health Belief Model construct in the fact that eating natural products that don't contain sugar helps to prevent unfavorable health outcomes due to the fact that most consumers have a basic understanding of these concepts. However, these two selling points of natural and sugar-free products also overlap with the perceived benefits one as well. The reason for this is that consumers are familiar with the benefits of eating natural products and less sugar without giving much thought to the health consequences. In other words, the idea of natural and sugar-free products is ingrained in consumers' minds as being a benefit regardless of the health outcomes that are prevented when these types of products are eaten. In the previous advertisements discussed, both constructs are used in each commercial as is the perceived barrier one.

The Food and Drug Administration (FDA) regulations for products labeled "no added sugar" must meet the following criteria:

1. No amount of sugars . . . or any other ingredient that contains sugars that functionally substitute for added sugars is added during processing or packaging; and
2. the product does not contain an ingredient containing added sugars such as jam, jelly, or concentrated fruit juice; and
3. the sugars content has not been increased above the amount present in the ingredients by some means such as the use of enzymes, except where the intended functional effect of the process is not to increase the sugars content of a food, and a functionally insignificant increase in sugars results (FDA Code of Federal Regulations Title 21 2024).

In addition to this, products may not use a reduced calorie label due to lower sugar content unless the product meets the FDA's requirements outlined for that designation. It's important to note that these regulations don't cover the addition of sugar alcohol or artificial sweeteners.

"Our Own Cereal"

A 2022 commercial used the Nutrition Health Halo with the no-sugar theme and the perceived benefits and perceived susceptibility Health Belief Model constructs to introduce a new product. The commercial opens with two men,

Gabi Lewis and Greg Sewit, sitting at a table surrounded by boxes of Magic Spoon Cereal with two heaping bowls full of the colorful cereal on the table in front of them. The camera flips the table over to reveal two younger boys while the adult versions tell how they "grew up loving cereal" and then "quickly realized how [their] favorite cereals were empty carbs and sugar" as the camera shows them in a college setting with boxes of cereal called "Sugar-Os" while looking distraught ("Magic Spoon TV Spot, 'Our Own Cereal' " 2022). They tell viewers how they decided to invent their own cereal by getting rid of "the sugar, grains and all the other junk" which they said left them with nothing but empty bowls with sad faces on them ("Magic Spoon TV Spot, 'Our Own Cereal' " 2022). The next shot is of them in the kitchen while they tell how they "recreated the magical taste, packed it with protein instead" as the words "12–14g of protein per serving" are shown on the screen after which they are pictured each holding one colorful o-shaped cereal nugget while saying "and gave it a classic cereal shape" while the text "4–5g of net carbs per serving" appear on the screen ("Magic Spoon TV Spot, 'Our Own Cereal' " 2022). Next, they are shown sitting at a table eating the cereal telling how they loved it and then looking at their phones while images of social media comments appear alongside of each of them while they say, "And everyone else seemed to love it, too. We called it Magic Spoon. Try the magic for yourself at magicspoon.com" ("Magic Spoon TV Spot, 'Our Own Cereal' " 2022).

Though in the commercial, the co-founders say that they "got rid of the sugar," in a 2023 interview with *Forbes* magazine, Gabi Lewis describes the cereal as having "less sugar" and the ingredients listed on the company's website include a "sweetener blend" that includes monk fruit, which they describe as native to Southeast Asia and cultivated by Buddhist monks who traditionally used it in herbal medicine, and allulose, a naturally occurring sugar from plants and fruits that adds a trivial amount of sugar per serving with the taste of sugar but no impact on blood sugar levels and almost no calories. In that same interview, Lewis notes that

> we discuss the concept of nostalgia and the product guardrails, such as having zero grams of sugar in all our products. We debate internally what it would mean if we were to add two grams of sugar to something. Is zero sugar really key to Magic Spoon, or is it just being meaningfully lower in sugar than traditional cereal or other products in the category we're in? (Knox 2023)

Also, noting that "the key intangibles for our brand are evoking joy and nostalgia, being fun and colorful, and being the antithesis of health food that takes itself too seriously" (Knox 2023). His description of the product as being "the antithesis of health food" (Knox 2023) directly opposes the company's use of the no-sugar-added theme and Health Belief Model constructs, both of which promise increased nutrition and avoidance of unfavorable health outcomes such as elevated blood sugar levels.

Use of the no-sugar-added theme in the Nutrition Health Halo and perceived benefits and perceived susceptibility constructs can also be seen on but not limited to the following cereal boxes: Kellogg's Zero No Sugar Added Cinnamon Flavor Special K, Alpen Muesli cereal, Poppins Corn Flakes, Cascadian Farm Organic Cinnamon Apple Granola, Kellogg's Muesli, Cascadian Farm Organic Blueberry Crunch cereal, Cascadian Farm Organic Vanilla Crisp cereal, Three Wishes Unsweetened cereal, Uncle Sam Original Wheat Berry Flakes, Shredded Wheat Original Big Biscuit, Fiber One Original cereal, Meijer Bountiful Morning Granola Cereal, Arrowhead Mills Puffed Wheat cereal, Grainfield's Corn Flakes, Heartland Corn Flakes, My Cereal Mix Sugar Free Vanilla Almond Granola, Familia Swiss Muesli, Simply Fuel Best Granola, Slurrp Farm Strawberry, and Ragi & Rice with Milk Cereal for Little Ones.

Zero Is the New Diet

Another product classified as an ultra-processed food uses the more modern term that includes the word "zero" instead of "no sugar added." In a campaign launched in 2021 to promote a new package design and recipe for Coca-Cola Zero Sugar, the company used artificial intelligence to create a font designed to allow the product to "speak for itself" (Ramos 2024). The company used "neural network object detection—a type of AI that finds out what objects are in an image—to identify letters within the bubbles, condensation, and fizz of a Coke Zero. This approach led to the creation of the font type called 'Coke Sans Sugar'" that was used in a series of advertisements anthropomorphizing the soda. One of the commercials begins with a close up shot of a bottle of the soda speaking in a male voice with the words below saying, "Allow me to describe the Effervescence and bubbles of Coke Zero. The caramel, liquid, ice cold temperatures, the taste" before being interrupted by a female voice asking what he is doing (Ramos 2024). The male bottle says he isn't doing anything except "hanging out" as the camera pulls away to reveal two women eating in a dinner-type setting with two bottles of Coke displayed prominently in front of them after which the female Coke says that it sounded to her as if the male soda was talking to himself (Ramos 2024). The male Coke asks her why he would talk to himself, and she insists that he does that sometimes, just before the camera cuts to a shot of the bottle being poured into a glass after which the male Coke bottle says he can't hear her, but she says he can. After they argue back and forth one more time, the camera cuts to the two women with the words, "Time to try the best Coke ever?" on the screen (Ramos 2024). In this commercial and in the larger campaign, the perceived severity and perceived benefits Health Belief Model constructs are used through the direction of attention on the lack of any sugar as a form of preventing illness and the perceived barriers construct is illustrated by the focus on good taste with the idea of the product being the best one ever.

The campaign, which launched globally had a strong presence on social media including TikTok on which an interactive filter was used to turn users into singing bottles of the soda (Ramos 2024). The ingredients in Coke Zero are almost identical to the company's Diet Coke soda launched in 1983. Under the Frequently Asked Questions at the company's UK website, they say that "Both drinks are sugar free and calorie free. Coca-Cola Zero Sugar looks and tastes more like Coca-Cola original taste, while Diet Coke has a different blend of flavours which gives it a lighter taste."

Animated Coke bottles aren't the only way the company promoted the new Coke Zero flavor. A 2023 commercial for the product features Maggie Rogers singing a song titled "Taste the Transformation" in what resembles a music video with quick cuts and lively music centered around the NCAA Final Four playoffs in Houston that year. Images include a young couple taking a selfie in front of a Coca-Cola Zero Sugar sign, the Final Four NCAA playoffs sign followed by another Coke Zero sign, a "Taste the Transformation" billboard, a Coca-Cola delivery truck, a billboard with basketball player Magic Johnson and the words "Best Coke Ever? #takeataste," various images of people with cans of Coke Zero, shots of women and men playing basketball both with and without Magic Johnson, all interspersed with images of Maggie Rogers in concert followed by the final shot of two bottles of Cokes made out of lights with the words "Best Coke Ever? #takeataste" over them ("Coca-Cola Zero Sugar TV Spot, 'Taste the Transformation' Song by Maggie Rogers" 2023). Though the backdrop of the commercial is the playoff game, the focus is on Coca-Cola Zero Sugar, which by its very name uses the Nutrition Health Halo and perceived severity and perceived benefits Health Belief Model constructs.

Another soda company launched a major advertising campaign promoting its zero-sugar product at the 2023 Super Bowl with two ads. In the first quarter of the game, viewers watch Ben Stiller in various acting roles, including a duel with a lizard-type man who he tells to leave his wife alone, after which he explains, "Acting is the art of making you believe what you're seeing is real," before the camera cuts to shots of him proposing to a woman, talking to an extra-terrestrial creature on a Mars-like planet, at a makeup mirror all the while talking about how the pain is real when the woman he proposes to accidentally kicks him in the face, how the friendship with the creature is real, and how "the real is real" while sitting at the makeup mirror before saying, "but it's not real. It's acting," at which point he takes a sip of Pepsi Zero Sugar and says, "Wow, that's like really good" ("Pepsi: 'Great Acting or Great Taste (Ben Stiller)?' " 2023a). In the final shot with him, he looks at the camera and says, "Or, was I just acting? Only way to know is to try it yourself," which is followed by shot of a can of Pepsi Zero Sugar with the words "ZERO NEVER TASTED SO GOOD #REALORACTING" ("Pepsi: 'Great Acting or Great Taste (Ben Stiller)?' " 2023a).

The company's second quarter Super Bowl LVII commercial featured actor Steve Martin. In the opening scene he is dressed in surgical attire and tells Miss Hastings that she will like her new nose, just as the camera pulls out to reveal that Miss Hastings is a dog. After that, he removes his surgical mask and looks into the camera saying, "As an actor, it's my job to make you believe that what you're seeing is real," before the camera cuts to him reaching the front of a long line as the window closes telling viewers, "That the frustration is real," and then in a restaurant where he receives a very small meal noting that the disappointment is real, followed by another scene with joy being real before he looks to the camera again and says, "But that's just acting" before taking a sip of Pepsi Zero and saying how fantastic it is ("Pepsi: 'Great Acting or Great Taste (Steve Martin)?' " 2023b). At that point, he asks viewers if he was just acting and as in the other commercial telling them to find out for themselves by trying the soda. Both commercials are examples of the use of the updated Nutrition Health Halo with the zero-sugar theme as well as the perceived severity, perceived benefits, and perceived barriers Health Belief Model constructs with the new twist of using the word "zero" rather than "no sugar added" to modernize it.

Inventions and Star Power

Soda companies aren't the only ultra-processed products highlighting their brands' zero-sugar content and thus using the Nutrition Health Halo. Both Tropicana, owned partially by PepsiCo, and Minute Maid, owned by the Coca-Cola company, recently released advertising campaigns focusing on the no-sugar-added benefits of their products. Tropicana launched "The Juice That Starts It All" campaign to remind consumers of the products' place in their lives, which includes a commercial that begins with a male announcer saying, "Sure, Tropicana may not have invented orange juice, but in 1954 we found a way to bring fresh tasting OJ to everyone" as images of a hand pouring a glass of orange juice on a counter are followed by workers in a field harvesting oranges (Ramos 2024). The announcer goes on to tell viewers that their oranges are picked when they are the tastiest and are squeezed within a day "and never add any sugar," which brings orange juice everywhere before telling viewers that even though they can't say they invented orange juice, they can say that "brunch wouldn't really be brunch without OJ," so they say they invented brunch, which is followed by an image of people drinking orange juice at a picnic table (Ramos 2024). The commercial goes on to say that the company also invented Saturday morning, fridge chugging, breakfast to-go, morning people, bffs, mimosas, and even grandmas but that they are not finished because they are "Tropicana, the juice that starts it all" (Ramos 2024). Though the commercial focuses on orange juice, which does not have sugar, the company also offers Zero Sugar Summer Splash Punch, Zero Sugar Lively Lemonade, and Zero Sugar Passionfruit Lemonade Escape. The words "ZERO SUGAR" are positioned in a green banner with white font directly below the Tropicana logo and above the juice flavor. The company also has a Tropicana Light product line feature on the company's website that has "50% less sugar, 50% fewer calories than regular orange juice. 100% great taste," which illustrates the use of the Nutrition Health Halo as well as the perceived severity, perceived benefits, and perceived barriers Health Belief Model constructs.

For their advertising campaign, Minute Maid employed Jon Hamm, best known for his role as Don Draper in the show *Mad Men*, to promote the product. A commercial for the zero-sugar product opens with the actor sitting in a chair across from his agent who asks whether he has read the script yet. The actor flips through the pages of the script and says, "There's literally nothing there" as the agent agrees and says that none of the pages have anything on them (Ramos 2024). Hamm says he doesn't know what they're asking him to do, to which the agent responds saying "Minute Maid Zero Sugar sells itself," after which the actor again says he has nothing to guide him (Ramos 2024). The agent says that if the actor isn't comfortable, he doesn't have to do it, and the agent can give it to one of his influencers to which Hamm says no before chugging a large bottle of Minute Maid Zero Sugar Lemonade. The agent tells him that it's too much and that if he gives them everything on the first commercial, they won't ask him to do another one, saying that the sequel is important before a final shot of the product in the actor's hands with the words "Great Taste. Zero Sugar. Sells Itself." appearing next to the product (Ramos 2024). In addition to the Zero Sugar Lemonade, Minute Maid also sells Zero Sugar Mango Passion, Zero Sugar Pink Lemonade, Zero Sugar Fruit Punch, Zero Sugar Pineapple, and Zero Sugar Strawberry Lemonade, all of which feature the words "zero sugar" under the Minute Maid logo and above the name of the flavor on the label.

The idea of promoting zero sugar is said to be driven by consumers. As Duane Stanford, editor and publisher of *Beverage Digest* notes, "People are kind of back to really moderating the sugar intake. If you want growth and younger consumers and health-conscious consumers, then you really need to make sure you have an option with less sugar" (Ramos 2024). It's important to note that the ingredients in the juice drinks, by definition, make the product ultra-processed. The following are the ingredients in Minute Maid Zero Sugar Lemonade as listed on the manufacturer's website: pure filtered water, lemon juice from concentrate**, less than 0.5 percent of: natural flavors, citric acid (provides tartness), vitamin c (ascorbic acid), potassium citrate (regulates tartness), glycerol ester of rosin, modified cornstarch, aspartame, acesulfame potassium. ** adds a negligible amount of sugar, phenylketonurics: contains phenylalanine. The product would not be classified as ultra-processed if the ingredients were lemons and water. Similarly, the ingredients listed on the manufacturer's website in Tropicana Zero Sugar Summer Splash Punch are water, lemon juice concentrate*, citric acid, potassium citrate, natural flavor, ascorbic acid (vitamin c), peach puree concentrate*, cherry juice concentrate*, red grape juice concentrate*, and steviol glycosides. *adds a negligible amount of sugar, which make this an ultra-processed product.

The use of the Nutrition Health Halo and perceived benefits and perceived susceptibility constructs can also be seen on, but are not limited to the following drink labels: Zero Sugar Snapple Apple, Zero Sugar Snapple Kiwi Strawberry,

Sparkling Ice Peach Nectarine Zero Sugar Flavored Water, Sparkling Ice Coconut Pineapple Zero Sugar Flavored Water, Sparkling Lemon Lime Zero Sugar Flavored Water, Kroger Zero Sugar Fruit Punch, Electromax Zero Sugar Electrolyte Drink, Vitamin Water Zero Sugar Shine Strawberry Lemonade, Lemon Perfect Zero Sugar Lemon Water, Lemon Perfect Zero Sugar Dragon Fruit Mango Lemon Water, Lemon Perfect Zero Sugar Peach Raspberry Lemon Water, Lemon Perfect Zero Sugar Watermelon Lemon Water, Naked No Sugar Added Non GMO Protein Double Berry Fruit Juice, Smirnoff Ice Zero Sugar Original Malt Beverage, Smirnoff Ice Zero Sugar Raspberry Malt Beverage, Smirnoff Ice Zero Sugar Red, White & Berry Malt Beverage, Smirnoff Ice Zero Sugar Pink Malt Beverage, Nature's Twist Sugar Free Lemonade, Great Value Zero Sugar Fruit Punch Sport Hydration Drink, Great Value Zero Sugar Lemon Lime Sport Hydration Drink, Great Value Zero Sugar Mixed Berry Sport Hydration Drink, Ocean Spray Zero Sugar Mixed Berry Juice Drink, Kroger Zero Sugar Blackberry Tea, and San Pellegrino Zero Sugar Pomegranate & Orange Italian Sparkling Drink.

Renovations, Sparkles, and Zero-Sugar Desserts

An iconic brand recently underwent a renovation, making the switch from using the words "sugar free" to "zero sugar" that same year. In addition to updated packaging with more fruit on the labels and a modernized 3-D looking logo, Jell-O changed the wording on its sugar-free products to zero sugar on all pudding and gelatin cups and boxes. The move was designed to "modernize . . . claims to further highlight Jell-O's permissibility and variety of options available to . . . consumers, like Zero Sugar" as a way to "resonate with younger generations and meet their evolving needs" (Wheless 2023). Though no specific advertisements were planned to highlight the word change and updating, the story was covered across many media outlets drawing its own type of publicity. On the packaging, the words "zero sugar" are in the upper left corner in a white background shaped in a semi-circle in blue font with the word "zero" in larger letters and the word "sugar" in smaller font in a half circle underneath the word zero, thus illustrating the zero-sugar theme and employing the perceived benefits and perceived susceptibility constructs to motivate consumers to purchase the product.

The same year, the company partnered with AHA Sparkling Water to bring "Sparkling Jell-O" to consumers during the months of May and June. In one advertisement, there is a sky-blue background with white stars and pink edges and large font with the word "sparkling" in white script and the word "Jell-O" in the company's logo colors of red and white. In the upper right corner is the same half-oval in white with the words "zero sugar" in blue. Underneath that are three boxes of Sparkling Jell-O with photos of the coordinating water flavor alongside the Jell-O flavors. The Sparkling Jell-O, which includes three flavors: Zero Sugar Lemon, Zero Sugar Lime, and Zero Sugar Strawberry, is meant to be paired with AHA Sparkling Water flavors of lime and watermelon, blueberry and pomegranate, and blackberry and lemon. The company also publicized its recipe through media outlets and press releases. "The recipe starts by adding one cup of boiling water to the Jell-O mix. Stir for about 2 minutes or until completely dissolved. Then, stir in one can of AHA Sparkling water. Refrigerate for four hours and you have—Sparkling Jell-O" (Kiner 2023).

In addition to the Zero Sugar Jell-O products, the company also offers zero-sugar pudding and pie filling. The design of the packaging is similar to the Jell-O flavors with the zero-sugar banner in the top left corner, the company's logo above the flavor, and a large photo of the pudding on the right side of the box. The ingredients in Zero Sugar Jell-O Chocolate Pudding and Pie Filling are cornstarch, cocoa (processed with alkali), modified cornstarch, salt, contains less than 2 percent of natural and artificial flavor, carrageenan, fumaric acid, aspartame* and acesulfame potassium (sweeteners), polysorbate 60, red 40, yellow 5, blue 2. *phenylketonurics: contains phenylalanine, the majority of which themselves are ultra-processed ingredients. Other flavors, with similar ingredients include zero-sugar banana cream, cheesecake, chocolate fudge, lemon, pistachio, white chocolate, and vanilla. For example, the cheesecake flavor lists the following ingredients on its box: modified cornstarch, maltodextrin, tetrasodium pyrophosphate, sodium phosphate, contains less than 2 percent of salt, artificial color, xanthan gum, aspartame (phenylketonurics: contains phenylalanine) (sweetener), natural and artificial flavors (contains barley), calcium sulfate, acesulfame potassium (sweetener), mono- and diglycerides, lactic acid, yellow 5, yellow 6.

Other dessert products using the zero-sugar theme in the Nutrition Health Halo and the perceived benefits and perceived susceptibility constructs can also be seen on, but are not limited to, the following: Russell Stover Sugar Free Peanut Butter Cup Chocolate Candy, Russell Stover Sugar Free Chocolate Candy, Hershey's Zero Sugar Chocolate Candy, Reese's Zero Sugar Chocolate Peanut Butter Cups, Voortman Sugar Free Shortbread Oatmeal Cookies, Snack Pack

Sugar-Free Chocolate Pudding Cups, Jolly Rancher Zero Sugar Fruit Flavored Candies, Pillsbury Zero Sugar Chocolate Fudge Flavored Brownie Mix, Pillsbury Zero Sugar Creamy Supreme Vanilla Premium Frosting, Pillsbury Zero Sugar Moist Supreme Yellow Premium Cake Mix, Breyer's No Sugar Added Vanilla Ice Cream, Klondike No Sugar Added Vanilla Ice Cream, Fudgsicle No Sugar Added Original Fudge Pops, Werther's Original Sugar Free Chewy Caramels, Turkey Hill No Sugar Added Vanilla Bean ice cream, and Murray Sugar Free Cookies.

It's important to note that while several different ultra-processed product types are highlighted in this section, the Nutrition Health Halo with the zero-sugar theme, as in previous and preceding chapters regarding all health halos discussed in this study, is not limited solely to these products. In fact, it can be seen on many different types of products, which include hot dogs (Garret Valley Farms Sugar Free Uncured Beef Franks, Wellshire Sugar-Free All Natural Uncured Beef Franks, Pedersen's No Sugar Added Uncured Beef Hot Dogs), sausages (Tillamook Zero Sugar Original Smoked Sausages, Applegate Naturals No Sugar Chicken & Herb Breakfast Sausage, Pedersen's No Sugar Added Ground Italian Sausage), condiments (Heinz No Sugar Added Tomato Ketchup, Smucker's Sugar Free Breakfast Syrup, G Hughes Sugar Free Honey Mustard Sauce), soups (Cook's Delight Zero Sugar Vegetable Base, Wild Zora Tuscan Chicken Soup, Cook's Delight Zero Sugar Chicken Base), and bread (Nature's Own Life Sugar-Free Whole Grain Bread, Private Selection Sugar Free 100% Whole Wheat Bread, Sola No Carb No Added Sugar Sweet & Buttery Sliced Bread).

Low Fat, High Risk

Ancel Keys completed his undergraduate degree at the University of California at Berkeley, earned his Ph.D. in biology six years later and then earned a second Ph.D. in physiology at the University of Cambridge before becoming a professor at the University of Minnesota where he would establish and direct the internationally renowned Laboratory of Physiological Hygiene, a research center for human physiology and nutrition (Sparling 2020). In the early 1950s he would spearhead the well-known Seven Countries Study, which involved decades of research across different countries to study diet-related diseases. The first phase of the study took place between 1958 and 1983 to determine "standardized lifestyle and risk factors . . . at baseline and after 5 and 10 years of follow-up in 16 cohorts of middle-aged men from seven countries" in which "teams of the local principal investigators . . . also collected the mortality data during 25 years" that was followed by a later phase during 1984–99 "by extending the cardiovascular surveys about different aspects of health in the elderly from nine European cohorts" with "50-year mortality data . . . collected up to 2014 in 13 of the 16 cohorts" (Seven Countries Study 2024). In the study, researchers concluded that "dietary patterns in the Mediterranean and in Japan in the 1960s were associated with low rates of coronary heart disease" and that "sufficient physical activity, non-smoking and moderate alcohol consumption also is associated with a low risk of cardiovascular disease" (Seven Countries Study 2024).

Keys and SnackWell's

On January 13, 1961, Ancel Keys would appear on the cover of *Time* magazine in a story about his efforts to determine the dietary causes of heart disease. The article would bring even greater attention to Keys's conclusion that a diet low in saturated fat and high in whole grains, fruits, and vegetables, what is now known as the Mediterranean diet, would prevent heart disease. And though his conclusion, which was based partly on data from his Seven Countries Study, would receive both criticism and praise through the years, it would, in the 1990s, be wrongly blamed for the unhealthy low-fat movement speared by what was called the SnackWell's Effect. Named after an American low-fat cookie brand, this phenomenon was first introduced to explain the sales frenzy around low-fat cookies, based on the idea that consumers ate more of the product since it was labeled low in fat, and spurred on by the release of the United States Department of Agriculture's (USDA) first food pyramid in 1992, which put fats, oils, and sweets at the top in the use-sparingly category, public demand for reduced-fat and fat-free products grew. Though the ramifications on addictive eating habits of this low-fat movement advertising have been discussed elsewhere (Danowski 2024, 116–19), it's important to note that, "Ancel Keys has been thrown under the bus by a clamoring crowd who claim his work led to the low-fat diets that had Americans living on SnackWell's, soda, and white bread" (Harriman 2017). Instead, it's noted that "nothing could be further from the truth; Keys promoted quality carbs, fats, and protein all around—long before this became fashionable" (Harriman 2017). The controversy surrounding Keys's work reached a turning point in 2017 when the True Health Initiative issued a white paper that reviewed data from Keys's study. In the paper, it was concluded that

> Misadventures in low-fat eating, to say nothing of low-fat junk foods, cannot legitimately be attributed to any position espoused by Keys over the course of his career. That there was a foray into misguided applications of a low-fat dietary approach with ramifications still relevant today is undeniable. Reasons for it are complex, contentious, and beyond the scope of this paper—and perhaps fodder for another. But it is clear that responsibility cannot legitimately be assigned either to Keys, or the Seven Countries Study. (Harriman 2017)

There are still some today who condemn Keys's research as "unscientific" and consider the Mediterranean diet to be "part wishful thinking, part wild guess" and that it is a "romantic theory about what we should eat" (Ede 2024, 22). As nutrition scientist Georgia Ede writes, "By blaming modern health epidemics such as obesity, type 2 diabetes, and heart disease on saturated fat and cholesterol, the U.S. Dietary Guidelines drove us away from nutritious whole foods like meat and eggs and right into the arms of the ultraprocessed *[sic]* food industry" (20).

"Okay about Being Bad"

A 2003 commercial for Subway low-fat sandwiches illustrates not only the SnackWell's effect but also the health appeal of low-fat products. The commercial opens with a woman and a man in a car. The man is driving, and he tells the woman that he is nervous about meeting her family as she tilts a box of chunky chocolate chip cookies into her mouth. He looks at her and asks, "Did you just eat that entire box of cookies?" to which she replies that it's okay since they had Subway last night (Play Pause Video 2018a). The man looks thoughtful as the camera cuts to a shot of Subway sandwiches with the words "Subway's 7 under 6 sandwiches" in white font across the shot as a male announcer says, "Subway's low fat sandwiches, a variety of delicious subs so you can feel good about being good and okay about being bad" as small print below tells viewers that the six grams of fat are in the six-inch sub "without cheese or non-low fat condiments such as mayonnaise" before the camera cuts to a shot of the man tackling the woman's grandfather (Play Pause Video 2018a). The crowd stares stunned at the man just as a football hits him in the crotch and the grandfather appears saying that it's okay and that it's second down, before a final shot of the company's logo is shown with the male announcer saying, "Subway, good so you don't always have to be" (Play Pause Video 2018a). The idea that consumers can eat a whole box of cookies if they eat a low-fat sandwich the night before speaks to the heart of the SnackWell's effect of eating more cookies because they are low in fat as well as an illustration of the Nutrition Health Halo with the low-fat theme and the perceived severity, perceived benefits, and perceived barriers Health Belief Model constructs.

Another commercial in this campaign from Subway also uses the SnackWell's effect as well as the low-fat theme and several constructs. The 2003 advertisement opens with a man and a woman at a picnic with another man dressed as cupid sitting in a tree above them. The man is eating a large piece of cake as the woman looks at him with disapproval. The man tells here that it's okay since he had Subway last night, just before the camera cuts to images of the sandwiches while a male announcer says, "Subway sandwiches thousands of customizable low-fat ways to feel good about being good and okay about being bad" (Play Pause Video2018b). The commercial ends with cupid shooting his arrow into an older woman's heart and a younger biker man who become an unlikely pair as another cupid looks on and the first cupid tells him that it's okay because he had Subway last night. Once again, this commercial speaks to the heart of the SnackWell's effect, encouraging consumers to eat more of the product because it is low in fat. It also illustrates the Nutrition Health Halo with the low-fat theme and the perceived severity, perceived benefits, and perceived barriers Health Belief Model constructs used in the promotion of ultra-processed foods.

Fat Shaming

Though used frequently in the late 1990s and early 2000s, in advertisements, the low-fat theme of the Nutrition Health Halo has taken a back seat in recent years to the zero-sugar theme. One area in which the reduced-fat theme is still used today in the advertising of ultra-processed foods, however, is in the fruit yogurt industry. Though there were many nonfat fruit yogurt commercials aired during the low-fat craze of the 1990s and 2000s, one stands out in infamy. The commercial, which is now labeled as the "1990 Dannon Light Yogurt Fat Shaming Commercial" on YouTube, opens with two women and two men with obesity looking at themselves in the mirror. Each has difficulty with the clothing they are wearing. For one woman, her dress is too short while another's zipper pops open, and one man can't button his pants while the other's shirt button pops off. Over these images, a male announcer says, "It's not always easy to feel good about how we look which is why Dannon is introducing Dannon Light, a delicious non-fat yogurt with NutraSweet and a mere 100 calories because how you feel is a reflection of how you look," after which a shot of the woman with obesity is shown with a shopping bag while looking at a thin woman trying on clothes (CRT Afterglow 2022). As the camera cuts to a shot of Dannon Light Strawberry yogurt, the announcer says, "New Dannon Light, the first light yogurt good enough to be called Dannon" (CRT Afterglow 2022). It's worth noting that this commercial employs all four of the Health Belief Model constructs, focusing especially on the perceived susceptibility one with the idea of preventing the disease of obesity yet at the same time, employing the use of the perceived benefits (low calorie), perceived severity (prevention of unfavorable outcome of feeling poorly), and perceived barriers (good taste in a low-calorie product) constructs.

The company, which was founded in 1942, continues to make Dannon Low Fat and Non Fat Yogurt and also produces several other brands of yogurt, one of which, Danimals, is targeted at kids. A commercial for this product opens with a mother dragging a refrigerator on her back to her son's school cafeteria where he is eating lunch. She hands him a yogurt and he thanks her. The boy sitting next to him says his mom freezes his Danimals Squeezables and puts them in his lunchbox in the morning. He says, "Just freeze it. Thaw it. And it's ready by lunch" just before a female announcer says, "New Danimals Squeezables Low Fat Yogurt. Squeeze more fun into your kid's lunch" as a shot of a lunch box with a sandwich, apple, and the yogurt is shown next to the product box (ALittleBitOfIrish 2015).

Also launched in the 1990s by Dannon was Oikos Low-Fat Greek Yogurt, which was rebranded and reformulated with more fruit and a creamier taste in 2021, which still remains popular today. Prior to this, the company employed *Full House* star John Stamos to promote its product. The partnership, which began in 2011, included a 2014 *Full House* reunion advertisement during that year's Super Bowl and lasted until 2015 when the brand replaced Stamos for Carolina Panthers' star Cam Newton in an attempt to appeal to a male audience. In a 2016 commercial, when the product was named Dannon Oikos Non-Fat Greek Yogurt, a woman is shown on a plane. She looks at her ticket to see that she is seated next to a man who is laughing loudly with headphones on. A stewardess who witnesses this tells her that the seat across the aisle is available. The woman smiles and says, "This is too good to be true" as she sits next to someone reading a magazine with John Stamos on it and the headline "The hottest Greek around" (Laurent 2016). The woman looks at the magazine just as the passenger pulls it down to reveal that it is John Stamos who introduces himself to her. The woman then, once again, says that, "This is too good to be true," as Stamos says, "Dannon Oikos Non-Fat Yogurt, delicious yet healthy" after which she repeats her too good to be true idea before a male announcer says, "There are things that are too good to be true such as Dannon Oikos, thick, creamy, with zero percent fat and twice the protein of regular low-fat yogurt" during which time the woman reaches over and kisses Stamos (Laurent 2016). The commercial ends with her tasting the yogurt from the kiss and taking it from Stamos before the other man says he wants an Oikos as the announcer says the product is "too delicious to be nutritious" (Laurent 2016).

It's worth noting that in the case of yogurt, the low-fat label is both a description of the product as well as a health halo and the three Health Belief Model constructs (perceived susceptivity, perceived severity, perceived benefits) used in the promotion of that product. As is the case with several of the products mentioned in this study, product description labeling morphs into a health halo and the use of the Health Belief Model constructs when other unhealthy ingredients also included in that product are ignored while the healthy one is highlighted in promoting it.

Yogurt products that use the reduced-fat theme of the Nutrition Health Halo and Health Belief Model constructs on their labels include, but are not limited to, the following: Chobani Strawberry on the Bottom Nonfat Greek yogurt, Lucerne Nonfat yogurt, Prairie Farms Fat Free Vanilla yogurt, Prairie Farms Strawberry Fat Free yogurt, Parmalat Fat Free Strawberry yogurt, Green Mountain Creamery Vanilla Greek Nonfat yogurt, Golden Acre Dairy Fat Free Strawberry yogurt, Trader Joe's Greek Yogurt Nonfat Vanilla Bean, Siggi's Vanilla 0% Milkfat yogurt, Onken 0% Fat Strawberry yogurt, Kemps Vanilla Nonfat yogurt, Dannon Light + Fit 0 Fat Greek Vanilla yogurt, Green Valley Organic Low Fat Blueberry yogurt, Publix Fat Free Light Peach yogurt, Activia 0% Fat Strawberry yogurt, Giant Food Greek Nonfat Strawberry yogurt, SKYR Fat Free Raspberry yogurt, Yoplait Light 0 Fat Cherry yogurt, Lactaid Nonfat Blueberry yogurt, Great Value Fat Free Vanilla Stirred yogurt, Anderson Erikson Low Fat Blueberry yogurt, Food Club Greek Nonfat Black Cherry yogurt, Nestle Fat Free Strawberry yogurt, Gogurt Fat Free Strawberry yogurt, Essential Everyday Fat Free Strawberry yogurt, Lactel Fat Free Mixed Berry yogurt, Yoplait Parfait

Pro Gluten Free Low Fat Blueberry yogurt, and Food Lion Original Nonfat Strawberry Banana Blended yogurt.

Fat Free But Not Light

Like the dairy industry, ice-cream manufacturers advertised their fat-free products heavily in the 1990s then tapered off to using the reduced-fat theme on product packages instead. One example of this is a 1990 commercial for Simple Pleasures Ice Cream, which opens with a shot of the camera moving through various ice-cream containers until it rests on a container of Fat Free Chocolate Simple Pleasures ice cream while a male announcer says, "Introducing the best news for ice cream lovers since ice cream began. New Simple Pleasures. It's everything you love about ice cream but no fat" (ewjxn 2018a). The camera cuts to close up shots of the ice cream as it's being scooped as the announcer continues, "New Simple Pleasures is unbelievably rich, incredibly creamy and absolutely delicious because new Simple Pleasures is made with all natural Simplesse instead of fat. New delicious all natural Simple Pleasures. There's never been an ice cream like it" (ewjxn 2018a). Simplesse is "formulated by microparticulation of egg white and/or cows' milk proteins and is used as a fat substitute in many fat-laden foods" (Sampson and Cooke 1992).

A year later, Baskin-Robbins aired a commercial introducing their new fat- and sugar-free ice-cream line. The commercial opens with a heterosexual couple being served ice cream at one of the company's establishments as a male announcer says, "Introducing the lighter side of Baskin-Robbins. New, fat-free, with no cholesterol, light, and sugar-free" before the camera cuts to the couple eating their ice cream as the woman says, "I can hardly tell the difference. Can you, Fred?" as the man is shown rising up to indicate the lightness of the product (Classic90sFan 2019). While the reduced-fat theme in the Nutrition Health Halo and the perceived benefits and perceived susceptibility constructs appear to be popular with both consumers and manufacturers, the use of the word "light" did not work for one company. In 2004, Dreyer's/Edy's introduced slow churned ice cream using the word "light" on the packaging. Customers didn't seem to like the word, and in 2007, the company discontinued advertising the product until 2012 in a campaign that emphasized "that Slow Churned ice cream is half the fat and one third of the calories of regular ice cream" without using the word light, which "had a lot of negative perception . . . because of the taste experience," since "taste is king, first and foremost" with consumers wanting "great taste and half the fat, rather than OK taste and no fat" (KTAR Newsroom 2012). Despite this, Ben & Jerry's currently has a line of "Lighten Up" ice-cream flavors that include chocolate cookie dough and vanilla brownie flavors that was introduced in 2018.

Additional ice-cream products that use the reduced-fat theme of the Nutrition Health Halo and perceived benefits and perceived susceptibility constructs on their labels include, but are not limited to, the following: Breyer's Delights Low Fat Vanilla Bean ice cream, Low Cow Low Fat Fudge ice cream, Halal Fat Free Chocolate ice cream, Edy's Fat Free Chocolate Fudge ice cream, Great Value Fat Free Vanilla ice cream, Blue Ribbon Classics Reduced Fat Vanilla ice cream, Blue Ribbon Classics Reduced Fat Butter Pecan ice cream, Blue Ribbon Classics Reduced Fat Golden Gaytime ice cream, Blue Ribbon Classics Reduced Fat Peanut Butter Brownie ice cream, Healthy Choice Praline & Caramel Premium Low Fat ice cream, Healthy Choice Chocolate Chocolate Chunk Premium Low Fat ice cream, Healthy Choice Rocky Road Premium Low Fat ice cream, Wegman's Black Raspberry Low Fat ice cream, Blue Bunny Reduced Fat Vanilla ice cream, Turkey Hill 50% Less Fat Chocolate Chip Cookie Dough ice cream, Turkey Hill Reduced Fat Moose Tracks ice cream, Hood Cow Chow Reduced Fat ice cream, Kroger Low Fat Fudge Bars, Skinny Cow Cookies 'n Cream Low Fat ice cream, Skinny Cow Chocolate Fudge Brownie Low Fat ice cream, Skinny Cow Cookies 'n Cream Truffle, Clemmy's Chocolate Fudge Low Fat ice cream, Weis Markets Reduced Fat Vanilla ice cream, Pierre's Slender Reduced Fat Moose Tracks ice cream, Pierre's Slender Reduced Fat Butter Pecan ice cream, Pierre's Slender Reduced Fat Mint Chocolate Chip ice cream, Pierre's Slender Reduced Fat Neapolitan ice cream, Creamie's Reduced Fat Chocolate ice cream bar, Creamie's Reduced Fat Banana ice cream bar, and Buon! Per Te Low Fat Mango Passionfruit ice cream.

Belly Dancing Crackers, Cookies That Exercise, and a Talking Cow

A few other examples of ultra-processed foods using the reduced-fat theme and perceived benefits and perceived susceptibility Health Belief Model constructs in advertisements during the 1990s include,

- A 1994 Reduced Fat Ritz Crackers commercial in which the crackers are animated to belly dance as an announcer introduces them and says there are "lots to choose from" as an image of four other low-fat products are shown in the last shot (ewjxn 2024). These products include Reduced Fat Oreos, Reduced Fat Better Cheddars, Reduced Fat Wheat Thins, and Reduced Fat Triscuits.
- A 1995 commercial featured Reduced Fat Oreos in an exercising class with an instructor telling them to twist as an announcer introduces them and says, "Less Fat. Loads of taste" (ewjxn 2018b).
- A 1995 Reduced Fat Pillsbury Chocolate Chips advertisement that begins with an announcer asking where a chocolate chip cookie with "all the taste you love and less fat" can be found as the camera shows first a closeup of a cookie with melting chocolate as it is torn apart and then a woman in a white dress lounging around eating them before the camera cuts to a woman in a kitchen sitting who answers, "In my dreams?" (Klaus-Tapes 2024). The company's mascot, the Pillsbury Doughboy, answers by saying, "No, in your oven" as the announcer goes on to introduce the product before the camera cuts to the woman enjoying a cookie as the Doughboy says, "A baking dream come true" before she pokes him in the stomach (Klaus-Tapes 2024).
- A 1996 Hershey's Syrup commercial featuring an animated white cow that turns to brown as he says, "Everyone knows that the best way to make chocolate milk is to add Hershey's Syrup but here's something you may not know. Hershey's Syrup is virtually fat free and believe it or not, it's always been that way" just before the camera cuts to a shot of a Hershey's Syrup container next to a glass of chocolate milk (IIRTVFan2, 2017).
- A 1998 Low Fat Eggo Waffles commercial that opens with a male announcer saying, "It's the Eggo everyone's waited for. New Eggo Low Fat Waffles" as a shot of two older women is shown at the breakfast table as an Eggo pops out of the toaster. One woman says to the other that she can have the waffle since she needs the low fat more. The other woman huffs in offense but does not reach for the waffle leaving it for the first woman who smiles as she takes it just before an announcer says, "So irresistible people are sinking to a new low to get their hands on one" (Ye Olde Commercials 2018). The scene shifts to a man and a woman at the table. As the man reaches for the waffle, the woman tells him he can have it since he needs the low fat more than she does. The

man says okay and takes the waffle leaving the woman perplexed. The announcer then asks, "How low will you go not to leggo?" as the camera cuts to the woman who let go of the Eggo snipping roses viciously and muttering "You need the low fat more than I do" (Ye Olde Commercials 2018).

"Stay Golden"

One product area where the reduced-fat theme and perceived benefits and perceived susceptibility Health Belief Model constructs are still used today in a few advertisements is the chip industry. A 2022 Baked Lay's commercial opens with a closeup of the product bag with the words "65% Less Fat Than Regular Potato Chips" positioned directly underneath the word "baked" in large font (Lay's 2022). Upbeat music plays as the camera cuts to a shot of a mother behind a counter in a modern space resembling a kitchen in which the cabinets are drawn on the wall. The mother is smiling exuberantly as she hands snack-size bags of Lay's potato chips to two girls who run toward her with backpacks on. A female announcer says, "Baked Lay's are made with 65% less fat than regular potato chips. The classic flavor of Lay's just baked. Lay's stay golden" as the mother is shown eating the chips from a larger bag and smiling (Lay's 2022). The final shot is of three different flavors of the product on a yellowish gold background with the words "Stay Golden" below the company's logo (Lay's 2022). Similarly, a 2023 commercial for Tayto Lentil Chips opens with a shot of a single chip on a black background and a female announcer saying, "Tayto Lentil Chips 40% less fat with the great taste of Tayto" as an image of a smiley face made from the chips is shown before the camera cuts to an image of three bags in three flavors of the chips with the words "40% less fat" underneath the name of the product to the right (Mr. Tayto 2023).

The reduced-fat theme is present throughout this advertisement illustrated first by the closeup of the bag and later the verbal reminder, boldly proclaiming that the product contains "65% Less Fat Than Regular Potato Chips" with the information on the bag positioned strategically underneath the word "baked." Use of this word employs the perceived severity construct since consumers are all too well aware of the dangers of unfavorable outcomes if they eat too much fried food. The idea of "staying golden" draws on a poem by Robert Frost, "Nothing Gold Can Stay," which suggests the temporary nature of youthful innocence. This concept was later adapted in S. E. Hinton's 1967 coming-of-age novel, *The Outsiders*, and the 1983 Frances Ford Coppola movie adaptation in which a dying Johnny tells Ponyboy to "stay gold" meaning to preserve his innocence and purity. The joining of the slogan, the "golden" chips, the yellow bag, and the concession to the term used in literature and film creates both a reduced-fat theme in the Nutrition Health Halo as well as the use of the perceived benefits and perceived severity Health Belief Model constructs by associating an ultra-processed food with purity and leading consumers to believe that the benefits will reduce the risk of illness and obesity.

Additional chip products that use the reduced-fat theme and Health Belief Model constructs on their labels include, but are not limited to, the following: Popchips 50% Less Fat Sea Salt Potato Snack, Cape Cod Potato Chips Less Fat Original Kettle Chips, Kettle Brand Himalayan Salt Air Fried 30% Less Fat Kettle Potato Chips, H-E-B Original Kettle Cooked Potato Chips—Reduced Fat, Kroger Kettle Cooked Original Reduced Fat Potato Chips, Herr's Less Fat Kettle Cooked Potato Chips, Ruffles Reduced Fat Potato Chips, Trader Joe's Reduced Guilt 33% Less Fat Kettle Cooked Potato Chips: Lightly Salted, Cape Cod Waves 40% Less Fat Potato Chips, Pringles Original Reduced Fat Potato Crisps, Utz Kettle Classics Reduced Fat Crunch Potato Chips, Snips 65% Less Fat Baked Potato Chips Hot Chili Flavor, Snips 65% Less Fat Baked Potato Chips Honey Mustard Flavor, Smart Fries Reduced Fat Potato Chips Aged White Cheddar Flavor, Smart Fries Reduced Fat Potato Chips Classic Sea Salt Flavor, Smart Fries Reduced Fat Potato Chips Original Barbeque Flavor, Smart Fries Reduced Fat Potato Chips Sweet Jalapeno Flavor, Tim's Reduced Fat All Natural Potato Chips, Stacy's Baked Pita Chips—No Artificial Flavor, No Artificial Color, Low Fat, Kettle Brand Sea Salt & Vinegar 40% Less Fat Potato Chips, Kettle Brand Sea Salt 40% Less Fat Potato Chips, Kettle Brand Salt & Fresh Ground Pepper 40% Less Fat Potato Chips, Miss Vickie's Original Recipe Reduced Fat Potato Chips, Glenny's Low Fat, Extra Protein Potato Chips, Terra Sana Indian Curry 40% Less Fat Lentil Chips, Tostitos Baked 50% Less Fat Tortilla Chips, Trader Joe's Low Fat Baked Blue Corn Tortilla Chips Salted, Doritos Reduced Fat Tortilla Chips, Flamas Flavored, and Cheetos 50% Less Fat Baked Crunchy Cheese Flavored Snacks.

Whole Grains Not Whole Health

A man reaches into a bag of grains, takes a handful, and lets it flow through his fingers. As he does this, he says, "Whole grain wheat, hard red spring wheat" before moving onto the next bag, also filled with grains at which point he says, "Whole grain rye" (Bionic Disco 2020). As he raises his hand to his face, he says, "Whole grain means that the wheat germ and rye germ are still there," before moving onto other containers where he introduces bran, "defatted flax seed," and "pure golden honey" and then pointing out that "all of these ingredients are in Roman Meal Bread," which he describes as "the good tasting, light brown bread with natural whole grain goodness," and then says, "The Roman Meal company thought you'd like to know" (Bionic Disco 2020). Though this may seem to be a commercial aired recently, it's not. It was aired in October of 1974 (Bionic Disco) a year that marked the resignation of President Richard Nixon due to the Watergate scandal, a boxing match between Muhammed Ali and George Foreman, and a recession that would result in consumers spending "41 cents for a quart of milk, or 53 cents for an ordinary loaf of bread" (Colamosca 1974, 205) as well as the introduction of a Food Pyramid in Sweden in which bread, legumes, potatoes, milk, and grains would form the base indicating recommendations to consumers to eat more of these types of foods. The United States wouldn't adapt the pyramid until 1992, the base of which would also be bread with the addition of pasta, rice, and cereal with a recommendation of six to eleven servings each day.

My Plate and Whole Grains

After a revision in the early 2000s, the Food Pyramid was replaced in the United States by the My Plate visual, which included fruits, grains, vegetables, and protein with larger portions of grains and vegetables and smaller portions of fruits and protein with a small circle above the plate for dairy. My Plate is still posted at the U.S. Department of Agriculture's website, which offers a list of grains including barley, cornmeal, wheat, rice, oats, and other cereal grains as well as tortillas, pasta, bread, cereals, grits, popcorn, oatmeal, and rice. In this section, the difference between whole grains and refined grains is explained:

> Whole grains have the entire grain kernel, which includes the bran, germ, and endosperm. Some whole-grain examples are whole-wheat flour, bulgur (cracked wheat), oatmeal, and brown rice.
>
> Refined grains have been milled, a process that removes the bran and germ. This is done to give grains a finer texture and improve their shelf life. But it also

> removes dietary fiber, iron, and many B vitamins. Some examples of refined grain products are white flour, corn grits, white bread, and white rice. (USDA website)

Following this, it is suggested that refined grains need to be enriched to be considered healthy, by a process that involves adding certain vitamins and iron yet not fiber, which should be designated as "enriched" on the package. The section ends with the reminder that, "Only foods that are made with 100% whole grains are considered a whole grain food" (USDA website).

Also included in this section is a list of the benefits of eating whole grains, which include helping to lessen the risk of heart disease, assisting with healthy digestion and weight management, and, if fortified with folic acid and eaten while pregnant could play a part in preventing birth defects. Similarly, at the Mayo Clinic website, whole grains are described as "good choices for a nutritious diet" that "provide fiber, vitamins, minerals and other nutrients" that can "help control cholesterol levels, weight and blood pressure" as well as "lower the risk of diabetes, heart disease and other conditions" (Mayo Clinic Staff 2024). An umbrella review of twenty-one meta-analyses "to review the effectiveness of the role of whole grain as a therapeutic agent in type 2 diabetes, cardiovascular disease, cancer, and obesity" concluded that "there is some evidence for dietary whole grain intake to be beneficial in the prevention of type 2 diabetes, cardiovascular disease, and colorectal, pancreatic, and gastric cancers. The potential benefits of these findings suggest that the consumption of 2 to 3 servings per day (~45 g) of whole grains may be a justifiable public health goal" (McRae 2017, 10).

Healthy or Not?

Over the last decade, however, several medical doctors with nutrition backgrounds have challenged the healthiness of wheat and other grains with the allegations that they contribute to poor health, digestive problems, and mental health issues, including schizophrenia, autism, dementia, high blood pressure, psoriasis, obesity, inflammation, arthritis, heart disease, and diabetes. Pointing to modern production methods of wheat as contributing to unforeseen physical and mental problems and "clever marketing ploys" used by food manufacturers as well as the inundation of advertisements for unhealthy foods, researchers have noted that many food companies pay for much of the "research" by dietitians and nutrition scientists that is "made even more difficult to ignore when the American Heart Association and other health organizations endorse their products" (Davis 2019, 194). It has also been noted that the confusion about whole grains may be due to the USDA's definition of whole grains that paves the way for "processed food manufacturers to blast a kernel of wheat to smithereens and still call it whole, so long as they add the right ration of its bits back into the product" and noting that "manufacturers are invested in using the term 'whole grain' on their products because whole grains are supposed to be healthier than refined grains" (Ede 2024, 93).

Bread, cereal, crackers, muffins, energy or cereal bars, and cookies using the whole-grain theme of the Nutrition Health Halo are classified as ultra-processed foods, which by definition are unhealthy and considered by some to have "the power to destroy . . . good mental and physical health" having so little nutrient value that they have to be enriched, because vitamins and minerals have been "stripped away," or need to be fortified, "with nutrients they never had to begin with," which ultimately does not change "the fact that they are brimming with toxic molecules that damage your brain's structure and metabolism over time, ultimately compromising its ability to generate energy" (Ede 2024, 89).

Bread and Nature

A 1987 commercial for Home Pride wheat and white bread uses both oral and visual connections to illustrate the whole-grain theme in the Nutrition Health Halo as well as several Health Belief Model constructs including perceived severity, perceived benefits, and perceived barriers. The commercial opens with a long shot of a vibrantly colored sky over a tractor cutting grains in a field over soft music after which there is a cut to a close up of the grains as a male announcer's voice says, "The rich whole grains of Home Pride butter-topped brand" as the camera cuts to a close up shot of bread slices falling out of a package as he continues "and the rich golden honey and then and then," after which is shown a shot of a man churning butter as he says, "the butter, fresh sweet creamery butter poured down the length of each loaf," when a shot of baking bread with butter being poured on it is shown (Member Berries 2017). The camera then cuts to a shot of a family having a picnic outside while the announcer continues, "These give Home Pride it's rich, noticeably rich taste. Quite simply, there is no taste like the rich taste of Home Pride White or Wheat" as various close-up shots are shown of family members eating sandwiches and a sandwich being made before a final shot of two loaves of bread as the announcer says, "There's no taste like the rich taste of Home Pride" with the same words at the bottom of the screen. The whole-grain theme is used in the words spoken by the announcer when he says, "rich whole grains" and then uses the word "rich" in association with both honey and the taste of the product. The establishing shot in the opening of the commercial with a tractor harvesting grains followed by a close up shot of the field which is then followed by a direct cut to the product creates a visual association between the product and the grains growing in the field that draws on the perceived susceptibility Health Belief Model construct by reminding consumers that eating "natural" food will help prevent illness or poor health. Though the word "healthy" was not used in association with the whole grains, the visual cues make it clear that the bread has a connection to nature, which is believed by many to be healthy.

Several decades later in 2009, another bread company would not be as subtle with its connection to nature. The commercial opens with several people picking vegetables and bringing them to a table set up outside as a female announcer says, "Foods that are best for you come straight from nature" at which point the camera cuts to a shot of two loaves of Nature's Own Bread with slices of bread next to them and then continues to focus on shots of the bread as the announcer continues "like our new specialty breads, healthy, nutritious all natural whole grain breads, some with organic flour" as the camera focuses on shots of people enjoying sandwiches outdoors (Nature's Own Bread 2009). The commercial ends with the announcer urging consumers to "give your family the best of nature" with the company's new specialty breads (Nature's Own Bread 2009). It's worth noting that in addition to the Nutrition Health Halo, and as in products mentioned in the previous section, the name of the product itself illustrates the use of the perceived severity and perceived benefits Health Belief Model constructs.

Another example of a bread commercial using the whole-grain theme and the two constructs in association with nature opens with a father and son walking through a grain field with wind energy towers in the background. A song is played and begins with the words "Oh, this is how it starts" and continues as the man picks up a strand of wheat and strips it to pour the seeds into his son's open hand ("Brownberry TV Spot" 2021). The son takes the wheat kernels and throws them up in the air as the camera shows them blowing in the wind past a wind energy tower with a barn in the background. The song continues with the words "brighter than the sun" as the camera shows a woman eating a sandwich on her front porch and a couple in their garden on top of a building in a city before returning to the father and son who are sitting on a picnic bench in the wheat field eating sandwiches as a male announcer says, "Brownberry Bread, gathering, baking, and delivering the goodness of nature from one generation to the next and from seed to slice" as the final shot focuses on three loaves of the product on a picnic table in the grain field with a sandwich next to it and the words "From Seed to Slice" shown to the left underneath the company's logo ("Brownberry TV Spot" 2021). A similar commercial from the company using the whole-grain theme and constructs with the nature theme was aired a year later and features *Full House* actor John Stamos. The commercial opens with a family having a picnic in a park. The man asks the woman what she has and there is a close up of Brownberry Whole Grains Healthy Multi-Grain bread on a red-and-white checked picnic blanket, surrounded by three sandwiches and lemonade in a mason jar. The man answers his own question by saying, "Oh, Brownberry Whole Grains. That's that nutritious bread, right?" just before actor John Stamos slides in between the couple and says, "That's right, picnic family. It's delicious, good nutrition for your balanced life" before telling them that he eats it every day ("Brownberry Whole Grains TV Spot" 2022). As Stamos slides out, the man tells the woman that that's the reason he looks so good. She quickly thrusts a sandwich in his direction and tells him to eat it. The final shot is of Stamos eating a sandwich while sliding in the park on green grass, surrounded by bushes and trees with a wind energy tower in the background. In the foreground are two loaves of the company's bread next to a sandwich and the company's logo to the left with the words "From Seed to Nutritious Slice" next to it ("Brownberry Whole Grains TV Spot" 2022). This particular commercial uses humor and celebrity in addition to leading viewers to believe that the product is healthy by its association with nature resulting in the use of the whole-grain theme in the Nutrition Health Halo and the perceived severity and perceived benefits Health Belief Model constructs. Also present in this advertisement is the perceived barriers Health Belief Model construct as evidenced by Stamos's emphasis on the "delicious, good nutrition for your balanced life." Use of the words "balanced life" indicate on some level the promise of relief from stress as illustrated by the abundant scenes in nature and the portrayal of a family activity that many in today's busy world do not have time for.

Additional ultra-processed bread products using the whole-grain theme and perceived susceptibility and perceived benefits constructs on their packaging include, but are not limited to, the following: Dave's Killer Bread Organic 21 Whole Grains and Seed Bread, Dave's Killer Bread Organic White Bread Done Right, Dave's Killer Bread Organic Seed Bread, Food for Life Ezekiel 4:9 Organic Frozen Sprouted Whole Grain Sesame Bread, Food for Life Ezekiel 4:9 Organic Frozen Sprouted Grain Bread, Udi's Gluten Free Frozen Whole Grain Bread, Arnold 12 Grain Bread, Arnold Oatnut Bread, Favorite Day Sliced Multgrain Bread, Schar Gluten-Free Artisan Baker 10 Grain & Seeds Bread, Pepperidge Farm Whole Grain 15 Grain Bread, Pepperidge Farm Whole Grain 100% Whole Wheat Bread, Nature's Own 100% Whole Wheat Bread, Nature's Own Honey Wheat Bread, Martin's 100% Whole Wheat Potato Bread, Market Pantry 100% Whole Wheat Bread, Gardenia High Fiber Whole Wheat Bread, Oroweat 100% Whole Wheat Small Slices Bread, Dempster's 100% Whole Wheat Bread, Stern's Bakery 100% Whole Wheat Bread, Stern's Bakery 12 Grain Bread, Stern's Bakery Choice Grain Bread, Sara Lee 100% Whole Wheat Bread, Canyon Bakehouse Gluten Free Heritage Style Whole Grain Bread, Lewis Bakeshop Whole Wheat Bread, Panera Bread 100% Whole Wheat, Panera Bread Whole Grain Multi-Grain, Panera Bread Whole Grain Baker's Grain, Panera Bread Whole Grain Hearty White, Beckman's Whole Wheat Sourdough, 365 Whole Foods Market Whole Wheat Sandwich Bread, Mrs. Baird Whole Grain White Bread, Milton's Craft Bakers Multi-Grain Bread, H-E-B Organics 100% Whole Wheat Plant Based Organic Bread, H-E-B Essential Grains 100% Whole Wheat Bread, H-E-B Essential Grains 100% Whole Wheat Multigrain Bread, Three Bakers Gluten Free 7 Ancient Grains Bread, Three Bakers Gluten Free Whole Grain Golden Flax Bread, Three Bakers Gluten Free MaxOmega Whole Grain Bread, Three Bakers Gluten Free White Whole Grain Frozen Bread, One Mighty Mill Mighty Whole Wheat Bread, One Mighty Mill Mighty Power Grains Whole Wheat Bread, One Mighty Mill Mighty Cinnamon Raisin Whole Wheat Bread, Sasko Low G.I. Seeded Whole Wheat Brown Bread, Schmidt Olde Tyme Omega Me Crazy! 100% Sprouted Whole Wheat Bread, and Schmidt Olde Tyme Omega Me Crazy! 21 Grain and Seeds Bread.

"The Whole, Whole Grain"

The whole-grain theme of the Nutrition Health Halo is used frequently in cereal commercials as a way to create a health halo over ultra-processed products while the Health Belief Model constructs are used to motivate purchase of the products.

As with bread advertisements, many cereal commercials and product labels include images of grain fields, individual grains, or nature. A 2014 commercial featuring chef Curtis Stone does all three. The commercial opens with the well-known chef standing in a field of wheat as he says, "Like many chefs today, I feel the best approach to food is to keep it whole for better nutrition and that's what they do with Great Grains cereal." As he finishes speaking, the camera focuses on a close up of a wheat kernel next to a flake of cereal at which point he says, "See the seam on the wheat grain," with his finger pointing to an indent in the middle of the kernel before continuing, "it's the same as the one on the flake because Great Grain steams and bakes the actual whole grain" at which point the words "whole grain" appear below the flake with the company's logo in the top of the frame (Burns Group 2014). After this, the chef encourages viewers to "check out the other guy's flake," which does not have a seam he says because it's more processed and then asks the viewer which they suppose has "better nutrition for you" as he is shown in the field eating a bowl of cereal (Burns Group 2014). Small text in white font at the bottom says, "Better nutrition means that our whole grains are not diluted with chemically modified fibers, isolated fibers, or artificial sweeteners" as the camera focuses on a close up of a spoon filled with the cereal and then pulls out to the chef eating the cereal (Burns Group 2014). The final shot is of a box of the cereal in front of the grain field with the words "The *Whole* Whole Grain Cereal" to the left (Burns Group 2014).

Though it may appear as if Stone makes a compelling argument for the healthiness of the cereal, the small text about the definition of better nutrition as the grains not being diluted, has nothing to do with the "whole, whole grain" while the ingredients listed on the box of the company's Crunch Pecan version of this cereal indicate a different message. The following ingredients are listed: whole-grain wheat, cane sugar, whole-grain rolled oats, pecans, wheat flour, malted barley flour, rice flour, expeller pressed canola oil, salt, rice syrup, molasses, bht, which is butylated hydroxytoluene, added to preserve freshness. Cane sugar, wheat flour, malted barley flour, rice flour expeller pressed canola oil, rice syrup, and bht, a lab-made chemical that is used as a preservative in foods, are all ultra-processed foods, and thus, unhealthy.

Similarly, the use of the perceived severity, perceived benefits, and perceived barriers Health Belief Model constructs is illustrated by first showing viewers the "seam" on the wheat grain that is said to be steamed and baked, which according to Stone means that it is less processed and has "better nutrition" (perceived severity). The fact that he is shown in a field while eating breakfast in a low-stress, natural environment illustrates the perceived benefits construct while the perceived barriers construct is employed by the inclusion of a well-known chef, who is known to have an exceptional palate to determine good taste, as shown eating the product. All these constructs work together to motivate consumers to purchase what is advertised as a healthier product on screen, yet they are not actually any more so than other cereals.

The idea of the "whole whole grain" may have been a reaction to a General Mills initiative to add more whole grains to its products. In a commercial released a few years prior to the Great Grains one, a family is shown eating breakfast from a box with a question mark on it. The camera focuses on the mother who has a spoon with cereal on it as a female announcer says, "If whole grain isn't the first ingredient in breakfast cereal, what is?" as the camera shows the cereal on the mother's spoon, which is in the shape of a question mark ("General Mills TV Spot" 2012). The camera cuts to a shot of five boxes of cereal on the counter with the family eating behind it as the female announcer says, "Now, in every box of General Mills Big G cereal, there's more whole grain than any other ingredient. That's why it's listed first" as white font appears at the bottom of the screen with the words, "As compared to any other single ingredient" before the camera focuses on an ingredient list on a box of cereal with the words "Whole Grain Oats" circled in red ("General Mills TV Spot" 2012). The next shots are of several family members eating the cereal with satisfied looks on their faces as the female announcer urges viewers to "Get more whole grain than any other ingredient" and white font appears at the bottom of the screen with the words "All Big G cereals have at least 8 grams of whole grain per serving; at least 48 grams recommended daily" before a final shot of the five boxes of cereal are shown with the announcer urging viewers to "Just look for the white check" as an image of a white checkmark appears over the products ("General Mills TV Spot" 2012). It's worth noting that in the close up shot of the ingredients listed on the box, sugar is the second ingredient followed by modified corn starch, brown sugar syrup, and canola and/or rice bran oil, all of which are ultra processed food ingredients.

Despite the unhealthy ingredients in the cereals, by focusing on the fact that whole grains are the first ingredient, the company is making use of the whole-grain theme in the Nutrition Health Halo as an attempt to promote unhealthy, ultra-processed foods as healthy. At the same time, the company is employing the perceived severity, perceived benefits, and perceived barriers Health Belief Model constructs to motivate viewers to purchase the cereal. By focusing on the number of whole grains in the cereal products, which has for years received great emphasis in the popular press as being healthy, the company is leading viewers to believe that if they eat this product, they will avoid unfavorable health outcomes (perceived severity). Images of healthy-looking family members who are of normal weight eating in a brightly lit beautiful eating area help to emphasize the perceived benefits of eating the product while the perceived barriers are addressed by the looks of satisfaction after eating spoonfuls of the cereals indicating good taste.

A recent UK Cheerios commercial highlights the tastiness of whole grains to appeal to consumers thus making use of the perceived benefits Health Belief Model construct. The commercial begins with time-lapsed shots of a seed in the ground to it growing to its full height as a female announcer says, "From the seed to the multigrain to the bowl to the crunch," as the camera focuses on a woman and young boy both eating cereal, tasty little Os, high in fiber from oats, wheat, and barely. "All the goodness of Cheerios multigrain made tasty" as the camera focuses on different grains and various people eating the cereal until there is a final shot of two boxes of Cheerios on a table next to milk and a bowl with the words "MULTIGRAIN MADE TASTY" in white font to the left of the screen (Cheerios UK 2024). Once again, use of the whole-grain theme as well as the connection with nature with images of a seed growing (perceived severity), emphasis on the good nutrition in the high fiber (perceived benefits), and the woman and boy clearly enjoying the taste of the cereal (perceived benefits) work to motivate consumers to purchase the product despite the fact that there is little health value in it.

Another commercial posted by the company to Pinterest that same year opens with various shots of parents and children eating Cheerios as a male announcer says, "You don't just eat Cheerios for you, you do it for them" before there is a final shot of three boxes of limited edition heart-shaped Cheerios with the words "Familia," "Dad," and "My Love" on each box as the announcer says, "Heart Healthy Cheerios" under which the words "Three grams of soluble fiber daily from whole grain oat foods, like Cheerios cereal, in a diet low in saturated fat and cholesterol, may reduce the risk of heart disease. Specially marked Cheerios varieties provide .75 grams per serving" appear below the boxes and in the post itself (Cheerios 2024). In addition to using the whole-grain theme and the previously mentioned constructs, this product also employs the perceived susceptibility Health Belief Model construct by promoting the product as a means of keeping "hearts healthy."

"Bubble Grains at Bedtime" and "A Meal in Every Muffet"

Though it may seem to be a recent phenomenon to use the whole-grain theme, an advertisement from the March 1920 issue of *Good Housekeeping* magazine indicates otherwise. The advertisement features an illustration of a woman's hand pouring Puffed Wheat and Puffed Rice cereal from a large cup into a bowl filled with milk, which is placed on a table next to a lamp with a chair behind it. The headline "Bubble Grains at Bedtime" is positioned directly below with the words "Foods Easy to Digest" directly underneath (Sheryl 2020). Below this are two paragraphs that begin with the words "Puffed Wheat and Puffed Rice are not for breakfast only" and then continues to urge readers to serve them for luncheon and supper, tells how they "float in every bowl," and that they "are bubble grains, airy, crisp, and toasted, puffed to eight times [their] normal size," which "makes the milk dish so enticing" (Sheryl 2020). Underneath this is a smaller headline with the words "Every Food Cell Blasted" followed by four paragraphs, which tell about how Puffed Wheat is "made delightful" through "Prof. Anderson's process," which "explodes" every food cell to make digestion easy and supply "whole wheat nutrition" that "does not tax the stomach" (Sheryl 2020). Another paragraph below this in bold lettering tells readers that "Puffed Grains are the greatest of grain foods and the most enticing" before including an advertisement for Puffed Rice Pancake Flour at the bottom quarter of the page below which the Quaker Oats Company is listed as the "Sole Maker" of these products (Sheryl 2020).

Though it's not possible to thoroughly understand the reference to "Prof. Anderson's process" of "exploding" food cells, it is more than likely that the advertisement refers to steam explosion, which is "a physicochemical pretreatment method to realize cell walls' physical rushing and thermal degradation under the action of high-temperature and high-pressure saturated steam" that ruptures cell walls of food making it easier to digest (Yu et al. 2023). The lack of explanation regarding this process, which is promoted coupled with the statement touting the grains as superior to all others, illustrates the use of the whole-grain theme in the Nutrition Health Halo as well as the perceived severity, perceived benefits, and perceived barriers constructs of the Health Belief Model.

An advertisement six years later from the company would introduce the new Pettijohn's Whole Wheat cereal with a housewife enticing title of "Men Welcome the Stimulation of a Steaming Breakfast Dish of the New Pettijohn's

Whole Wheat Cereal," which features an image of a breakfast table with a bowl of the cereal at the top, six paragraphs of text underneath the title, an image of the product, an outlined paragraph titled "In brief," and the company's logo at the bottom all surrounded by a border with images of wheat drawn into it (Period Paper 2016). The text in the middle notes that "bran is only part of the whole wheat story," which they say makes the cereal popular due to the "White Montana Wheat—rich in mineral salts, protein and energy content" due to an "exclusive milling process [that] retains . . . health giving vitamins and brings out its distinctive flavor" making it "nourishing" and "an effective laxative" (Period Paper 2016). The "In brief" box highlights the "palatable" taste and vitamins and minerals "of the Wheat Berry and all the Natural Bran" ending with the idea that "With milk, it forms one of the best balanced food combinations known to dieticians" and reminding readers that "It cooks in 3 to 5 minutes" (Period Paper 2016). It's also worth noting that the box includes a reminder to consumers that the product is whole wheat, "each flake an entire grain of natural wheat freed from the indigestible outer covering, unmutilated in making ready for use, palatable, easily digested and assimilated, and supplies all the necessary ingredients requisite for the development of a strong, healthy constitution" (MSU Libraries 2024).

An advertisement in the January 1928 issue of *Good Housekeeping* magazine employs a subtler approach to using the whole-grain theme and constructs. At the top of the page is the name of the product—Muffets—with an image of five of the toasted whole-wheat cereal topped with various things, including fruit, cream, and vegetables. The subheading below the picture says, "Not only a cereal, but a real help in serving other foods" (Houseofblair 2024). In the middle of the page is an image of the product box with one column of text on each side and the words "There's a Meal in Every Muffet" underneath (Houseofblair 2024). It is in the text where the whole-grain health halo is used to describe the product as "flaky, tender, wound into a shape that makes for perfect spoonwork" as well as a "new, different, and better toasted whole-wheat cereal" that is "rich in vital food elements" and part of the "grown-up age of cereals" (Houseofblair 2024). The text goes on to describe how satisfying, easily digestible, and "rich in vital food elements" the cereal is (Houseofblair 2024). The text on the right side of the page highlights five suggestions about how to serve the product, which include eating it as traditional cereal with milk, adding diced chicken, topping with raspberry jam, hollowing out and filling with vegetables, or topping with asparagus and hollandaise sauce.

In addition to using the whole-grain theme of the Nutrition Health Halo, both of these advertisements use three of the Health Belief Model constructs by convincing readers that use of the products advertised will help them to prevent health problems (perceived severity), increase nutrition (perceived benefits), and taste good (perceived barriers). The Pettijohn's Whole Wheat cereal advertisement also uses the perceived susceptibility construct by touting the product as a way to avoid constipation.

In 1906, the Pure Food & Drugs Act prevented false or misleading information on food labels but did not require ingredient lists. In 1966, the Fair Labeling & Packaging Act mandated that products participating in interstate commerce needed to list the ingredients. It wasn't until 1990 with the Nutrition & Labeling Education Act, however, when all companies were required to list ingredients and nutritional information in a standardized panel that included calories, fat, cholesterol, sodium, carbohydrates, and protein, as well as select vitamins and minerals.

Whole Grains, Constructs, and War

During the Second World War, the whole-grain theme was used in advertisements as a way to win the war. A 1943 advertisement for Shredded Ralston breakfast cereal features a headline of "Give me a Shredded Ralston breakfast, I've got a job to do" above an image of a soldier and a youngster dressed in a soldier's uniform over which the words "That Goes for Me, Too!" appear (Lofty Life Ads 2024). To the right is an image of a large bowl of the cereal above the product box. Text underneath the image says, "Everyone has a job to do today . . . to help win the war. Seeing the job through takes energy and that's what you get in Shredded Ralston. Whole-wheat energy and a hearty hit-the-spot flavor that's made Shredded Ralston a national favorite. Enjoy Shredded Ralston often—it's nourishing—it's plentiful—it's not rationed" (Lofty Life Ads 2024). Similarly, a 1940s era advertisement published in *Life* magazine also uses the whole-grain health halo. At the top of the page, there's an image of a female soldier who is saluting under which is a headline "Salute . . . This Morning Energy Breakfast" with a subheading below saying, "Nabisco Shredded Wheat's the Best Part—Crisp as Toast, High in Food Energy" (oddzenenz254, 2024). There are two paragraphs of text below that encourages mothers to "keep the family fit" and to "make breakfast count" since the product will cause them to "greet it with a smile" and "eat it with delight" (oddzenenz254, 2024). The paragraph underneath that tells readers that Nabisco Shredded Wheat is "made from 100% whole wheat," which is "one of the Basic 7 foods our Government advises for good health in wartime" while a sidebar to the left outlines how the product contributes essential food elements including "proteins for strength," "carbohydrates for energy," vitamin B1 which "aids in digestion, "iron for blood-building," and "phosphorous for strong bones" (oddzenenz254, 2024). Another advertisement for the same product during this time includes an image of a woman with the headline "My Man's Fitness Is One of My War Jobs" before going on to describe how the product benefits everyone in the family with "men working harder" and "children taking over some of Dad's duties" because it's made of "100% whole wheat" made of "rich whole grain" that "helps convert foods into keen, live-wire energy for the whole family" (American Century Shop 2024b). Readers are also reminded that Nabisco Shredded Wheat is "a good source of Vitamin B1 as *Nature* provides it" and that it is "recommended in the Nutrition Food Rules" (American Century Shop 2024b; emphasis in the original).

One cereal company using the whole-grain theme presented its product as the solution to wartime food rationing. A 1943 Quaker Oats newspaper advertisement featured an image of a woman to the left with the words "How Meat Rationing Turned Me to Whole-Grain Quaker Oats for My Family's Breakfast" under which there are three comic book like squares with illustrated images and text (Quaker Oats Rationing Ad [1943] 2024). In the first square is a woman looking at a piece of meat and wondering what the vital elements in it are only to realize that it's protein that she found in "delicious whole-grain Quaker Oat" (Quaker Oats Rationing Ad [1943] 2024). In the second box, she is shown with her son and wonders whether protein is important only to realize that "Children can't grow normally without it" and that "Oatmeal leads every other cereal—hot or cold—in Protein" because "The best authorities say so!" (Quaker Oats Rationing Ad [1943] 2024). The final box shows the woman and her husband as she thinks "HIS STAMINA MUST BE PROTECTED" since they are both "working harder than ever" (Quaker Oats Rationing Ad [1943] 2024). A box to the right of this resembling a newspaper story has a headline of "Authorities Agree Oatmeal Leads All Cereals in Great Vitality Element Protein" under which the text notes how many foods are rationed but the "delicious Whole Grain Oatmeal" is "rich in so many vital elements that wartime America needs" because it "leads all cereals in protein," which is "meat's basic vitality element" (Quaker Oats Rationing Ad [1943] 2024). At the bottom of the advertisement, underneath the name of the company are the words "100% Real Whole-Grain Oats" (Quaker Oats Rationing Ad [1943] 2024).

All of these wartime advertisements work in a similar manner to convince consumers not only of the value of their products by preventing health problems (perceived severity), increasing nutrition (perceived benefits), and tasting good (perceived barriers) as the ones described prior, but outline the perceived susceptibility of acquiring poor nutrition or lack of energy and strength during a time of food rationing. This combination of using the Nutrition Health Halo with Health Belief Model constructs to motivate consumers to purchase these products under the veil of patriotism provides powerful persuasion for those left at home to eat these unhealthy ultra-processed products as a way of supporting soldiers.

More "Whole Grain Goodness" Than Ever

One company took the whole-grain theme a little further in the introduction of its line of cereals in the early 2000s. The advertisement features a close up of a spoon filled with cereal flakes and dripping milk. Above the image is the headline "No spoon has ever held more whole grain goodness" while below it in large font are the words "Introducing Nutri-Grain. The first line of flaked, whole grain cereal with no sugar added" (Mustard 2009). The cereal is touted as "a whole grain different" in the advertisement (Mustard 2009). It's worth noting that in addition to the whole-grain health halo, this product also used the no-sugar-added one discussed in Chapter 4 as well. However, the company now produces a high protein, fiber, and multigrain line of cereals known as Iron Man Food, which they advertise at their website as "Packed with fibre, multigrains (wheat, oat, and corn), B vitamins and iron, Kellogg's® Nutri-Grain® breakfast cereal has essential nutrients to fuel the active bodies*. It has the iconic malty taste and crunch that families love. *Contains 650 kJ of energy per serve, plus a source of B vitamins and iron," which lists sugar as the fourth ingredient. The ingredients listed are as follows in the format at the company's website: cereals (51 percent) (wheat flour, oatmeal (contains oats), maize flour), sugar, wheat protein, maltodextrin, molasses, oat fiber, vegetable gum (acacia gum), salt, barley malt extract, minerals (calcium carbonate, iron, zinc oxide), raising agent (potassium bicarbonate), natural flavors, natural colors (paprika, turmeric), vitamins (niacin, vitamin B6, riboflavin, folate). As previously discussed, in addition to sugar, wheat flour, maize flour, wheat protein, maltodextrin, molasses, oat fiber, vegetable gum, barley malt extract, natural flavors, and natural colors are all ultra-processed foods. The inclusion of a percentage after the ingredient "cereals" appears to be an attempt to indicate the large number of whole grains in the product; however, wheat flour and maize flour, the second and third ingredients following cereal, as well as those listed above are unhealthy ultra-processed foods thus creating a perfect illustration of the whole-grain theme and constructs even in the list of ingredients on the cereal box.

Additional cereal products using the whole-grain theme and constructs include, but are not limited to, the following: Total, Weetabix, Cheerios, Multi-Grain Cheerios, Honey Nut Cheerios, Cheerios Oat Crunch Cinnamon, Raisin Bran, All Bran, Bran Flakes, Ezekiel 4:9 Sprouted Crunchy Cereal, Ezekiel 4:9 Golden Flax Cereal, Ezekiel 4:9 Almond Cereal, Ezekiel 4:9 Cinnamon Raisin Cereal, Holle Organic 4-Grain Whole Grain Cereal, Holle Organic Oat Whole Grain Cereal, Holle Organic 3-Grain Whole Grain Cereal, Holle Organic Semolina Whole Grain Cereal, Holle Organic Spelt Whole Grain Cereal, Alpen Muesli Original, Alpen Muesli No Sugar Added, Alpen Muesli Triple Berry, Kashi Organic Berry Fruitful, Kashi Organic Cinnamon Harvest, Kashi Organic Island Vanilla, Kashi Honey Sunshine, Kashi Go Crunch, Kashi Go Toasted Berry Crunch, Kashi Go Chocolate Crunch, Fiber One, Grain Berry Multi-Grain Flakes, H-E-B Multi-Grain Flakes with Fruit & Nuts, H-E-B Fruit & Grain with Nuts, Woodstock 5 Grain Cereal, Woodstock Organic Traditional Rolled Oats, Original Shredded Wheat, Big Biscuit Shredded Wheat, Spoon Size Shredded Wheat & Bran, Spoon Size Shredded Wheat Honey & Nut, Spoon Size Shredded Wheat Vanilla Almond, Honey Nut Clusters, Frosted Mini Wheats Cinnamon Roll, Cream of Wheat Whole Grain Hot Cereal, Bob's Red Mill Organic Whole Grain High Fiber Hot Cereal, Bob's Red Mill 7 Grain Hot Cereal, Bob's Red Mill 10 Grain Hot Cereal, Bob's Red Mill Organic 6 Grain Hot Cereal, Alpha Bits, Grape-Nuts, and Golden Krisp.

Strong Bones, High Protein, Low Nutrition

In 1924, iodine was added to salt to prevent goiters, then in 1933, vitamin D was introduced into milk followed by "in 1940 the Committee on Food and Nutrition (now the Food and Nutrition Board (FNB)) recommend[ing] the addition of thiamin, niacin, riboflavin, and iron to flour" that would soon after carry the label of "enriched" through the establishment of "using a standard of identity, which establishes the specific type and level of fortification required for [a] particular staple food to be labeled as enriched" with "standards . . . amended over the years, but . . . continue as the basis for the addition of thiamin, niacin, riboflavin, folic acid, and iron to enriched flour, with the addition of calcium as optional" (Institute of Medicine (US) Committee on Use of Dietary Reference Intakes in Nutrition Labeling 2003). Today, "marketers blitz supermarkets with new fortified products: so many items are spiked with calcium, for instance—juice, cereal, snack bars and even waffles—that nutrition experts are debating whether enough is enough" (*Chicago Tribune* 2021). Additionally, "misleading advertising of UPPs [ultra-processed products] with added micronutrients and with excessive content of sugar, fat, and salt might increase the consumption of such products, giving them a 'health halo effect' that leads consumers to overestimate their nutritional quality and healthfulness" (Kroker-Lobos et al. 2022). The fortification theme of the Nutrition Health Halo is used regularly in many different products and has been for many years.

"The Peppy Bran Food" and "Builder Upper Vitamins"

The 1940s would bring the introduction of many vitamin-fortified, ultra-processed foods, with one of the most popular being vitamin-and-mineral-fortified breakfast cereals. The first of these, according to its product maker's website was introduced in 1938 as outlined by the company at its website: "Kellogg's recognized that fortification with micronutrients played a vital role in achieving optimal health for all the family and has been voluntarily adding vitamins and minerals to breakfast cereals for over 70 years. In 1938, Kellogg's launched 'Pep,' the first cereal to be fortified with B vitamins and vitamin D." However, a 1933 advertisement for the product published in the April 1933 issue of *Good Housekeeping* magazine featured an illustration of a man driving a car with a woman by his side and the headline underneath with a red background in white text, "Keep Going with Pep!" (Vintage Paper Ads 2024). Four paragraphs of text next to an image of the product begin with saying that young people "dash from one busy hour to the next" and "need spirit and energy" that come from "Kellogg's Pep Bran Flakes," which "gives all the goodness of health-giving grain" (Vintage Paper Ads 2024). Though this advertisement and subsequent ones did not contain the words "enriched" or "fortified," they did highlight the vitamins in the product. This advertisement, for example, includes the following: "Wheat is nature's storehouse of energy and nourishment. Vitamin B. Proteins. Healthful minerals" (Vintage Paper Ads 2024), thus illustrating the use of the fortification theme as well as the perceived severity, perceived benefits, and perceived barrier constructs of the Health Belief Model through the promise of healthful minerals (perceived severity), increased energy (perceived benefits), and good taste (perceived barriers).

Prior to this, the product was advertised as "the Peppy Bran Food" with little or no mention of vitamins and minerals except for the image of the product. A 1926 advertisement encourages readers to "Help Yourself to Health" with a signature of W. K. Kellogg next to it and the word "Pep" in large red letters with an image of a young woman getting ready to dive off a diving board (dustystuffsantabarbara 2024). The text underneath the image says, "Takes *pep* to make that graceful flashing dive!" with six small paragraphs of text below telling readers that "PEP is a wonder" that "fills you with glorious pep" and "builds health, stamina, and strength" and is "packed with nature's own health-bringing elements . . . keep[ing] you robust, alert, alive!" (dustystuffsantabarbara 2024; emphasis in the original). The next paragraph talks about how Pep is "mildly laxative" and helps to keep children "regular" and "in romping health" with the words "the peppy bran food" underneath the block of text (dustystuffsantabarbara 2024). On the image of the box of cereal in the advertisement are the words, "A Laxative Bran Food Rich in Food" on the first line with the following words below it: "Iron, Lime and Other Mineral Salts" (dustystuffsantabarbara 2024). In addition to the use of the fortification theme as well as the perceived severity, perceived benefits, and perceived barrier constructs of the Health Belief Model through the promise of health (perceived severity), increased stamina and strength (perceived benefits), and good taste (perceived barriers), this advertisement also employes the perceived susceptivity construct through its promotion as using this product as a laxative.

By the 1950s, the added vitamins appear to have taken a more prominent role in the company's advertisements. A 1951 advertisement features an illustration of a mother who is holding the flexed muscle her daughter is making with a large image of a bowl of cereal underneath and a headline interwoven between the two that says, "Mother's helper thrives on Pep the Build-Up wheat cereal!" (Lost in Time Vintage Ads 2024). Four paragraphs in smaller text begin with the words, "Kellogg's PEP has more 'builder-upper' vitamins than any *other* wheat flakes cereal. Helps build muscles, bones and teeth. Of all wheat flakes, only PEP is richer in Vitamin B1 than whole wheat itself. A *full day's* needs of 'Sunshine' Vitamin D in every one-ounce bowlful. Food experts call it 'the mighty ounce'!" (Lost in Time Vintage Ads 2024; emphases in the original). Both the visual image of a mother holding her daughter's flexed muscle as well as the text promising "builder upper" vitamins by eating the product indicate the presence of the fortification theme as well as all four constructs used to advertise an ultra-processed food product.

"It's a Bird. It's a Plane!" It's Pep Cereal!

Kellogg's Pep cereal would join with one of the strongest pop culture characters of the time to promote its product while simultaneously using the fortification theme and constructs in its advertising. "Born" on April 18, 1938, in the pages of *Action Comics*, (TRAVSD 2018a), appearing in a newspaper comic strip in 1939 followed by a radio show that same year that would run into the early 1950s, the character of Superman epitomized health and strength. It is, no doubt for this reason, that Kellogg's put forth Pep cereal as a sponsor of the popular *Superman* radio show. In one particular advertisement, an illustration of Superman is shown with a bowl of cereal in front of him and a spoon filled with the product in his hand on the left side. Above him in a dialogue box pointing in his direction are the words "Mmm! Rich Golden Wheat Flakes with That Sunny Flavor—That's Kellogg's Pep!" with an illustration of a sun with the words "The Sunshine Cereal" in it and above an illustration of the product box (TRAVSD 2018b). To the left of the box are the words "Listen to Superman Monday through Friday" while underneath in a ribbon across the bottom of the advertisement is a "Special to Mom!" that tells readers, "Better nutrition than whole wheat—one bowlful gives a day's need of sunshine vitamin D. Kids love PEP!" (TRAVSD 2018b). In another advertisement featuring Superman, "Boys!" and "Girls!" are encouraged to "Eat the Super Cereal You Hear All about on the *Superman Radio Program*" and told to "Get Hep to Swell-Tasting Kellogg's Pep That's so Mighty Good for You, Too!" (Pop Culture Safari 2015; emphasis in the original). Smaller text directed at "kids" notes that "Pep is *extra* good for you" and "Gives you *more* vitamins B1 and D than any other nationally advertised wheat-flakes cereal," which are needed for "growth, steady nerves, strong bones and teeth" for " 'blockbuster' energy" (Pop Culture Safari 2015; emphases in the original).

It's worth noting that "Superman reached a radio audience of millions; in 1946, the *Adventures of Superman* aired five times a week nationwide on the Mutual network and regularly attracted the highest juvenile audience of any show, according to contemporary Hooper ratings" (Goodrum 2008). Some media scholars have dubbed Superman as "one of the most popular fictions in the USA" (Goodrum 2008), no doubt based in part on the character's legacy, which includes not only the newspaper comic strip, the comic books, and the radio program but also subsequent films and television series as well. The character's association with an ultra-processed food employing the fortification theme and constructs is no accident. Superman is internationally known for his superior strength and stamina, which may lead children and even adults to believe that the product he is advertising is healthier than it actually is. Further taking into consideration the lack of savvy about advertising techniques by the general public during this time period, it becomes clear exactly how solidified with vitamins, health, and well-being this cereal was.

"When You Eat Candy, Eat Right!"

Though there are many other cereal brands using the fortification theme and constructs, a few of which will be discussed later in this chapter, it's worthwhile noting that during this time period, there appears to be liberal use of the theme in all types of products, including, for example, candy bars. A 1943 advertisement for Baby Ruth candy bars shows an illustration of one young boy holding a baseball bat with another behind him wearing a baseball glove. Both are smiling. The headline above them reads, "Today's Meals Make Tomorrow's Men," while below the illustration it says, "Balanced Diet Is Important to the Future Strength of Your Children—Follow Uncle Sam's Nutrition Program Now" with a chart describing the nutritional needs of the United States to the right (buy sites 2021). Smaller text goes on to describe "the basics groups of food—protein, fat, carbohydrates, minerals and vitamins" that "supply all our nutritional needs" and then noting that "your Government *[sic]* prepared an official food chart" to plan meals and make sure everyone receives "adequate nutrition" (buy sites 2021). In a box underneath is an illustration of the candy bar with text telling consumers that the product is "a wonderful energy food to add to your regular diet," which "contains the most wholesome of ingredients" and "tastes delicious" noting that "because it's rich in Dextrose—the sugar your body uses directly for energy—Baby Ruth helps overcome fatigue when body sugars are low" (buy sites 2021). The idea of fortifying candy with dextrose, a form of sugar, seems absurd in today's time, yet it was commonplace to advertise sugar and dextrose as nutritionally beneficial during this time period.

Another candy bar takes the fortification theme a step further. An advertisement in the 1946 issue of *The Saturday Evening Post* features an illustration of a woman pointing to images of three large candy bars with the headline, "When You Eat Candy . . . Eat Right!" with the final two words in a larger red font (Mister Cola 2024). The first candy bar illustration is of Shotwell's Almond Shur-Mac, which in the small text next to it is said to have "almonds, nougat, caramel, chocolate coating . . . plus Vitamins B1, B2, D, calcium, phosphate, niacin and iron" while the middle candy bar illustration is of Shotwell's Almond Big Yank, which according to the description includes "Almonds, marshmallow, fudge chocolate coating . . . plus Vitamins B1, B2, D, calcium, phosphate, niacin and iron," and the third illustration is for Shotwell's High-Mac that includes "nougat, caramel, chocolate coating, plus Vitamins B1, B2, D, calcium, phosphate, niacin and iron" (Mister Cola 2024). In three paragraphs of small text to the left of the final candy bar, consumers are told that "it's vital to *eat right*" and that eating the "Shotwell candies shown on this page" ensures getting "the *right* vitamins and minerals for *right* eating" (Mister Cola 2024; emphases in the original). In the text, the vitamins and minerals are described as "added 'extras'" in the candy so "you can eat right today!" (Mister Cola 2024).

Though use of the words "fortified with" are not explicitly used, the implication of "added 'extras'" can be taken as use of the fortification theme as well as the perceived severity construct, either through the practice of fortification or the highlighting of the vitamins and minerals contained in the ingredients. Another advertisement published a year later for the Hi-Mac candy bar would confirm this. In the advertisement, the headline says, "Eat Showell's 'High-Mac' and eat right!" with the words, "Contains Needed Vitamins and Minerals" next to an illustration of a couple at the top of the page to the right of the headline (The Jumping Frog 2024). Underneath this is an image of a woman at a table with her daughter and the words "Right for food balance" below which is an image of a man with a hat on with the words "Right for a lift," and then an image of a young girl holding a book titled *Better Nutrition* and the smaller headline which says, "Right for Taste! Right for Nutrition!" next to her (The Jumping Frog 2024).

Doughnuts with Vitamins?

In what some call "a notorious case in the history of misleading advertising," Vitamin Donuts were introduced in 1941 by the Doughnut Corporation of America (Museum of Hoaxes 2014). In an early advertisement for the product, an illustration of a young boy holding a doughnut with a bite out of it is show in the right corner with the words "For Pep and Vigor" in the left corner across from him and above the words "Vitamin Donuts" with the word "vitamin" in red text and the word "donuts" in blue over a bright yellow background (Museum of Hoaxes 2014). Beneath this is an illustration of a young girl smiling while looking at an image of a large white plate with two doughnuts on it with a smaller image of two chefs in white with a dark blue background and the words "Mark of" above them in white font and "Tested" on one chef's hat and "Quality" on the other's hat (Museum of Hoaxes 2014). Underneath the plate and the girl is a dark blue ribbon across the bottom of the advertisement with the words "Each Donut Fortified with a minimum of 25 units of Vitamin B1" (Museum of Hoaxes 2014).

Though "the name was justified, so the Doughnut Corporation believed, because the donuts were made with flour fortified with thiamine (Vitamin B1)," the Nutrition Division of the War Food Administration did not agree, saying that "the name was misleading, because it was only the flour that was enriched with vitamins, not the entire donut" (Museum of Hoaxes 2014). They also noted that if Vitamin Donuts were approved, "then anything made with enriched flour could theoretically be a Vitamin product—Vitamin Cake, Vitamin Bread, Vitamin Cookies, etc." (Museum of Hoaxes 2014). The Nutrition Division told the company to use "Enriched Flour Donuts" instead, "but the Doughnut Corporation didn't think this sounded appetizing, so they dropped the product entirely" (Museum of Hoaxes 2014). It's also worth noting that the "the flour in modern donuts has far more vitamins in it than the flour in Vitamin Donuts did" (Museum of Hoaxes 2014). Though discontinued, the importance of this product in the history of the Nutrition Health Halo should not be underestimated.

Fortification and Bread

While the temptation to fortify many different kinds of foods to evoke a health halo exists, "one of the basic criteria concerning food fortification is the selection of the right vehicle, which should be a food that is commonly eaten by the target population group, is economically affordable and available all year long" (Roseli 2008, 336). One of the most commonly fortified foods, in addition to breakfast cereals, is bread due to the fact that "flour and by extension bread, is one of the best vehicles for food fortification because it meets" the requirements mentioned above (Roseli 2008, 336). A 1952 commercial for a well-known bread product, which dubbed itself the first sliced bread in 1930, explains each of the eight vitamins added into the product. The commercial opens with the words "Help Build Strong Bodies 8 Ways" with an announcer saying the same words before the number "8" turns into a character with a face in the top portion of the number, a chef's hat and arms holding a loaf of Wonder Bread, who encourages viewers to eat the product (TV Toy Memories 2012). The character goes to ask a young boy whether he wants to grow strong to which the boy answers affirmatively before the Number 8 character tells him that if he eats a sandwich every day and two slices of Wonder Bread with each meal, he will get the vitamins he needs before going on to describe each element, which includes "as much muscle-building protein as roast beef," "as much calcium for bones and teeth as cottage cheese," "as much phosphorous for cell metabolism as this egg," "as much iron for red blood as three lamb chops," "as much Vitamin B-1 for appetites as fried liver," "as much Vitamin B-2 for growth as this much cheese" (three slices), "as much niacin for mental health as six sardines," "as much energy as two glasses of milk" (TV Toy Memories 2012). As he describes each vitamin, images of the food he mentions are shown and then put into the loaf of bread. He then tells the boy that this is how he can help himself "grow bigger and stronger 8 ways" by eating the bread as the boy is shown growing before an announcer urges viewers to buy the bread (TV Toy Memories 2012). The emphasis in this advertisement with specifically naming the eight vitamins in the bread clearly indicates the use of the perceived severity Health Belief Model construct as a means to avoid poor nutrition in growing children, a problem that was common during and following the Second World War.

In a similar print advertisement, an illustration of a young boy is shown holding a piece of bread with a bite taken out of it. The headline says, "Wonder Bread Builds Strong Bodies 8 Ways!" in red text (*Star Tribune* 2024). To the right of the boy is a numbered list with eight entries, the top of which says, "All these remarkable food values are supplied by 2 slices at each meal and one sandwich between meals daily" (*Star Tribune* 2024). Within the list are headings that describe each value including (1) "Muscle," (2) "Bones and Teeth," (3) "Body Cells," (4) "Blood," (5) "Appetite," (6) "Growth," (7) "Brain," and (8) "Energy" with the same comparisons to the foods mentioned in the previously described commercial (*Star Tribune* 2024). Underneath the boy is an illustration of the product with a red circle and the words "Doubly Fresh!" in white text touching the bottom of the loaf of bread. In a twist on the idea of eight vitamins, a 1966 advertisement for the product read, "Make the most of their 'Wonder Years' above a collage of photos of children playing with text below that said, "The 'Wonder Years'—one through twelve—are the formative years when you can do the most for your child's growth" (Vintage Paper Ads 2, 2024). A small paragraph of text notes that children will "grow to 90% of their adult height" during these years and that "Wonder Bread is carefully enriched with foods for growing bodies and minds" after which consumers are encouraged to "Serve your children nutritious Wonder Bread" (Vintage Paper Ads 2, 2024). At the bottom of the advertisement in the center in bolded print are the words "Wonder Bread helps build strong bodies 12 ways" (Vintage Paper Ads 2, 2024). Though it's not possible to determine whether or not the intention of the company is to infer that there are twelve vitamins in its product, given the focus on the number eight in previous decades, it is not outside the realm of possibilities. In either case, the company's advertisements during this time indicate a clear use of the fortification theme of the Nutrition Health Halo and the perceived susceptibility and perceived benefits Health Belief Model constructs.

Despite a consumer backlash against unhealthy white bread and a slip in sales, Wonder Bread still manages to garner a good portion of the bread market. "From January to mid-August 2023 . . . the brand's sales surpassed $300 million, and about 55 million loaves of Wonder Bread were sold" with "Wonder Bread's 2022 sales total[ing] $484 million" leading one analysist to note that "while Wonder Bread has somewhat fallen out of favor, people do still eat white bread, and Wonder Bread remains . . . profitable" (Baker 2023).

In 1981, another bread product was advertised as having "five extra vitamins and minerals" (ewjxn 2023). The commercial begins with an announcer saying, "Introducing Butternut Super White" as the logo flies into the frame in white text over a dark red background before the camera cuts to a shot of a mechanic telling viewers that the product "has more vitamins and minerals than ordinary white bread and makes me feel like a man of steel" as he is shown lifting a car up (ewjxn 2023). The camera then cuts to a shot of a woman sitting on a bench eating lunch who says that the product is "the most nutritious white and it gives me x-ray vision" as she giggles and looks at two men who walk in front of her before a shot of the bread is shown as the announcer says, "Butternut Super

White, five extra vitamins and minerals and 100% vegetable oil" as the words fly in onto a circle on the wrapper of the bread (ewjxn 2023). Following this is a shot of a skinny boy with glasses lifting a dumbbell bar with many weights on it who says, "I eat Super White just for the taste" as the camera zooms out to show two men, one on each side of the bar lifting it up along with him before the announcer says, "The most nutritious white is Butternut Super White" (ewjxn 2023).

A 1990s bread commercial focused its product and commercial on kids. The commercial opens with a woman driving and then cuts to a child and then another woman who in piecemeal say, "Why I like Iron Kids Bread" before showing a young African American boy holding a guitar and saying, "I just like the taste of white bread," then to a shot of what appears to be his mother saying, "He loves white bread" then back to the woman driving who says "I like wheat bread," and then to what appears to be her young daughter saying "I only like white bread," who then imitates her mother as she tells viewers, "I can hear her now" as the camera moves back to the woman who starts to say "Iron Kids Bread has . . ." before going back to the girl who is pointing her finger ". . . many important nutrients" (Midnight Munchies 2018). The camera continues to go back and forth between the mothers and their children as the mothers point out that the bread is nutritious, and the kids say they like the taste as an announcer tells viewers, "It's the bread parents and kids can agree on" (Midnight Munchies 2018). The name of the product, which is associated with a necessary nutrient, as well as several mothers pointing out how nutritious the product is clearly illustrate the use of the fortification theme and the perceived susceptibility and perceived benefits constructs.

Additional bread products using the Nutrition Health Halo and perceived severity and perceived benefits constructs on their packaging include, but is not limited to, the following: Kings Mill 50/50 Vitamin Boost bread, X-treme Wheat bread, Gardenia High Fiber Wheat bread, Gardenia Super Soft & Fine Enriched Wholemeal White Bread, Gardenia Multi-Grain bread, Gardenia 600 Jumbo Enriched White Bread, Wonder High Fiber Vitamins & Minerals White Toast Bread, Wonder Sandwich White Vitamins & Minerals bread, Wonder Gluten Free Soft White Vitamins & Minerals bread, Baker's Life Viva Wholemeal Vitamins & Minerals bread, Baker's Life Viva White Vitamins & Minerals White bread, Baker's Life Viva High Fiber White Vitamins & Minerals bread, Stonemill Bakehouse 12-Grain bread, Stonemill Bakehouse Naturally Fermented Plant-Based Protein bread, Stonemill Bakehouse Naturally Fermented Sprouted Rye & 12 Grains bread, Tip Top Bakery the One White Slice Bread, Nature's Own

Whitewheat Healthy White Enriched bread, H-E-B Round Top Large White Enriched Bread, H-E-B Extra Think Enriched White Bread, H-E-B Split Top Enriched White Bread, Sunshine Enriched Corn & Bran Bread, Holsum Pan Club Enriched White Bread, Super Atta Enriched Bread, Top-One Enriched Wholemeal Bread, Top-One Enriched Multi-Grain Bread, and Top-One Enriched White Bread.

12 versus 22

As previously mentioned, breakfast cereals are one of the most popular ultra-processed foods to use the fortification theme and perceived susceptibility and perceived benefits constructs. While many cereal manufacturers advertise their products as being healthy, there are a few who claim superiority even in the fortification process. A 1990 commercial for Total cereal is evidence of this. The commercial begins with a man at a counter with four boxes of cereal and a large bowl who says, "I'll just add two shakes of this . . ." before a male announcer interrupts him to say, "So, you think you can mix a bowl of cereal with more vitamin and mineral nutrition than Total?" to which the man replies, "Well, how about this?" as he pours a different box of cereal into the mixture (ewjxn 2022). The announcer says to the man, "Sorry, one bowl of Whole Wheat Total has 100% of 12 essential vitamins and minerals. For all this nutrition, nothing can top Total. Nothing," as the camera cuts to a shot of a box of the cereal with the words "Nothing can top Total" to the left of the screen with the word "nothing" underlined in red (ewjxn 2022).

A recent seven-second social media advertisement takes the idea of twelve essential vitamins and minerals and nearly doubles it in their recent promotion. The commercial opens with milk and cereal being poured across the screen while an announcer says, "With 22 vitamins and minerals from Vector, be ready for sports" as the camera cuts to a shot of the Kellogg's cereal box on a bench with a bowl full of the product to the right and a glass jar of milk to the left (Kellogg's Vector 2023). Above the bowl of cereal are the words "22 Vitamins & Minerals" (Kellogg's Vector 2023). The manufacturer's website advertises the Vector cereal products as "specifically formulated to help fuel your active lifestyle" with both the Vector Maple Crunch and Vector Apple Cinnamon cereals containing eleven vitamins and minerals while the original flavored one, which is advertised as a "meal replacement" contains twenty-two vitamins and minerals.

Another social media advertisement begins with energetic music and a shot of the Cheerios Honey Nut Honey cereal mascot, Buzz the Bee, twirling a box of that cereal on one lifted hand with the words, "Now with 2× the Vitamin D" in large text next to him ("General Mills TV Spot, 'The Cereals You Love, Now with Twice the Vitamin D'" 2023). All but the "2×" are in light blue while the "2×" is in red colored font. The camera cuts to a shot of six squares within the large screen. In each square is a cereal mascot, which include Buzz the Bea, the Trix Rabbit (Trix cereal), Sonny the Cuckoo Bird (Cocoa Puffs cereal), Lucky the Leprechaun (Lucky Charms cereal), Chip the Wolf (Cookie Crips cereal), and one of the Crazy Squares (Cinnamon Toast Crunch cereal). Each mascot is shown dancing around in their square before they each hold up a portion of the words "Now with 2× the Vitamin D" across the screen after which a swirl of blue is shown and then the Bee and the Leprechaun are pictured dancing next to each other with the words "Vitamin D Helps Build Strong Bones" in the middle of them in yellow-colored text ("General Mills TV Spot, 'The Cereals You Love, Now with Twice the Vitamin D'" 2023). The next shot is of the Leprechaun, the Wolf, the Rabbit, and the Cuckoo Bird each in a square with the same words about the vitamin and the benefits to bones. The final shot is of the Leprechaun putting his box of cereal next to a line of the other cereal with the words "The Cereals You Love Now with 2× the Vitamin D" above, as a female announcer says the same words and the Leprechaun reappears to put his arms up in a cheering motion ("General Mills TV Spot, 'The Cereals You Love, Now with Twice the Vitamin D'" 2023). The repeated reminder of the cereals containing twice as much Vitamin D as well as the various company mascots expressing joy about this illustrate a blatant use of the fortification theme and perceived severity construct in products that are, by definition, unhealthy.

Additional cereal products using the fortification theme and perceived susceptibility and perceived benefits constructs on their packaging include, but is not limited to, the following: Multi-Grain Cheerios, Cheerios Veggie Blends Blueberry Banana Flavored Cereal, Cheerios Oat Crunch Oats Honey Cereal, Cheerios Oat Crunch Cinnamon Cereal, Honey Bunches of Oats Cereal with Almonds, Honey Bunches of Oats Cereal, Special K Cereal, Raisin Bran Crunch Original Cereal, Kellogg's Corn Flakes, Grape-Nuts, Life Cereal, Basic 4 Cereal, Farina Hot Wheat Cereal, Kix Cereal, Cinnamon Toast Crunch Loaded Cereal, Purely Elizabeth Super Food Cereal Vanilla Blueberry Almond Cereal, Purely Elizabeth Cinnamon Raisin Almond Superfood Cereal, Purely Elizabeth Honey Peanut Butter Superfood Cereal, King Vitamin Cereal, Kashi Cinnamon Walnut

Vitamin D Cereal, Cream of Wheat Hot Cereal, Cream of Wheat Mixed Berry Cereal, Cream of Wheat Bananas & Cream Hot Cereal, Cream of Wheat Maple Brown Sugar Hot Cereal, Cream of Wheat Cinnabon Hot Cereal.

Rice Krispies Treats Cereal, Honey Stars Cereal, Apple Jax Cereal, Hill Country Fare Berry Crunch Cereal, Stater Bros. Berry Crunch Cereal, Kaboom Cereal, Count Chocula Cereal, Gerber Single Grain Oatmeal Cereal for Babies, Gerber Oatmeal & Banana Cereal for Babies, Nestle Milo Cereal, Stop & Shop Oats & O's Multigrain Cereal, Kemach Multi-Grain Toasted Oats Cereal, Great Value Toasted O's Breakfast Cereal, Fruity Pebbles, Tesco Fruit & Fibre Fruity Crunch Cereal, Tesco Corn Flakes, Tesco Frosted Flakes, Reese's Puffs Cereal, H-E-B Flakes with Strawberries, Gold Honey Flakes, Gold Honey & Banana Flakes, Crazy Cow Strawberry Milk Flavored Cereal, Crazy Cow Chocolate Milk Flavored Cereal, Kellogg's Frosted Flakes, Kellogg's Maple Cinnamon Frosted Flakes, Kellogg's Strawberry Milkshake Frosted Flakes, and Bitsy's Brainfood Organic Fruit & Veggie 123 Cereal.

"A Rousing Tonic"

Food products aren't the only ultra-processed items employing the fortification theme and perceived susceptibility and perceived benefits constructs. When taken into consideration the previously mentioned definition of ultra-processed foods as containing "either food substances never or rarely used in kitchens (such as high-fructose corn syrup, hydrogenated or interesterified oils, and hydrolysed proteins), or classes of additives designed to make the final product palatable or more appealing (such as flavors, flavor enhancers, colors, emulsifiers, emulsifying salts, sweeteners, thickeners, and antifoaming, bulking, carbonating, foaming, gelling and glazing agents)," it's clear that many liquid products, including sodas, fall into this category. However, one drink product segment has specifically grown over time to market products containing vitamins and thus making great use of the fortification theme and perceived susceptibility and perceived benefits constructs. One such product, first introduced in 1895 by the Anheuser-Busch Company, known as Malt-Nutrine is the focus of an advertisement from 1908 in which a large half-page illustrated image of a farmer with a pitchfork loading hay into a wagon filled with bales of hay is shown. The headline below the image says, "The Health of the Farmer" in larger bold text with the words "is proverbial" below which begins a paragraph of text telling readers that "health is there" on the farm and "blows in its breezes" with "strength of character . . . bestowed by Nature's elemental forces breathing across its bending harvests" (Period Paper 2016a). In the middle of the page is the name of the product with an image of a bottle of it to the right of page. Another paragraph below says that the product "contains nothing whatever but the combined juices of germinated barely and selected Saazer Hops," which the copy claims will infuse "life into the blood" and sustain "all the vital powers" to those who are "feeble, aged, and run down" making it a "veritable restorer of recreative and soothing potency" (Period Paper 2016a). Consumers are urged to order the product from "Druggists or Grocers" (Period Paper 2016a). On the label of the illustrated product, it states that it is "a non intoxicant sparkling highly concentrated liquid extract" (Period Paper 2016a).

Despite this proclamation, Anheuser-Busch's Malt-Nutrine did contain alcohol up until Prohibition from 1920 to 1933 and was "considered a 'tonic,' 'malt extract' or 'liquid bread' with its main ingredients of barley, malt and hops. The drink . . . had less than 1.9% alcohol" and was advertised as providing health "for nursing mothers, and for people with insomnia or who were ill, distributed through drug stores and grocery stores, and served at health resorts" (The Antique Advertising Expert 2024). A previous advertisement for the product in 1895 promoted the product as "A rousing tonic. To the nursing mother it is nourishment for herself and babe. To consumptives and sufferers from wasting diseases, to all who are thin and sickly, it means more flesh and greater strength" (The Antique Advertising Expert 2024). An advertisement from 1911 features an illustration of a woman smiling in a grain field, with a man standing in front of a barn in the distance and a headline below saying "Barley Brings Health and Vigor" with smaller text continuing "when ably malted and fermented with the tonic properties of Saazer Hops as in Anheuser-Busch's Malt-Nutrine" with the product logo in the middle of the page (Free Carpet Store 2021). Below this, the text says, "Thousands of women will testify to its food and tonic qualities" with the words "Declared by the U.S. Revenue Department A Pure Malt Product and not an alcoholic beverage. Sold by druggists and grocers" (Free Carpet Store 2021). The product was discontinued in 1942 due to a decline in sales once the alcohol was lessened to "less than half of one percent" during Prohibition (The Antique Advertising Expert 2024).

These advertisements use the perceived susceptibility, perceived benefits, and perceived barriers Health Belief Model constructs. By promising to give "life" to those who are "feeble, aged, and run down," the construct of perceived susceptibility is employed to prevent the unfavorable outcome of loss of strength while the promise of health and vitality illustrates the perceived benefits construct as does the assurance to nursing mothers that they are providing nourishment to both themselves and their babies. Images of farming, hay, barely, and nature use the perceived barriers construct, which is designed to assure consumers of the product's lack of alcohol and "naturalness" to make them feel better.

"Drink Your Vitamins and Like 'Em!"

The 1940s would bring the introduction of Borden's Hemo drink, which was introduced as a new way to drink milk, with its deep, rich, malty flavor. It was fortified with vitamins and minerals and was positioned as a family drink that fights fatigue, renews energy and vitality, with the name supposedly taken from hemoglobin since the product "contains vitamin B11 or folic acid, folate and Iron which is good for the blood and for anemic people" (Castro 2020). Elsie the Borden Cow was featured in many of the advertisements for the product. One of the first shows Elsie in a boat with her young cow son fishing while a bull pushes the boat. In a dialogue box about her, she says, "We Don't Need an Outboard Motor Now That We've Got Elmor Drinking Hemo!" with the product name in red font (Kristen's Vintage Paper 2024). In red font under the nearly half-page illustration are the words "Get your Hemo everyday—Drink your vitamins and like 'em!" with the word "your" underlined (Kristen's Vintage Paper 2024). Below this to the right are eight paragraphs of text that tell readers how their son, known as little Beulah, wanted his father to push the boat again with the bull replying that he needs something to drink and Elsie suggesting Hemo, which she says "is wonderful for everyone—especially in these days of food shortages and rationing" since "Government authorities say that 3 out of 4 Americans may not get enough vitamins with their meals" (Kristen's Vintage Paper 2024). Elsie then talks about how happy she is about the product and the vitamins it contains while Elmer says he's hungry to which Elsie replies that they can stop for lunch and a nice thermos full of Hemo if he pushes them another mile.

To the right of the advertisement is a chart outlining the vitamins contained in one class of the product, which include the equivalent of vitamin A "in three boiled eggs," vitamin B1 "in 4 slices of whole wheat bread," vitamin B2 "in 4 servings of spinach," vitamin D "in 3 servings of beef liver," niacin "in 3 servings of carrots," iron "in ½ pound of beef," and calcium plus phosphorous "in 2 servings of cauliflower and 1 serving of cooked green beans combined" (Kristen's Vintage Paper 2024). At the bottom of the page is an image of the product.

A similar advertisement from the time period also features Elsie but this time she is illustrated as a teacher standing in front of and pointing to a blackboard in a classroom of six children. The headline in red text says, "Drink Your Vitamins and Like 'Em," next to which in much smaller black text it says, "Says Elsie the Borden Cow" (American Century Shop 2024a). A dialogue box above Elsie says that "just one glass of Hemo gives you:" with the word "one" underlined and the same chart as in the previous advertisement pictured on the blackboard she is pointing to (American Century Shop 2024a). Five paragraphs of text to the left below the illustration begin with "You know you need vitamins . . . BUT . . . you can eat till you're ready to pop—and still not get *enough* vitamins and minerals!" before talking about the same vitamin deficiency as the previous ad and then going on the describe the vitamins and minerals in the product (American Century Shop 2024a; emphasis in the original). The advertisement continues saying that consumers can get the vitamins they need "not in expensive patent medicines—but in a grand tasting drink!" that costs "only 2½¢" per glass (American Century Shop 2024a). Near this is an illustration of a young couple in front of a counter being given a Hemo milkshake from a man dressed as a soda fountain worker with the caption urging consumers to "ask for Hemo made up like a malted milk in any flavor you like," which is next to an illustration of two filled glasses of the product next to a can of Hemo with a sign by it saying that it costs 59¢ for a pound, which makes twenty-four drinks with a caption telling consumers to follow the instructions on the can and that it's only 2½¢ per glass.

The ingredients listed on a jar of the product dated 1941 are as follows:

> Vacuumed dried combination of whole milk modified by malt enzymes, dextrose, sugar extract from converted infusion of malted barley and whole wheat flour, cocoa and salt. The natural vitamin and mineral content has been supplemented by addition of vitamin A from fish liver oil, vitamins B1, B2 (G), D (irradiated ergosterol), and P-P (niacin amide), calcium phosphate, iron pyrophosphate, artificial flavor (vanillin) and vanilla. (bobobill21, 2024)

Though a formal definition of ultra-processed foods was not created until much later, the inclusion of vacuumed-dried milk and malt enzymes, dextrose, and sugar extract in the ingredients of this product would qualify it for designation as an ultra-processed food according to the NOVA system. The contents of the advertisements, most notably the chart outlining the equivalences as well as the repeated association to "health" and vigor," are clear indications of the fortification theme in the Nutrition Health Halo as well as the perceived susceptibility, perceived benefits, and perceived barriers Health Belief Model constructs. The idea of obtaining a large number of vitamins (perceived benefits) by drinking a Hemo malted milkshake, which according to the advertisements tastes good (perceived barriers), to prevent illness (perceived susceptibility) clearly illustrates the three Health Belief Model constructs.

"The New Way to Take Vitamins"

Despite the long history of vitamin- and mineral-infused ultra-processed drinks, one company declared its product to be a novel way to take vitamins in a 1946 advertisement that promotes the solution as taking "them in fortified food—the Ovaltine way!" (the*maxx 2024). The advertisement includes six paragraphs of text followed by three lines of text and then a large illustration of a smiling mother in the background holding a glass of Ovaltine watching a smiling female child also holding a glass of Ovaltine in front next to a chart. In the six paragraphs, readers are told that "the whole subject of vitamins is new" and that many are learning "a new and better way" to take them, which the text says is by taking them in fortified food, which makes them work more effectively in combination with vitamin A needing protein to build cells as well as vitamin D, calcium, and phosphorous needing each other to be more effective (the*maxx 2024). Ovaltine is said to be the solution.

In three lines of text below these paragraphs, it says that "3 out of every 4 people," according to reports from the government need more vitamins and minerals due to loss and deficiencies of "modern food" in storage, cooking, and shipping (the*maxx 2024). In the chart, which tells consumers what vitamins and minerals are in two glasses of the product, it says that the following are contained:

> More food energy than 2 dishes of ice cream. More iron than 3 servings of spinach. More vitamin D than 10 ounces of butter. More protein than 3 eggs. More vitamin A than 2 servings of peas. More vitamin G than ¾ pound of sirloin steak. More niacin than 6 slices of enriched bread. More vitamin B1 than 3 servings of oatmeal. More calcium and phosphorus than 2½ servings of American cheese. (the*maxx 2024)

A medical doctor writing about the ingredients in Ovaltine and the idea of vitamins and minerals as a selling point of the product sarcastically said, "It's a good thing for Ovaltine that no one makes ice cream with multivitamins in it because that would be direct competition. Everyone knows ice cream would be a great choice if there were multi-vitamins included!" (Freedhoff 2006).

Ovaltine is listed for sale at the Twinings' website in the UK and the Nestle's website in the United States. The UK site proclaims that "Ovaltine is now enjoyed in over 54 countries worldwide. It's the perfect comforting and tasty drink for the busy lives we live today." On the U.S. website the product is described as

> chocolatey, malty, and yummy all in one, *Ovaltine* has a rich, 110-year heritage as a trusted provider of great tasting, good for you flavored milk deliciousness. *Ovaltine* makes milk work harder by providing a good source of 12 vitamins and minerals in every serving, including 40% of the recommended daily value of Calcium when *Ovaltine* is mixed with a 8 ounce cup of milk. *Ovaltine* delivers great taste with no artificial flavors or artificial sweeteners,

and consumers are encouraged to purchase the product at the Amazon or Walmart websites. The ingredients in Ovaltine are as follows: sugar, whey, corn maltodextrin, malt extract (malted barley, barley, caramel color, soy lecithin), nonfat milk, caramel color, beet juice color, natural flavors, soy lecithin, salt, molasses. Vitamins and minerals: calcium carbonate, magnesium hydroxide, vitamin C (sodium ascorbate), ferric orthophosphate (iron), zinc sulfate, vitamin E acetate, niacinamide, copper gluconate, vitamin A palmitate, vitamin B6 (pyridoxine hydrochloride), vitamin B1 (thiamine hydrochloride), biotin, vitamin D3. It's also worth noting that the package label includes the words "Good source of 12 Vitamins & Minerals" as well as "Good source of Iron, Zinc & Vitamins A, C, D & E," thus further establishing the product's use of the fortification theme. Similar to the Hemo advertisements, three of the Health Belief Model constructs are employed in these advertisements. The idea of obtaining a large number of vitamins (perceived benefits) by drinking Ovaltine, which according to the advertisements tastes good (perceived barriers), to prevent illness (perceived susceptibility) clearly illustrates the three Health Belief Model constructs.

Additional ultra-processed drink products using the fortification theme and perceived susceptibility and perceived benefits constructs on their packaging include, but is not limited to, the following: Vitaminwater Essential Electrolyte Enhanced Water W/ Vitamins Orange-Orange Drink, Vitaminwater Zero Sugar with Love Raspberry Dark Chocolate, Vitaminwater Zero Sugar Forever You

Coconut Lime, Vitaminwater Zero Sugar XXX Acai Blueberry Pomegranate, Vitaminwater Zero Sugar Shine Strawberry Lemonade, Vitaminwater Zero Sugar Rise Orange, Vitaminwater Zero Sugar Power-C Dragonfruit, Vitaminwater Zero Sugar Gutsy Watermelon Peach, Vitaminwater Zero Sugar Squeezed Lemonade, Ensure Original Vanilla Liquid Nutrition Shake, Ensure Original Milk Chocolate Liquid Nutrition Shake, Ensure Original Strawberry Liquid Nutrition Shake, Ensure Original Butter Pecan Liquid Nutrition Shake, Ensure Original Dark Chocolate Liquid Nutrition Shake, Ensure Original Banana Nut Liquid Nutrition Shake, Ensure Original Coffee Latte Liquid Nutrition Shake, Ensure Max Protein Shake (All Seven Flavors), Ensure Plus with Fiber (Both Flavors), Ensure Complete (All Three Flavors), Ensure Plant (Both Flavors), Ensure High Protein with Fiber (Both Flavors), Hi-C Flashin' Fruit Punch, Hi-C Orange Lava Burst, Hi-C Torrential Tropical Punch, Hi-C Boppin' Strawberry, Hi-C Grabbin' Grape, Hi-C Strawberry Kiwi Kraze, Hi-C Mashin' Mango Melon Drink Mix, Hi-C Flashin' Fruit Punch Drink Mix, and Hi-C Grabbin' Grape Drink Mix.

Tang Orange Instant Drink Mix, Tang Mango Instant Drink Mix, Tang Lemon Instant Drink Mix, Tang On the Go! Zero Sugar Instant Drink Mix, Naked Juice Superfood Green Machine, Nestle Health Science Boost Plus Vanilla, Nestle Health Science Boost Plus Chocolate, Nestle Health Science Boost Plus Strawberry, Vitamin Energy Focus+ Berry, Carnation Breakfast Essentials High Protein Nutritional Powder Drink Mix Rich Milk Chocolate, Carnation Breakfast Essentials High Protein Nutritional Powder Drink Mix Classic French Vanilla, Carnation Breakfast Essentials Complete Nutrition Drink Mix Strawberry, Carnation Breakfast Essentials Complete Nutritional Drink Vanilla, Carnation Breakfast Essentials Complete Nutritional Drink Milk Chocolate, VIT HIT Naturally Sweetened Low-Calorie Drink with Tea, Juice, Water, and a Hit of Vitamins ACTIVITEA, VIT HIT Naturally Sweetened Low-Calorie Drink with Tea, Juice, Water, and a Hit of Vitamins IMMUNITEA, VIT HIT Naturally Sweetened Low-Calorie Drink with Tea, Juice, Water, and a Hit of Vitamins LEAN & GREEN, Activia+ Immune System Strawberry Yogurt Drink, Activia+ Immune System Peach Yogurt Drink and Activia+ Immune System Raspberry Yogurt Drink.

Gluten Free, Health Free

At seventeen years old, Anna had experienced more pain than many adults twice her age. A lifelong sufferer of stomach problems, when she reached her teenage years, her abdominal pains often kept her awake at nights which meant that she would need to go to the nurse to sleep during school. Assuming she was lactose intolerant, she stopped eating foods that contained dairy. Her stomach pain did not, however, go away. While she was awaiting test results for potential food sensitivities, her pediatric gastroenterologist suggested that she remove gluten from her diet. As she describes, "After a week or so of being gluten-free, I felt so much better, I had more energy, and my stomach hurt less" (Children's Hospital of Philadelphia 2021). Anna was diagnosed with celiac disease, which is "an autoimmune response to gluten that causes the body to attack the small intestine, causing belly pain, nausea, bloating or diarrhea" leaving those with celiac disease unable to "tolerate gluten in any form . . . [and needing] to follow a gluten-free diet for the rest of their lives" (Rajagopal 2024). Another condition called "non-celiac gluten sensitivity, sometimes called gluten intolerance" also results in those afflicted needing to avoid gluten products (Rajagopal 2024). Some symptoms of both conditions include bloating, constipation or diarrhea, fatigue, gas, and stomach pain (Rajagopal 2024).

Over the past fifty years, "celiac disease has increased fivefold" (Karlis 2023) while "the global gluten-free products market size was estimated at USD [United States dollars] 6.45 billion in 2022 and is expected to grow at a compound annual growth rate . . . of 9.8% from 2023 to 2030," which some say can be attributed to

> the rising prevalence of celiac and other diseases [as well as] unhealthy lifestyles . . . [and] prevention of health disorders, such as heart disease, diabetes, obesity, chronic pulmonary disease, and metabolic syndrome, [which was driven by] the advent of the COVID-19 pandemic . . . [in a] surge . . . attributed to the increased health and wellness concerns among consumers during this period [giving rise to an] interest in the nutritional functioning of foods. (Grand View Research 2024)

Despite the "increased health and wellness concerns" of consumers, many mistakenly purchase gluten-free foods believing they are healthy. However, "some processed gluten-free foods contain high amounts of unhealthy ingredients such as sodium, sugar and fat," the consumption of which "can lead to weight gain, blood sugar swings, high blood pressure and other problems. So, a gluten-free label doesn't necessarily make a food healthy" (Rajagopal 2024). It is this belief in the health of gluten-free products that creates the gluten-free theme in the Nutrition Health Halo.

Gluten-Free Designation and Popular Foods

The U.S. Food and Drug Administration set forth criteria for foods labeled as gluten free and with similar terms such as without gluten, free of gluten, and no gluten in August 2013 and August 2020 (U.S. Food & Drug Administration 2024). As outlined in the criteria, foods carrying the gluten-free designation must

> limit the unavoidable presence of gluten to less than 20 ppm, and not contain an ingredient that is any type of wheat, rye, barley, or crossbreeds of these grains or an ingredient derived from these grains, and that has not been processed to remove gluten or an ingredient derived from these grains that has been processed to remove gluten, if it results in the food containing 20 or more ppm gluten. (U.S. Food & Drug Administration 2024)

It's also noted that food products that are "inherently gluten-free" including "bottled spring water, fruits and vegetables, and eggs can also" carry the gluten-free label "provided any gluten that came in contact with the food is less than 20 ppm" (U.S. Food & Drug Administration 2024).

Some of the most popular gluten-free products, known as "key product categories," include "baking mixes, cold cereal, cookies, crackers, dough, flour, fresh bread, pasta, and salty snacks" (Freedonia Group 2023). The bakery product category, which includes breads, rolls, cakes, pastries, cookies, tortillas, and pretzels, "held the largest share of 28.5% of the overall revenue [for gluten-free products] in 2022" and is expected to grow the most at a rate "of 11.0% from 2023 to 2030 owing to the combination of affordable pricing and a diverse range of products" (Grand View Research 2023). In addition to this, gluten-free breakfast cereals and pastas are expected to increase in sales as well (Grand View Research 2023). While gluten-free products are increasing, the advertisement of these products is mostly limited to brief announcements about the availability of gluten-free offerings released mainly after the first decade of the turn of the century.

Being Able to Say "Yes" and Eat Breakfast Together

A 2011 commercial for Chex cereals, however, offers a little more than an announcement. The commercial opens with images of a family in shadows outdoors with one child doing a cartwheel as the mother says, "Can a little bowl of cereal change your life? I think it can." as images of the children playing are shown with soft music in the background (GlutenFreeville 2011). The camera cuts to a shot of a young girl smiling while eating a bowl of cereal with a box of the product next to her as the mother continues, "One of the challenges for Kala being gluten free is actually finding choices the whole family will love" as the camera pulls out to reveal the family eating cereal with boxes of Chex on the table while laughing (GlutenFreeville 2011). The camera cuts to a closeup shot of a young girl reaching for a box of cereal as the mother says, "Then we discovered Chex cereals. Five flavors of Chex cereals are gluten-free including the honey nut flavor and that's amazing to a mom like me. As a parent, you don't want to have to tell your kids no all the time," as the camera shows the family outdoors again with the two girls hanging from a large tree and then riding bicycles as the mother continues, "It's nice for me to be able to say yes to something that they want to eat" (GlutenFreeville 2011). The camera cuts to a shot of the two girls putting two boxes of Chex cereal on top of three others before a final shot of five boxes of cereal with the words "Chex Cereal. Five Flavors. Gluten Free" above and a reminder that the other flavors the company makes, Wheat Chex and Multi-Bran Chex, contain gluten (GlutenFreeville 2011).

In a similar commercial for Cheerios produced in 2015, an engineer "on the Cheerios team" introduces himself and says that he has been working there for about fifty years as the camera first shows a shot of a woman holding a child, then the engineer working, and then him with the young boy running around (Cheerios 2015). The camera pulls out to show a woman next to the boy as both are playing with blocks on a table while Phil, the engineer, watches and introduces the woman as his daughter-in-law. Phil tells consumers that "a few years ago, I found out that if Joyce eats anything with gluten in it, she feels pretty darn sick, so I thought oats don't contain gluten and Cheerios are made of oats so how about some Cheerios?" as the camera first shows oats and then a field of oats (Cheerios 2015). Phil tells viewers to "hold on" because "it's not that simple" since "sometimes grains with gluten in them get mixed in with the oats" as an image of grains in small containers in a metal cabinet is shown (Cheerios 2015). An image of a grain separator with Phil watching a man using it is shown as he says, "So, I got to thinking. What if we could take the grains that contain gluten out and make Cheerios gluten free?" as Phil then cheers saying "Gluten-free oats!" (Cheerios 2015). The camera then cuts to his daughter-in-law who says that "Dad" called her and said he was going to give her box number one before a shot of Phil in a kitchen is shown as he says more people can now have Cheerios as the camera pulls out to show him eating with Joyce as he tells viewers that he can now have breakfast with her. The final shot is of five boxes of Cheerios on a table with two empty bowls, one inside the other and two empty spoons next to a glass container filled with milk and the words, "Cheerios. Now gluten free" in white text above (Cheerios 2015).

Both advertisements rely on the gluten-free theme in the Nutrition Health Halo to create a belief that the products advertised are healthy while using strong emotion and family ties to reinforce the point. In the first one, the mother talks about a bowl of cereal changing her life and how nice it is to not have to say no to her daughter all the time. In the second one, the father-in-law discusses wanting to have breakfast with his daughter-in-law and working to create a cereal to make that happen. Both scenarios are emotionally charged leaving viewers with positive feelings about the product advertised due to the happy ending portrayed in the commercials. The perceived susceptibility Health Belief Model construct is the primary motivation portrayed in these commercials as a means to prevent the symptoms associated with gluten intolerance by eating the cereals. In both advertisements, the use of the product is associated with avoiding the symptoms and "getting pretty darn sick," which employs the perceived severity construct while the perceived benefits are shown by those affected with gluten intolerance smiling with energy and happy. The perceived barriers construct is used by reminding viewers of the good taste of the product as well as the images of happiness and satisfaction while eating the products.

A recent content analysis by UK researchers of gluten-free products found that "23 out of the 25 GF [gluten free] products analysed contained more sugar than their 25 gluten-containing counterparts." Among the three food groups studied, which included breakfast cereals, bakery items, and ready-to-eat meats, it was determined that "all contained 1.3× greater sugar . . . than the gluten-containing products" (Rothburn, Fairchild and Morgan 2022). The researchers also examined "emotive language" on product labeling and packaging concluding that "the majority of the GF products used emotive language in order to persuade the consumer to buy the product," which includes such examples as " 'food for health conscious people too busy to cook,' 'just because its gluten free, it doesn't need to be fun free,' 'all natural ingredients,' 'this is genius,' 'freedom to enjoy the food you love' and 'deliciously gluten free,' " which according to the researchers result in the companies targeting both those medically needing to eat gluten-free products as well as those who do not, a phenomenon they identified as "hiding beneath a 'health halo' " (Rothburn, Fairchild and Morgan 2022).

Additional ultra-processed cereal products using the gluten-free theme in the Nutrition Health Halo and perceived susceptibility and perceived benefits constructs on their packaging include, but is not limited to, the following: Cascadian Farm Organic Honey Nut Vanilla Crunch, Cascadian Farm Organic Fruitful O's, Nature's Path Organic Sunrise Crunchy Maple, Nature's Path Organic Sunrise Crunchy Vanilla, Nature's Path Organic Fruit Juice Corn Flakes, Nature's Path Organic Honey'D Corn Flakes, Nature's Path Sunrise Crunch Cinnamon, Arrowhead Mills Organic Maple Buckwheat Flakes, Van's Natural Foods Cinnamon Heaven, Freedom Foods Maple Crunch, Freedom Foods Cocoa Crunch, Barbara's Bakery Brown Rice Crips, Barbara's Bakery Multi-Grain Puffins, Kellogg's Corn Flakes, Kellogg's Special K, Kellogg's Gluten Free Rice Crispies, Kellogg's Coco Pops, Kellogg's Organic Puffed Corn Cereal, Nestle Gluten Free Honey Flakes, Nestle Go Free Rice Pops, Annie's Organic Cinnamon Roll, Annie's Organic Cinnabunnies, Three Wishes Cinnamon Grain Free Cereal, Three Wishes Honey Grain Free Cereal, Three Wishes Horchata Grain Free Cereal, Three Wishes Vanilla Frosted Grain Free Cereal, Three Wishes Cocoa Grain Free Cereal, Three Wishes Chocolate-Covered Strawberry Grain Free Cereal, Three Wishes Gingerbread Grain Free Cereal, Three Wishes Smores Grain Free Cereal, Three Wishes Strawberry Grain Free Cereal.

Inno Foods Almond Fruit Crunch Cereal, 365 Whole Foods Market Berry Crisp Pillows, True Goodness Organic Honey Nut Toasted Oats, True Goodness Organic Frosted Corn Flakes, True Goodness Organic Bran Flakes, Vitabella Organic Traditional Corn Flakes, Vitabella Organic High Fiber Multi-Grain Flakes, Vitabella Organic Choco Crispies, Vitabella Organic Chocolate Hazelnut Pillows Snack, Organ Rice & Millet Wildberry Flavor O's, Organ Multi-Grain O's with Quinoa, Post Fruity Pebbles, Lieber's Crunchy Fruit Rings, Lucky Charms, Trader Joe's Crunchy Almond Butter Cereal, Trader Joe's Crunchy Maple Ladder Cereal, Purely Elizabeth Honey Peanut Butter Superfood Cereal, Purely Elizabeth Vanilla Blueberry Almond Superfood Cereal, Purely Elizabeth Chocolate Almond Superfood Cereal, Purely Elizabeth Cinnamon Raison Almond Superfood Cereal, Love Grown Cinnamon Lion Hearts, Love Grown Truly Fruity Sea Stars, Love Grown Chocolate Comet Crispies, Freee Organic Fruit & Fibre Flakes, Freee Organic Fibre Flakes, Freee Organic Cereal Flakes, Bob's Red Mill Mighty Tasty Hot Cereal, Bob's Red Mill Organic Creamy Buckwheat Hot Cereal, and Bob's Red Mill Organic Brown Rice Farina Hot Cereal.

"The Best Things in Life"

Gluten-free breads were introduced in the mid- to late 1990s as part of "the first wave of modern low and no-carb trends in the mid- to late 1990s" that changed "the script on the low-fat craze of the 1980s" and "the protein and fat-heavy Atkins" diets, which would eventually turn into the ketogenic or "keto" diets currently popular (Kapadia 2023). However, during this time, the breads were "once relegated to fringe diets and health food stores, [with] wheatless bread and products—most are high in carbohydrates, a stark contrast to the gluten-free diet's low-carb origins—began to develop a mainstream audience as the focus shifted from low-carb to no gluten" (Kapadia 2023). This would lead to a company named Schär introducing what would turn into the first packaged gluten-free foods (Kapadia 2023). This was followed by several other smaller companies introducing gluten-free breads until 2015 when Trader Joe's would introduce "gluten-free bread to the masses, selling well-received sandwich loaves . . . and in 2016 . . . burger chain Shake Shack . . . baking its own gluten-free buns and offering them at all locations around" the world (Kapadia 2023).

Though many gluten-free bread commercials are limited to a simple introduction of the product, there are some that include more. For example, a Schär bread commercial opens with a shot of a modern kitchen as a woman says, "The best things in life. A split second of calm and the storm follows" as a father is shown chasing a young boy through the house (Schär 2017). "Being surrounded by family and still doing it all by yourself" as the father straps the young boy into a high chair and a young girl is shown putting jam on her bread before the mother continues saying, "An extra smooch" as she is shown kissing her child then leaving with a suitcase with the next shot of her on the plane eating a Honeygrams cracker saying, "A moment just for you" (Schär 2017). The family is shown video conferencing with the mother as she says, "When you think less about gluten, you can savor more of life's best things" as an image of the mother in a hotel room on a bed eating a sandwich is shown before a final image of the company's logo with the words "Best in Gluten Free" are shown above the company's website address (Schär 2017).

While the gluten-free theme of the Nutrition Health Halo is clearly evident in this commercial, it's also important to recognize the use of the Health Belief Model constructs to motivate consumers to purchase the product. The emotional images of family members interacting together under the premise of being "the best things in life" are portrayed in the advertisement as being the result of thinking less about gluten while ironically the entire commercial is about a gluten-free product. The perceived susceptibility and perceived severity constructs are shown by the seriousness by which the gluten-free theme is portrayed yet with a positive spin by inferring that none of the activities would be possible without this particular gluten-free product, thus strongly urging consumption of it. The perceived benefits construct is shown through the happiness, love, and health as well as the idea that the mother is able to think less about gluten and "savor more of life's best things." The perceived barriers to purchasing a product that some fear may not taste good are addressed through the manner in which family members are shown savoring the product.

In a shorter commercial that was designed for social media use, a gluten-free Wonder Bread ad opens with a dark pink and lighter pink bottom background as a female announcer says, "Introducing the new Wonder gluten-free bread" as two loaves of the product, one soft wholemeal and the other soft white bread, fall from the top into the screen with the word "NEW" in blue font with a bright yellow background as the female announcer continues saying, "It's wonderfully soft, wonderfully tasty, wonderfully dairy free and wonderfully very high in fibre" as the words move in and out of the screen next to the bread (Wonder 2022). The next shot is of the two loaves of bread to the right of the screen as the female announcer says, "New Wonder gluten free. It's wonderful" as the company's logo is shown at the top next to the word "NEW" in blue font and bright yellow background with the words "Wonder-full and gluten free" in large white font and the words "Full of Softness and Taste" in smaller yellow font below (Wonder 2022). Another social media ad from the I Heart Publix Facebook site advertised Against the Grain bread. In the advertisement, the Against the Grain Gourmet logo is at the top in the middle of the post against a shade of blue background. The logo covers a portion of a blue napkin that is surrounded by two halves of a sandwich, a few potato chips in the foreground, and an image of the Original Baguettes product to the right. To the left of the image are the words, in white text, "Gluten-Free & Grain-Free Bread" in large font and then in smaller text below, "made with real, simple ingredients. No Gums. No Seed oils. No Preservatives. No Grains" (I Heart Publix 2024). Below this are the words "Shop, Upload & Earn" in blue font with a white background in an elongated oval shape (I Heart Publix 2024). Underneath this are the words "SAVE $5.00" in large white text with an arrow pointing to the oval shape (I Heart Publix 2024).

Though the advertisements are brief, the promise in both is that those who are gluten intolerant will avoid the undesirable outcome of the affliction's symptoms (perceived susceptibility) by taking action to purchase the products (perceived severity), which are promoted as eliminating these symptoms (perceived benefits) while tasting good (perceived barriers).

Additional ultra-processed bread products using the gluten-free theme and the perceived susceptibility and perceived benefits constructs on their packaging include, but is not limited to, the following: Canyon Bakehouse Gluten Free 7-Grain bread, Canyon Bakehouse Gluten Free Country White bread, Canyon Bakehouse Gluten Free Heritage Style Whole Grain bread, Canyon Bakehouse Mountain White bread, Canyon Bakehouse Multigrain bread, Canyon Bakehouse Gluten Free Heritage Style Whole Grain bread, Canyon Bakehouse Gluten Free Hearty Oat bread, Udi's Gluten Free Whole Grain bread, Udi's Gluten Free White Sandwich bread, Udi's Gluten Free Soft White bread, Udi's Gluten Free Everything Bagels, Udi's Gluten Free Frozen Plain Bagels, Udi's Gluten Free Ancient Grain Omega Flax & Fiber bread, Udi's Gluten Free Cinnamon Raisin Bread, Trader Joe's Gluten Free White Sandwich Bread, Trader Joe's Gluten Free Italian Bread, Trader Joe's Gluten Free Multigrain Bread, Trader Joe's Gluten Free Whole Grain Bread, Trader Joe's Gluten Free Cinnamon Raisin Bread, Franz Bakery Gluten Free Seven Grain bread, Franz Bakery Gluten Free Mountain White bread, Katz Gluten Free Egg-Free Bread, Katz Gluten Free White Bread, Kats Gluten Free Challah Bread, Katz Gluten Free Everything Bread, Katz Gluten Free Whole Grain Bread, Three Bakers Gluten Free White bread, Three Bakers Gluten Free 7 Ancient Grains bread, Three Bakers Gluten Free Large Slices Golden Flax bread, Three Bakers Gluten Free Rye Style bread, Three Bakers Gluten Free Great Seed bread, Three Bakers Gluten Free Max Omega bread, Sami's Bakery Vegan Gluten Free Millet Bread, Sami's Bakery Vegan Gluten Free Bagels, Sami's Bakery Gluten Free Low Carb Bread, Sami's Bakery Gluten Free Cinnamon Bread, Sami's Bakery Gluten Free Sourdough Bread.

AWG Bakery Gluten & Grain Free Everyday Loaf, AWG Bakery Gluten & Grain Free Everyday Bread, AWG Bakery Gluten & Grain Free Everyday Rounds, AWG Bakery Gluten & Grain Free Everyday Bagels, AWG Bakery Gluten & Grain Free Everyday Minis, AWG Bakery Gluten & Grain Free Everything Bread, AWG Bakery Gluten & Grain Free Everything Bagels, AWG Bakery Gluten & Grain Free Everything Loaf, AWG Bakery Gluten & Grain Free Rosemary Bread, AWG Bakery Gluten & Grain Free Rosemary Loaf, AWG Bakery Gluten & Grain Free Rosemary Minis, AWG Bakery Gluten & Grain Free CinnaSpice

Bread, AWG Bakery Gluten & Grain Free CinnaSpice Loaf, BFree Wheat & Gluten Free Soft White Loaf, BFree Wheat & Gluten Free Sandwich Loaf, BFree Wheat & Gluten Free Brown Seeded Sandwich Loaf, BFree White Sourdough Loaf, Helga's Gluten Free Wholemeal bread, Helga's Gluten Free 5 Seeds bread, Helga's Gluten Free Soft White Bread, Sam's Choice Gluten Free Multigrain Bread, Sam's Choice Gluten Free White Bread, Sam's Choice Gluten Free Classic White Bread, Rudi's Bakery Gluten Free Brioche Bread, Rudi's Bakery Gluten Free Sourdough White Bread, Rudi's Bakery Gluten Free Brioche Burger Buns, Rudi's Bakery Gluten Free Homestyle Multigrain Bread, Simple Truth Gluten Free Frozen White Sandwich Bread, Kroger Gluten Free 7 Multigrain Bread.

Bob's Red Mill Gluten Free Homemade Wonderful Bread Mix, Seitenbacher Gluten Free Bread Mix, Seitenbacher Gluten Free Oat Bread Easy Baking Mix, Pamela's Product's Gluten Free Bread Mix, gfJules Certified Gluten Free Bread Baking Mix, gfJules Certified Gluten Free Pizza Crust Mix, King Arthur Gluten Free Bread Flour, Vivian's Gluten Free Bread & Roll Mix, Authentic Foods Steve's Gluten Free Flour, Scotty's Gluten Free Keto Bread Low Carb Bread Mix, Molly and You Gluten Free American Original Beer Bread Mix, Williams Sonoma Gluten Free Quick Bread Mix, Williams Sonoma Gluten Free Coffee Cake Quick Bread Mix, Chebe Bread Gluten Free Pizza Crust Mix, Namaste Foods Organic Gluten Free Quick Bread & Muffin Mix, Addi's Gluten Free Super Moist Banana Bread Mix, Great Value Gluten Free All-Purpose Flour, Glutino Gluten Free Pantry Favorite Sandwich Bread Mix, Simple Truth Organic Gluten Free Corn Bread Baking Mix, Mom's Place Gluten Free I Can't Believe It's Not Wheat Bread Mix, Arnels Original Gluten Free Buckwheat Bread Mix, Well & Good Gluten, Nut & Dairy Free Crusty Bread Mix, Healtheries Gluten Free Bread Mix, Marie Callender's Gluten-Free Corn Bread Mix, Martha White Gluten Free Sweet Yellow Cornbread Mix, and LiveGfree Gluten Free Cornbread Mix.

"A Little Bake Shop in Every Bite"

Another popular area where the use of the gluten-free theme can be seen is in advertisements and product labels for cookies, and by extension, cookie dough. Though full advertisements for gluten-free products appear to be less frequent, some companies distribute information about new products to the news media hoping for coverage. For example, one product managed to garner a twenty-second mention on a southwest Florida Fox affiliate. The twenty-second mention was showcased as a news story that featured a large image of a gluten-free Oreo cookie package with seven cookies stacked in front of it as a female announcer told viewers that the company was coming out with a gluten-free version next year and that "the cookie [would] be available in both regular and double stuffed versions" before telling viewers that "gluten-free products are made to help those with some immune or intestinal disorders associated with gluten such as celiac disease" and that "gluten is the glue-like protein in some cereal grains like wheat" (Fox 4 Now 2020). It's important to note that when a food manufacturer introduces a new product, most times the company will issue a press release in the hopes that media will cover the story, resulting in what is sometimes called "free advertising" but offers no guarantees about how the media outlet presents the story unlike company-produced advertisements that have complete control over the message.

A commercial for a bakeshop using the gluten-free theme to promote its products begins with an image of an older two-story house painted in white and green with white trim as a female announcer says, "There's a little bake shop in South Hampton, New York, called Tate's . . ." as the camera zeros into a sign for the store which is outside the house ". . . that became legendary with people far and wide for introducing its buttery delicious chocolate chip cookies" as the camera goes inside the building and zeros in on a plate filled with cookies, and then one which spins as the announcer continues, "thin, crisp and craft baked with simple real ingredients and a dedication to quality" as the camera shows ingredients in bowls with a rolling pin in the background (Tate's Bake Shop 2020). The next shot is of shelves filled with packaged cookies as the announcer urges consumers to "Try any one of our variety of flavors including gluten free and taste for yourself what we mean when we say 'there's a little bake shop in every bite' " as the same words appear above a plate filled with cookies next to a package of the product (Tate's Bake Shop 2020). With what appears to be many different types of cookie varieties, it's worth noting that this shop emphasized its gluten-free products in the commercial, thus reinforcing the popularity of using the gluten-free theme and the perceived susceptibility, perceived severity, perceived benefits, and perceived barriers Health Belief Model constructs by ultra-processed food manufacturers. Ingredients in the Tate's Bake Shop Gluten-Free Chocolate Chip Cookies include sugar, soy lecithin, cane sugar, brown cane sugar, xanthan gum, and natural flavors, which, by definition, classifies them as an ultra-processed food product.

"Let's Be Taste Buds"

Similarly, the gluten-free theme and the Health Belief Model constructs are also used in advertisements and on product labels for cookie dough products. A commercial for a plant-based cookie dough begins with two women each eating a cookie and laughing against a blue background before the camera cuts to another woman eating a cookie looking directly into the camera against a pink background as a female announcer says, "We all have one thing in common" as the camera cuts to the words "Taste Buds" in large white font over a dark pink background before the announcer continues, "At Sweet Loren's, we're for the food lovers, those who devour life by the mouthful or plateful" during which time images of the various flavors of the product, cookies, and people dancing and eating them are shown (Sweet Loren's 2021). Images of the cookies on a baking rack and cookie sheet are shown as the announcer continues, "Everyone with an appetite for delicious without any compromise" as an image is shown of cookies falling against a pink background with first the words "Non GMO" followed by "Plant Based," then "Gluten & Dairy Free" in large white text with the word "Free" being the largest (Sweet Loren's 2021). An image of fifteen packages of the product with four off to the sides are shown as the announcer says, "Introducing the clean ingredient cookie dough that everybody with tastebuds can love" as more images of people dancing with cookies are shown before the words "Let's Be Taste Buds" with the first two words in white font and the last two in pink against a yellow background are shown before a final shot of cookies floating against a pink background with the company's logo in white above the words "Crafted with Only *clean* Ingredients" underneath which viewers are told to find the product in the refrigerated section (Sweet Loren's 2021; emphasis in the original).

The idea of "clean ingredients" that do not contain gluten represents the perceived susceptibility and perceived severity Health Belief Model constructs by including images of healthy people involved in various activities, including dancing, which is physical and not possible if one was suffering from gluten intolerance symptoms. This also portrays the perceived benefits while the perceived barriers are addressed by reminders about everyone having "an appetite for delicious without any compromise."

Additional ultra-processed cookie and cookie dough/mix products using the gluten-free theme and the perceived susceptibility and perceived benefits constructs on their packaging include, but are not limited to, the following: Simple Truth Gluten Free Vanilla Sandwich Cookies, Simple Truth Gluten Free Chocolate Sandwich Cookies, Simple Truth Gluten Free Chocolate Chip Cookies, Partake Vegan & Gluten Free Chocolate Chip Crunchy Cookies, Partake Vegan & Gluten Free Double Chocolate Brownie Soft Cookies, Partake Vegan & Gluten Free Birthday Cake Crunchy Cookies, Partake Vegan & Gluten Free Vanilla Wafers, Partake Vegan & Gluten Free Classic Grahams cookies, Kroger Gluten Free Kaleidos, Simple Mills Gluten Free Sweet Thins Mint Chocolate Cookies, Simple Mills Gluten Free Sweet Thins Chocolate Brownie Cookies, Simple Mills Gluten Free Sweet Things Honey Cinnamon Cookies, Homefree Gluten Free Mini Double Chocolate Chip Cookies, Homefree Gluten Free Mini Vanilla Cookies, Highkey Gluten Free Vanilla Wafers, Cybele's Free to Eat Gluten-Free & Vegan Chocolate Chip Cookies, Glutino Gluten Free Chocolate Vanilla Crème Sandwich Cookies, Glutino Gluten Free Chocolate Chip Cookies, Chips Ahoy! Original Crunchy Gluten Free Chocolate Chip Cookies, Annie's Homegrown Gluten Free Cocoa & Vanilla Bunny Cookies, Golden Gluten Free Oreo cookies, Mint Crème Gluten Free Oreo cookies..

Wow Gluten Free Soft Baked Lemon Burst Cookies, Wow Gluten Free Soft Baked Key Lime White Chocolate Cookies, Pamela's Products Gluten Free Figgies & Jammies Cookies, Walker's Gluten Free All-Butter Shortbread Rounds, Krusteaz Gluten Free Chocolate Chip Cookie Mix, King Arthur Gluten Free Sugar Cookie Mix, Betty Crocker Gluten Free Chocolate Chip Cookie Mix, Pillsbury Gluten Free Chocolate Chip Cookie Mix, Bob's Red Mill Gluten Free Chocolate Chip Cookie Mix, Bob's Red Mill Gluten Free Biscuit & Baking Mix, Meli's Gluten Free Chocolate Chip Cookie Mix, Meli's Gluten Free Original Monster Cookie Mix, Meli's Gluten Free Oatey Raisin Cookie Mix, Thrive Market Gluten Free Chocolate Chip Cookie Mix, Williams Sonoma Gluten Free Chocolate Chip Cookie Mix, Williams Sonoma Gluten Free Sugar Cookie Mix, Miss Jones Baking Company Gluten Free Monster Cookie Mix, Miss Jones Baking Company Gluten Free Sea Salt Caramel Double Chocolate Cookie Mix, Nature's Promise Gluten Free Chocolate Chip Cookie Mix, LillyBean Gluten Free Maple Shortbread Cookie Mix, Mom's Place Gluten Free Soft Molasses Cookie Mix, Mom's Place Gluten Free Sugar Cookie Mix, Cooggies Gluten Free Chocolate Chip Cookie Bake Mix, Wegmans Gluten Free Soft & Sweet Cookie Mix, gfJules Gluten Free Cut-Out Cookie Mix, Belly Gluten Free Chocolate Chip Cookie Mix, Jessica's Natural Foods Gluten Free Chocolate Chip Mix, Namaste Foods Gluten Free Vegan Ginger Molasses Cookie Mix, Namaste Foods Gluten

Free Mochaccino Cookie Mix, Magnolia Mixes Gluten Free Sugar Cookie Mix, and Magnolia Mixes Gluten Free Chocolate Chip Cookie Mix.

Gluten-Free Website Advertising

It's worth noting that while many ultra-processed food manufacturers may not use the gluten-free theme in their advertisements, many still do promote their gluten-free offerings on their websites. An example of this is the Hershey website that promotes its gluten-free cocoa, syrup, and chocolate items including several different versions of Reese's Peanut Butter Cups, York Peppermint Patties, Hershey's Nuggets, Chocolate Kisses, Hershey's Milk Chocolate, Payday Candy Bars, Health Bars, Almond Joy candy bars, SkinnyPop popcorn, Mounds Candy Bars, Rolo Candy, and Milk Duds. Similarly, at the Barilla Pasta website, which proclaims itself "The #1 Gluten Free Pasta Brand*" based "in part on data reported by NielsenIQ through its Connect Ad-hoc Analysis for the Dry Pasta Category, 52 week period ending 11.26.22 for the Total US xAOC," there are six gluten-free products promoted. These include Gluten Free Elbows Pasta, Gluten Free Fettuccini, Gluten Free Oven Ready Lasagne *[sic]*, Gluten Free Pene, Gluten Free Rotini, and Gluten Free Spaghetti.

As previously noted, though advertising of gluten-free products has been limited up to this point, it's not difficult to imagine an increase over the next few years considering the explosive growth predicted for these types of products over the next decade.

4

Identity Health Halo

The Identity Health Halo is defined as the use of text, colors, or images associated with consumers' desires to present themselves in a certain way, shape their sense of belonging, or express their values through food choices in the advertising or labeling of a product that creates a false perception of healthiness about the item. Some examples of this health halo include the use of such words as "diet" and "low calorie" as well as foods marketed as vegan or vegetarian and those that include images of exercise, playing sports, and healthy activities.

Diet Food and Reduced Calories

"The world is unfair to a dieter," a man's deep voice announces as a black and white image of a plate with a few vegetables is shown before the man continues, "Who can stay on a diet when this is all there is to eating" as the camera zooms into the sparse plate (Vintage Fanatic 2013). The camera then cuts to a bowl filled with beef stew as the announcer says, "Now, from the Edward Dalton Company comes today's new way to diet, Good Measure, the world's first 300 calorie diet dinners" as the camera focuses on a can of the product before the announcer continues, "Now, you can actually eat full meals like meat, potatoes, gravy, twice a day and still lose as much weight as you would with the well-known liquid diets" as the camera shows close ups of the stew (Vintage Fanatic 2013). The announcer goes on to tell viewers how the company learned how to control calories in "full meals" to make them exactly 300 calories and "as nutritionally complete as can be" as an image of a man and a woman at a table is shown with the woman smiling as she takes a bite before the announcer goes on to describe the diet that's "easy to stick" to and consists of eating "an average breakfast" and one can each of Good Measure "beef stew, chicken with noodles, or chili con carne" while still losing weight similar to that on liquid diets (Vintage Fanatic

2013). The commercial ends with a shot of three cans of the product and the announcer encouraging "Dieters rejoice with Good Measure Diet Dinners" (Vintage Fanatic 2013).

This commercial illustrates the reduced-calorie theme of the Identity Health Halo well as the use of all four Health Belief Model constructs. The association of an ultra-processed food, which promises large portions (perceived benefits) and good taste (perceived barriers), with a healthy body size and being thin (perceived susceptibility) are powerful draws for consumers who are struggling with being overweight or obesity (perceived severity). As with other health halos used in advertisements and on product labels, the promise of health by eating ultra-processed food results in the justification needed to purchase that food even though it is, by definition, unhealthy. As noted in a recent *New York Times* editorial, the "haze of aggressive marketing—words like 'low fat,' 'gluten-free,' 'paleo,' 'keto-friendly' and 'a good source of fiber' " don't "answer the fundamental question: Is this food good for me?" (Morgan and Bittman 2024). Arguably, the reduced-calorie theme can be a very powerful motivator for consumers to purchase products they believe to be healthy that will also help them to lose weight or maintain a healthy body size.

Another commercial for the Good Measures product, which uses the same theme and constructs, opens with a shot of a woman breaking a thin cracker in half and a carton of skim milk being poured into a glass as a male announcer says, "How long before you fall off your diet" as a shot of a cucumber being peeled is shown (spuzzlightyeartoo 2012). The announcer continues as a plate with two tomato slices, a few leaves of lettuce, and vegetable sticks are shown, "when this is all there is to eating" before the camera cuts to a shot of a bowl filled with beef stew as the announcer says, "Dieters, welcome back to eating. Today, there's a new way to diet" before introducing the product and continuing with a similar ending as in the previously described commercial and ending with the same directive for dieters to rejoice about being able to enjoy "full meals" and still lose "as much weight as with the well-known liquid diets" (spuzzlightyeartoo 2012).

"A Little Bit of Willpower" and "A Metrecal Steak"

The Edward Dalton Company was a division of the Mead & Johnson Company, "devoted exclusively" to the company's distinctive weight-loss product, which contained "proportionately more protein than its predecessors" with the "first shipments [leaving] Evansville in September 1959" at which point "sales took off" (Martin 2010). Originally, the company offered a vanilla-flavored powder to mix with water but then introduced a chocolate- and butterscotch-flavored liquid product that "was marketed as nutritional, with gobs of vitamins and minerals" causing *Life* magazine to say in 1960 "that one weight-reduction product had never combined so much" (Martin 2010). Print advertisements for the product in the early 1960s would ask leading questions. One would feature a photo of a woman looking at the small size of another woman's body with the caption, "Is this the day you finally do something about your weight? All it takes is a little bit of will power *[sic]* . . . and Metrecal" (Edelstein 2015). Another would feature a can of the product with an open belt wrapped around it and the words "The goal: weight loss, the product: Metrecal" (Edelstein 2015). Similar to the previous commercial using the reduced-calorie theme, these also employ all four of the Health Belief Model constructs by promising more protein and "gobs of vitamins and minerals" (perceived benefits), delicious vanilla, chocolate, and butterscotch flavors (perceived barriers), help with willpower (perceived susceptibility), and freedom from weight issues or obesity (perceived severity).

A television advertisement introducing the product began with a glass being placed on a countertop as white powder is poured into it while a male announcer says, "Milk will never be the same again" as milk is poured into the glass over the powder (Flaviano 2011). The announcer continues, "because now you can turn cold, fresh milk into a delicious diet meal" as first the mixture is stirred and then an image of the product is shown as the announcer introduces it as "New Metrecal fresh milkshake" before telling viewers that the product comes in an envelope with crystals that are "flavor charged" with flavor that is "locked in" as the camera continues to show images of the shake being mixed (Flaviano 2011). The camera then cuts to a shot of the milk being added as the announcer says, "Add fresh, cold milk and it explodes with flavor. Rich deep flavor. It's the newest, most delicious way to have a complete breakfast or lunch with all the protein of a meal like this but only 225 calories" as an image of a meal with meat, a potato, and vegetables is shown (Flaviano 2011). This is followed by the announcer urging viewers to try it as a woman is shown drinking a shake from a straw. The announcer promises, "You'll love the way you feel, the beautiful way you look" and that they will "love that great, new Metrecal feeling" as an image of the woman running on the beach is shown (Flaviano 2011). The announcer then tells consumers that the product comes in "four fabulous flavors" as images of the product are shown (Flaviano 2011). The shake powder was "a mix of skim milk powder, soybean flour, corn oil, minerals and vitamins" (Edelstein 2015) and would be considered an ultra-processed food in today's time period, according to the definition outlined in the NOVA study.

The product line would be expanded to include different flavors and would eventually be marketed to men. A two-page ad shows a man flipping a large steak on the grill on one side and a bowl filled with reddish liquid by a can of strawberry-flavored Metrecal with the headline, "The Metrecal Steak" (Edelstein 2015). Text above the large headline tells readers that a can of the product provides "the nutrition of steak, potatoes, peas and carrots. But not the calories" (Edelstein 2015). The text continues to say that the product comes in fourteen flavors and that consumers should have two cans per day. If they wanted to have three, the text says, they may disappear.

Once again, the reduced-calorie theme is illustrated in these advertisements as are all four Health Belief Model constructs through promises of high nutrition (perceived benefits), delicious flavors (perceived barriers), low calories and weight loss (perceived susceptibility), and freedom from excess weight or obesity (perceived severity).

Subsequent commercials would encourage dieters to freeze the product resulting in "a summer treat for dieters," and encourage them to "take Metrecal anywhere" in an advertisement featuring a man drinking the product on a plane (Pam 2013). By following the suggested Metrecal diet, consumers were ingesting only 900 calories per day, which sometimes resulted in hunger pains. The company's response to this was to tell consumers that the hunger pains would go away in a few days. Even though some claimed that the liquid product was "disgusting," the craze continued for several years with resourceful dieters adding liquor to their shakes for better taste (Pam 2013).

"Metrecal was so successful it spawned nearly 40 imitators from other large companies: Sears Roebuck brought out Bal-Cal, Quaker Oat's pitched Quota, Jewel Tea Company had Diet-Cal; even deep discounter Korvette's hawked Kor-Val, to name just a few" (Edelstein 2015). Included in this deluge was Borden's ready diet drink that was promoted in advertisements as "the happiest tasting diet drink" that would "make sticking to a diet so much easier" as well as SEGO liquid diet food that was advertised as being able to help "you through the temptation hours" and "so good tasting you'll forget you're dieting. Almost" (Edelstein 2015). The liquid diet drink craze continued until the late 1970s when "the Food and Drug Administration declared them dangerous due to 59 reported deaths connected to liquid protein products" (Pam 2013).

Eat Sugar to Lose Weight

While eating diet food in a can or drinking a liquid shake to lose weight may not seem all that removed from today's weight-loss methods, another ultra-processed food advertised for weight loss is very far away from anything advertised today. During the 1950s and through the 1970s, sugar was advertised as a means of losing weight. A 1950s print advertisement for Domino's Pure Cane Sugar features an illustration of a man and a woman seated at a table across from each other and eating breakfast. The man is taller, dressed in a pale green suit and tie, and is seated to the left in the advertisement. He is eating an apple. The woman has a cup of coffee in a bright yellow-colored cup and saucer and a matching creamer and sugar bowl, all matching the yellow color on the product package. Between them and to the left there is a fruit bowl with bananas, a pineapple, a bunch of grapes, and an apple. The woman is wearing a light mint-colored dress and is spooning sugar into her coffee. Dialogue from the man, in red text, says, "Sure, I love sugar but I'm watching my weight" while dialogue from the woman, in black text, says, "You need sugar for energy! And even three teaspoons of Domino Sugar contain *fewer calories* than your apple!" (Montone 2009; emphasis in the original). To the right of the woman is a large image of a package of Domino Sugar. Underneath the entire image in black text are the words, "It's *smart* to stay slim and trim and get Domino's 'Energy Lift' too!" (Montone 2009; emphasis in the original). The word "smart" is underlined in red.

Another advertisement for the product, which appeared in the November 1958 issue of *McCall's* magazine, features a large headline in red text that reads, "Which Is Less Fattening?" under which in smaller text are the words, "This Grapefruit? Or *Domino* Sugar?" (saltycotton 2010; emphasis in the original). Below this is a large image of half a grapefruit and three heaping teaspoons of sugar with a blue background that is bordered by a tape measure. Small text in black font underneath the grapefruit image says, "75 calories in half a medium grapefruit" while corresponding text underneath the teaspoons of sugar reads, "54 calories in 3 level teaspoons of Domino Sugar" (saltycotton 2010). Text below the images tells consumers that there's "Only 18 calories per teaspoon in Domino Pure Cane Sugar . . . and they're all quick energy!" which the copy says "your body needs everyday" since "it's a scientific fact that sugar give you energy faster than any other food" (saltycotton 2010). The paragraph of text ends with encouraging consumers that "while you hold down your weight, lift up your energy with Domino Sugar!" (saltycotton 2010). To the left of the text and wrapped in the tape measure that serves as a border for the large image is a woman dressed in a bathing suit holding a hat in one hand and touching her hair with the other and smiling. To the left of that is a large image of the product. Below the woman is a small advertisement for Domino's Confectioner's 10-X Powdered Sugar to make icing for cakes. At the bottom of the page in the center are the words "more women use Domino than any other sugar!" (saltycotton 2010).

The practice of promoting sugar as a means of providing energy and weight loss directly illustrates the Health Belief Model construct of perceived benefits with touches of the perceived susceptibility and perceived severity constructs as well. The notion that sugar is superior in weight loss, taste, and providing energy to traditional weight-loss foods such as apples, grapefruits, and other fruit addresses the perceived barriers many dieters have to foods they believe don't taste as good as foods with sugar in them.

Domino wasn't the only sugar company using the reduced-calorie theme and the Health Belief Model constructs to advertise its product. A 1950s era advertisement from the Great Western Sugar Company features an image of a whole orange with another sliced half next to it. The whole orange has a metal plate on it that reads, "Contents: Sugar Your Purest Energy Food" with a bottle of orange liquid behind the two oranges (Friedman 2014). To the right is a headline that says, "Sugar is Nature's essential element" below which is a paragraph of text that reads, "'Sugar-less' fad foods and so-called diet drinks deprive you of sugar's nutrition, energy, natural flavor and taste blending—a combination for which there is no substitute!" (Friedman 2014). Underneath that is the reminder that "Sugar is a vital factor in a healthy diet" (Friedman 2014). An image of the product is to the right, which is positioned to be almost exactly perpendicular to the images of the oranges and slightly taller thus making a clear association between the natural sugar in the fruit and the ultra-processed one, which results in the use of the reduced-calorie theme in the Identity Health Halo as well as all four Health Belief Model constructs. The idea of being deprived of "sugar's nutrition, energy and natural flavor" from diet foods employs the perceived susceptibility, perceived severity, and perceived benefits constructs while the promotion of the product's good taste addresses the perceived barriers of weight loss.

Nearly two decades later, an advertisement from the sugar industry would appear in a 1970 issue of *Life* magazine with the headline, "The 'fat time of the day:' that's any time you overeat. Sugar's instant energy can slip you past" below which is a photo of a man and a woman eating with a quote next to it that says, "I think of sugar as extra willpower" (Friedman 2014). Six short paragraphs below go on to explain that the " 'fat time of day' is when you're really hungry and ready to eat, and eat, and eat" and that the message is from "your tuned up appestat," which is described in small text from *Webster's Dictionary* as "a neural center in the hypothalamus believed to regulate appetite" (Friedman 2014). The text promises that "you can turn it down before mealtime" by eating something with sugar in it such as "a soft drink, a couple of cookies or a candy bar," which will turn "into energy in minutes" and help you get "past the 'fat time of day' in the sweetest way possible" (Friedman 2014). There is also a reminder about the fact that there are only eighteen calories in a teaspoon of sugar, which is "all energy" at the bottom of the page (Friedman 2014).

One of the boldest advertisements from the sugar industry was published in the 1970s with the headline, "If sugar is so fattening, how come so many kids are thin?" with a large image of a glass of soda with ice and a straw (Itzler 2024). Below the headline in white font against a red background, the text goes on to say, "Kids eat and drink more things made with sugar than anybody. But how many fat kids do you see?" before going on to explain that if you eat more food than your body needs, "you'll probably get fat;" however, "if you eat a balanced diet in moderation, you probably won't. And sugar in moderation has a place in a balanced diet" (Itzler 2024). The text continues by noting that "For kids, eating or drinking something with sugar in it can mean a new supply of body fuel," which "can be used in not too many minutes" and then noting the psychological benefit that "sugar is like a little reward that promotes a sense of satisfaction and well-being" and that "sugar is an important carbohydrate," which "isn't just good flavor, it's good food" (Itzler 2024).

"Skinny" Is the New Low Calorie

While the words "diet" and "low calorie" were used frequently on product labels and in advertisements several decades ago, they became less popular, replaced by the use of weight-loss associations in the names of products, so much so that industry news publication *Ad Age* declared "skinny" to be "the hottest marketing phrase" in a 2013 article noting that "Brands have put the label on everything from cocktails to popcorn to give foods a low-cal sheen for consumers that are watching their waistlines" (Schultz 2013). In the article, it's noted that the word "skinny" is "on foods normally seen as indulgent, such as Skinnygirl Cocktails and Nestle's Skinny Cow brand, which was one of the early adopters of the term when it launched in 1994 as ice cream" and that "Andrew Friedman, who co-founded SkinnyPop popcorn in 2010, said he chose the term to suggest 'few ingredients, better-for-you and a lifestyle' " (Schultz 2013). It's worth noting that in addition to using the Identity Health Halo, the idea of including the word "skinny" in product names directly illustrates the perceived benefits Health Belief Model construct while the pairing of this word with "indulgent" products draws on the perceived barriers of the Health Belief Model construct, all of which are designed to motivate consumers to purchase products that, in almost all cases, do not directly result in weight loss.

A 2024 commercial for SkinnyPop popcorn opens with a businesswoman sitting at her desk with a view of a city outside her window. She has a large bowl of popcorn in front of her while her male assistant is holding a bag of SkinnyPop popcorn. As the woman lifts a kernel of popcorn up to her mouth, she says, "This SkinnyPop popcorn is so delicious" to which her assistant replies, "And only three simple ingredients" as he pours more popcorn from the bag into her bowl ("SkinnyPop TV Spot, 'Never Have to Stop' " 2024). The woman then says, "I never have to stop" as she pushes her phone toward the assistant and tells him to hold all her calls, then throws her cell phone to him telling him to hold her texts, too, before handing her laptop to him and telling him to hold her emails ("SkinnyPop TV Spot, 'Never Have to Stop' " 2024). He struggles to hold everything while still holding the bag as she sits with her feet up on the desk eating popcorn and telling him not to leave. The final shot is of popcorn being poured into a bowl next to a bag of the product while a female announcer says, "SkinnyPop, endlessly delicious" ("SkinnyPop TV Spot, 'Never Have to Stop' " 2024). One of the "three simple ingredients" in SkinnyPop original popcorn is sunflower oil, which is an ultra-processed food ingredient thus illustrating the use of the reduced-calorie theme in both the name of the product and the message in the commercial as well as the perceived benefits, perceived susceptibility, and perceived barriers of the Health Belief Model constructs.

A similar commercial in the "Freedom to Snack" campaign released the same year features a woman and a man in a hot air balloon. She is eating popcorn out of a bowl, and he is eating out of a bag of SkinnyPop original popcorn. The woman says, "Mmm, this SkinnyPop is delicious" as the man pours more popcorn into her bowl and replies, "And only three simple ingredients" ("SkinnyPop TV Spot,

'Hot Air Balloon'" 2024). The woman looks excited as she says, "We never have to stop" before the man reaches for a handle on the bottom of the balloon to make it go higher ("SkinnyPop TV Spot, 'Hot Air Balloon'" 2024). The next shot is of a pilot and co-pilot in an airplane. The pilot asks the other man if he's seeing what he sees as the camera moves out to show the plane window with the hot air balloon in it. The man asks the woman whether the plane is too low or the hot air balloon too high, to which the woman replies that they are too high. The final shot is of the popcorn being poured into a bowl next to a bag of the product with a female announcer saying, "SkinnyPop, endlessly delicious" ("SkinnyPop TV Spot, 'Hot Air Balloon'" 2024). The idea of "never having to stop" as well as the visual illustration of the hot air balloon being "light" enough to rise to new heights in addition to the name of the product work together to create the use of the reduced-calorie theme in the Identity Health Halo as well as the perceived benefits, perceived susceptibility, and perceived barriers constructs of the Health Belief Model.

At the Hershey website, which is the manufacturer of SkinnyPop popcorn, the "Freedom to Snack" campaign is described as being created "with real snackers in mind—and the epiphany we all have when we find a salty treat that doesn't actually have to be a treat," which focuses on the "idea that SkinnyPop popcorn isn't strictly a better-for-you option, and it's not just a snack either. It's about eating one piece of popcorn after another to keep snackers satisfied" with the advertisements driving "home the moment the snackers realize that they can continue snacking to their heart's desire."

Similarly, a commercial for low-calorie chocolates uses both the Identity Halo and the weight-loss association in its product name. The commercial opens with a woman on a massage table eating chocolate from a box of chocolates in front of her. She says, "New Skinny Cow Divine Filled Chocolates are so divine" as a man begins massaging her and asks whether the chocolates are more divine than the massage he is giving her to which she replies, "Three pieces of chocolate filled with caramel or peanut butter cream, oh yeah" ("Skinny Cow Divine Filled Chocolates TV Spot, 'Massage'" 2013). He says, "How about this?" as he turns into a vampire though she is so focused on her candy that she doesn't notice and replies, "Ah, nothin' beats 130 calories" as she smiles lovingly at the piece of candy she is holding ("Skinny Cow Divine Filled Chocolates TV Spot, 'Massage'" 2013). Next, a woman's voice says, "Sharon?" as the camera cuts to the woman who is actually on the front area of a display of the product in a grocery store as she is being watched by the other woman and her son. The woman is embarrassed and begins to slide off the display as the camera cuts to a shot of three chocolate squares being poured out of a box while a female announcer says, "New Skinny Cow Divine Filled Chocolates, luscious chocolate filled with caramel or peanut butter cream, three pieces just 130 calories" as the camera first shows a candy being broken in half to feature the filled center and then cuts to a shot of three pieces of chocolate on a white dish with two boxes of the product behind it and the words "Find us in the candy aisle" below ("Skinny Cow Divine Filled Chocolates TV Spot, 'Massage'" 2013). Once again, the name of the product directly uses the perceived benefits and perceived barriers Health Belief Model constructs to motivate consumers to purchase the product. Pairing of the words "skinny" and "chocolate," thus creating a belief that eating chocolate will result in losing weight is a clear illustration of the reduced-calorie theme and the perceived benefits construct used to sell an unhealthy ultra-processed food.

Fat Shaming Was First

Though the use of the word "skinny" is still popular today, one technique used in the 1930s through the 1950s by some food manufacturers, known as "fat shaming," is not popular today. One of the most ardent of these companies was Ry-Krisp, which was founded by two Swedish immigrants who later sold the company to Purina in 1926. The advertisements, many of which promoted the "Famous Ry-Krisp Reducing Plan on Every Package" were mainly targeted at women, preying on their fear of not being thin enough. One early advertisement features an illustration of a couple ice skating. The woman is drawn as overweight while the man is fit. The man is smiling as he looks at a thin woman putting her ice skates on while sitting on a bench while the woman he is with is looking at him with concern. The headline above the image reads, "Don't Get Left . . . Get Ry-Krisp!" while below the illustration are the words, "Make Your Bread Ry-Krisp!" (Rare Historical Photos 2024). Below this is an illustration of the product next to the words "Famous Reducing Plan on every package" and above a calorie comparison chart that tells readers that "1 double-square wafter" of Ry-Krisp contains 21 calories, a slice of bread 63 calories, a plain bun or roll 118 calories, and a muffin or biscuit 129 calories (Rare Historical Photos 2024). A small paragraph to the left of the chart describes the product as "filling, far more hunger-satisfying than soft, quickly eat breads. Whole-grain rich in vitamins, minerals, and B-vitamins. Delicious!" (Rare Historical Photos 2024).

Another advertisement with the exact same layout changes only the illustration to show a woman with obesity sitting at a counter eating while the man with her is leaning over to stand closely and smile at another woman who is also smiling. A third advertisement in the series with the same layout features a woman with obesity in a bathing suit sitting on a dock watching a man in a boat rowing a thin woman in a bikini and smiling at her. In two of the three advertisements, the "Don't Get Left" portion of the dialogue is "spoken" by a nearby bird, while in the restaurant one it is spoken by a man in the background. Subsequent advertisements would feature the headline "Someone Ought to Tell Her about Ry-Krisp," with illustrations of a man kissing a thin woman and readers being urged to "lose ugly fat," a lifeguard struggling to carry a woman with obesity out of the water, and two thin girls massaging a woman with obesity. One particular advertisement features an illustration of a bride and a groom leaving the church while a woman with obesity holding a bouquet of flowers looks on. The headline "Fated not to be mated . . . Better reduce the Ry-Krisp way!" includes text below that goes on to say, "Alter your figure—it may be the first step to the altar!" as well as an image of a suggested meal that includes skim milk, peach halves, a salad with carrots and watercress, a plate with peas, cauliflower, and a tuna souffle all next to a box of the product (Rare Historical Photos 2024).

Similarly, an advertisement that also includes an image of a suggested meal has an illustration of a slim woman and man kissing while a woman with obesity looks at them. The headline reads, "If it's kissin' you're missin' Better reduce the Ry-Krisp way" (aikyastore.life 2024). A paragraph underneath urges readers to "Be Slim! Get the Ry-Krisp plan for the normal overweight—cut calories—have delicious meals like that shown here" (aikyastore.life 2024). A third advertisement in this series that includes an image of a suggested meal at the bottom has an illustration of a woman with obesity breaking a chair that she was sitting in while a thin woman looks on. The headline reads, "Too much on too little? Better reduce the Ry-Krisp way!" with text underneath that says, "If 'too fat' is your downfall . . . send for the Ry-Krisp plan! So simple for any normal overweight to lose pounds, gain sparkle" (aikyastore.life 2024). The meal is described as including "shrimp creole, baked potato, broccoli, apple-celery salad, skim milk, Ry-Krisp" (aikyastore.life 2024). A fourth advertisement to feature an illustration of a meal shows one of a woman with obesity sitting at a makeup table looking in a mirror as she has a powder puff in front of her chin and a surprised look on her face. The headline says, "'Takin' it on the chin? Better reduce the Ry-Krisp way!" with a paragraph below beginning with "Delicious Food! Slimmer Figure" and then describing the illustrated meal consisting of "chicken, two vegetables, Ry-Krisp plus salad, dessert!" (aikyastore.life 2024).

These previously mentioned advertisements for Ry-Krisp use the reduced-calorie theme in the Identity Health Halo to promise consumers better lives if they lose weight by eating their product, which also results in employing the perceived benefits construct of the Health Belief Model. The idea of being "left" or unpopular due to being overweight illustrates the use of the perceived susceptibility and perceived severity constructs while the idea of delicious taste addresses the perceived barriers associated with the bad taste of weight-loss products. While it's easy to see the deceitful nature of these promises looking back in the current year, it is not possible to understand the impact these advertisements may have had on women during the 1930s through the 1950s as well as the ideas and attitudes passed down through generations. It's not beyond reason to suppose that much of the drive for thinness and perfection occurring decades later and even today has its roots in these types of advertisements.

"Flaky-Thin" Saltines

Though the fat-shaming advertising techniques used by Ry-Krisp are rarely, if ever, seen in today's food advertisements, the practice of using the word "thin" in ultra-processed food advertisements is still present. One well-known cracker company began using the word "thin" in its advertisements in a 1940s campaign. An advertisement for Sunshine Saltines featured in this campaign showed an illustration of a thin, young girl wearing a red dress with matching bows on her two pigtails sitting at a table with a bowl of soup and a glass of milk while holding a cracker in her hand and smiling at it. The headline above her reads, "No wonder they call 'em Flaky Thin" while just below her on the white tablecloth are the words "Always More Delicious because they're Flaky Thin," under which is an illustration of the product with the following words: "all through the meal!" (Comicstrips 2024). In the larger text at the top, the word "Thin" is underlined in red while in the middle text, the words "More" and "Thin" are underlined in red to draw more attention to them. It's also worth noting that the red underlining matches the girl's dress; thus, it's not difficult to infer that the veiled message in the advertisement says that consumers will be "more thin" similar to the girl if they eat this product.

Several other advertisements from this time period would employ the use of the reduced-calorie theme as well as the perceived benefits and perceived susceptibility Health Belief Model constructs through the use of the word "thin" in promoting their products. Of these is one advertisement featuring a similar, or perhaps a slightly older, version of the girl in the previous advertisement with a bowl of soup in front of her and a character of the Sunshine baker holding a plate with a stack of saltines rising from it, which the girl is looking up at. The headline says, "More 'Krispy' More Crackers! . . . because they're the Flaky-Thin Saltine!" with the words "more" and "the" underlined in red and the words "flaky-thin" in red font (Comicstrips 2024). Though many of the subsequent advertisements would contain similar messages, the content of two in this series is worth mentioning. In one, a young Gigi Perreau, who is noted as staring in a Samuel Goldwyn Production of the 1949 film *Roseanna McCoy*, is shown at a table with a red-and-white checkered tablecloth. She is spreading peanut butter on a saltine and with a jar of jam in front of her. An illustration of the Sunshine Baker is standing next to her holding a plate full of saltines. In a dialogue bubble coming from the baker are the words, "The Flaky-Thin Cracker Stars at Everybody's Table!" with the words "Flaky-Thin" larger and in red text (Comicstrips 2024). The second advertisement worth mentioning in this series shows an illustration of a young boy leaning on a counter with a cash register on it. He has a baseball glove attached to his waist and a sling shot in his pocket. He is pointing with his thumb at the young girl next to him who is thin and dressed in a red-checked skirt with a blue sweater over it and matching red socks and bow in her hair. The dialogue from him says, "Krispy's for the lady . . . and make 'em Flaky Thin!" with the word "thin" and the exclamation point in red text (Comicstrips 2024). In this series of advertisements, there appears to be an inferred but subtle promise of thinness, the opposite of which is not being overweight (perceived susceptibility), for those who eat the saltines evidenced by the focus through red-colored text on the word "thin," which coordinates with the outfits of the thin, young girls thus illustrating both through text and visuals the reduced-calorie theme and the perceived benefits and perceived susceptibility constructs.

Trend Setter and Popped

Around the same time these advertisements were appearing in newspapers and magazines, Nabisco introduced another product that took advantage of both the reduced-calorie theme and the perceived benefits construct through the use of the word "thin" by including it directly in the product name and, for a time, contracting with a popular actress known for her thin physique. The year 1947 would mark the debut of Wheat Thins crackers. Though advertising for the product would gain some attention, it wasn't until the mid-1970s that the company's advertising campaigns began to receive increased popularity due to the contracting of actress Sandy Duncan, best known for her long Broadway run as Peter Pan and her role in the television sitcom *The Hogan Family*, who advertised the product throughout the 1980s. One of these commercials opens with Duncan in an outside setting near a fence with green grass and a large tree to the side and behind her. She holds up a box of Wheat Thins and says, "Call me a trend setter but I was eating Wheat Thins before people knew they were baked and not fried. Now, everybody knows. Who needs a greasy chip, right?" as the camera zooms in closer to her (Internet Lurker 2008). She continues to say, "Besides, Wheat Thins are delicious. Delicious is still in, isn't it?" as text below her appears saying, "Great taste without the guilt" before a final shot of her smiling and taking a bite of a cracker (Internet Lurker 2008).

A 1983 advertisement features Duncan at the Nabisco Bakers' Picnic where she is coaching a group of men to sing a song that begins with the lyrics "We bake our Wheat Thins thinner" as she tells the men to "Really hit the word thinner. That's important because the thinner the Wheat Thins, the better the taste" as she puts a cracker in one man's mouth (Dailymotion 1983). She then tells the men to continue with their practicing while she will "keep eating Wheat Thins, one after the other" as she laughs before the men sing "We bake our Wheat Thins thinner to get a better taste" and Duncan exclaims "Yes!" as she turns to congratulate the men and an announcer once again tells viewers that "the thinner the Wheat Thins, the better the taste" (Dailymotion 1983). Once again, the inference about a "thin" cracker resulting in a thin body size is implicit in both the name of the product and the advertising of it thus illustrating the use of the reduced-calorie theme and the perceived benefits and perceived susceptibility constructs.

A more recent commercial for another version of the product takes the idea of thinness in a different direction. The 2014 commercial opens with a shot of a man frantically eating Wheat Thins Popped in a hot air balloon while looking behind him as a siren sounds briefly and a man's voice comes through a megaphone saying, "We're not gonna ask you again, sir. Pull over" before the camera reveals two policemen in a hot air balloon behind him with a Metro Police emblem on the side ("Wheat Thins Popped TV Spot, 'Air Chase'" 2014). One of the officers says, "You got Wheat Thins, hand them over" before the man in the first hot air balloon shouts, "No!" after which the other officer urges him to "Just share a couple. They're so light and airy" at which point the camera shows a close up of the product with the man's hand in it ("Wheat Thins Popped TV Spot, 'Air Chase'" 2014). The man again refuses and the officers tell him to stop because they "want those whole grains" before one suggests they call for backup at which point there is another officer in a balloon behind them with a dog who says he's there as the dog barks and the camera zooms out to show all three balloons in a line with the first one yellow colored and the words "Wheat Thins Popped" on it ("Wheat Thins Popped TV Spot, 'Air Chase'" 2014). After that, the camera cuts to a yellow background where the word "Must!" appears followed by the word "Have!" and then a final image of the product ("Wheat Thins Popped TV Spot, 'Air Chase'" 2014). The association of Wheat Thins with being "light and airy" as well as the visual of "light" hot air balloons creates an Identity Health Halo and uses the perceived benefits and perceived susceptibility Health Belief Model constructs.

Other ultra-processed food products using versions of the reduced-calorie theme and perceived benefits and perceived susceptibility constructs include, but are not limited to, the following: Thin Slim Foods Zero Net Carb Plain Bread, Thin Slim Foods Zero Net Carb Cinnamon Bread, Thin Slim Foods Zero Net Carb Everything Inside Bread, Thin Slim Foods Zero Carb Honey Bread, The Skinny Food Co. Low Carb High Protein Wheat Bread, The Skinny Food Co. Low Carb High Protein Banquettes, The Skinny Food Co. Keto Gluten Free Hamburger Buns, The Skinny Food Company Chocoholic Drops, The Skinny Food Company Chocoholic Peanuts, The Skinny Food Company Duo Bar, The Skinny Food Company Chocoholic Snack Pot, Real Foods Sesame Corn Thins, The Skinny Food Company Spaghetti Noodles, The Skinny Food Company Low Carb Noodles, Real Foods Multigrain Corn Thins, Real Foods Sour Cream & Chives Corn Thins, Real Foods Tasty Cheese Corn Thins, Real Foods Soy, Linseed & Chia Corn Thins, Real Foods Wholegrain Rice Thins, Real Food Ancient Grains Rice Thins, ThinSlim Foods Zero Net Carb Pizza Crust, Mission Restaurant Style Thin & Crispy Tortilla Chips, Lundberg Family Farms Thin Stackers Brown Rice Flavor Puffed Grain Cakes, Lundberg Family Farms Thin Stackers Red Rice & Quinoa Flavor Puffed Grain Cakes, Lundberg Family Farms Thin Stackers Organic Fine Herbs Flavor Puffed Rice Cakes, Lundberg Family Farms Thin Stackers Organic Five Grain Flavor Puffed Grain Cakes, Kraft Singles Extra Thin American Cheese Slices, DiGiorno Pepperoni & Sausage Thin & Crispy Stuffed Crust Pizza, DiGiorno Supreme Thin Crust Pizza, DiGiorno

Four Meat Thin Crust Pizza, Girl Scouts Thin Mints, Boulder Canyon Thin & Crispy Cheddar Sour Cream Flavored Potato Chips, Boulder Canyon Thin & Crispy Classic Sea Salt Potato Chips, Herr's Extra Thin Pretzels, Utz Extra Thins Pretzels, Rold Gold Thins Minces Pretzels, Rold Gold Thins, Rold Gold Tiny Twists, and Pillsbury Thin & Crispy Pizza Crust Mix.

It's important to note that there are far more products using the reduced-calorie theme and the perceived benefits and perceived susceptibility constructs than there is room to include here.

Vegan, Vegetarian, Vegetables, Veils

"NUT FOODS Agree with Your Stomach, Are Very Fattening, Prevent and Cure Dyspepsia" reads an advertisement from the Newbro Drug Company on North Main Street in Butte, Montana, promoting the Battle Creek Sanitarium products carried in their establishment, and published in *The Anaconda Standard* on the morning of January 30, 1898 (Montana Historical Society 1898). Products listed in the one-column advertisement include Bromose, "a combination of carefully blanched and thoroughly cooked and sterilized nut meats with predigested cereals," maltol, a nut oil, malted Nuts, "just the thing for feeble invalids and infants," ambrosia that "melts in the mouth, is delicious, and very fattening," nut butter that "makes blood as well as fat—a great delicacy" and Nuttose, which "resembles meat so closely as to be called vegetable meat . . . is fattening, blood making and very wholesome [making it a] capital food for diabetics and rheumatics" (Montana Historical Society 1898). Consumers are encouraged in the advertisement to "Ask for Pamphlet" (Montana Historical Society 1898).

Nuttose is believed to be the "first Sanitarium product to be marketed as a meat alternative" (Terrell 2020), thus creating a foundation for ultra-processed food manufacturers to use the vegetarian theme in the Identity Health Halo as well as the perceived benefits and perceived susceptibility Health Belief Model constructs. Developed under the leadership of John Harvey Kellogg, director of the Battle Creek Medical Surgical Sanitarium, "one of the most popular health resorts in the United States, growing to more than thirty buildings on thirty acres of land in Battle Creek, Michigan," the product was born of Kellogg's theory that "eating bland, vegetable and grain-based foods reduced the risk of a range of health issues" (Terrell 2020). While director of the sanitarium, Kellogg would incorporate the Sanitas Nut Food Company, a mail-order business called The

Battle Creek Food Company, which would offer many products including the now-famous toasted corn flakes and another meat substitute product made from grains and nuts called Protose, which became available around 1899 (Terrell 2020). The company would in later years focus solely on breakfast cereals.

"The Most Remarkable Dietetic Discovery of Recent Years"

An early all-text, five-paragraph advertisement for Protose would promote the product as "The Most Remarkable Dietetic Discovery of Recent Years" and "almost identical with flesh-food in composition, appearance, and flavor" that is made only of vegetables making it "free from the many objections raised by eminent scientists against the use of meats" (Vegetarian History Blog 2010). The advertisement continues by saying that "progressive physicians" have sought a meat substitute to use in "cases of chronic rheumatism, Bright's disease, diabetes, and the long list of nervous affections" now use the product with "marked success" before going on to describe an August 26, 1899, analysis of Protose in the *Lancet*, a respected medical journal that stated that the product is made up of "64:22 per cent *[sic]*" moisture, "21:30 per cent *[sic]*" proteins, "10:23 per cent *[sic]*" fat, "1:40 per cent *[sic]*" mineral matter, and "2:85 per cent *[sic]*" carbohydrates making it "chemically . . . the composition of animal tissue, beef or mutton" (Vegetarian History Blog 2010). The advertisement further noted that the analysis found that "the fat exhibited a low melting point and was easily saponified" and "probably . . . readily digested" with a flavor that "is not unpleasant and somewhat meaty" before declaring the product to be unique and having "some merit" (Vegetarian History Blog 2010). In addition to the vegetarian theme, this advertisement employs all four of the Health Belief Model constructs by touting the product as a preventative for specific illness (perceived susceptibility), easily digested (perceived severity), free from scientific objections (perceived benefits), and "somewhat meaty" (perceived barriers).

A group of people in Worthington, Ohio, who were fans of Protose, which was "a combination of wheat gluten, peanuts, and soy," would add seasonings used in meat and make the product resemble meat leading to the creation of Worthington Foods, a company that introduced two vegetarian meat products: Soyloin Steaks and Meatless Wieners, also sold in cans (Smith 2015). The company would eventually be sold to Miles Laboratories that would create a sister establishment called Morningstar Farms, which is now owned once again by Kellogg's and still sells vegetarian meat products today. Though the NOVA food classification system was not yet invented, the ingredients in Protose, which include "pure wheat gluten (now known as seitan) and soybean curd (better known as tofu)" (Smith 2015), meet the established criteria for designation as an ultra-processed food while the emphasis on the vegetable properties in advertisements and on labels work together to create an Identity Health Halo with the use of the perceived benefits construct. The perceived susceptibility construct is also illustrated by highlighting the vegetable properties since eating meat during the 1920s and 1930s though seen as a necessity and luxury by many was also viewed by some as unhealthy resulting in diseases.

An advertisement from 1930 published in the December British issue of *Good Health* from Granose Foods Ltd. of Watford begins with the headline "Christmas—The Family Dinner!" and included an illustration of a can of Nuttolene, which is labeled as "The Choice Nutmeat" on the left side and a can of Protose, identified as "The Standard Nutmeat" on the right (Adventist Archives 2017). Two paragraphs of text begin with, "CHRISTMAS—A time of goodwill and gladness for everyone" then go on to discuss "the anxiety of wisely choosing good things for the dinner" since children and guests need to be considered who "eat for health as well as enjoyment" (Adventist Archives 2017). The copy continues by asking, "Why not provide a repast founded upon true health principles? With PROTOSE or NUTTOLENE forming the main savoury dish a delightful dinner can be yours" all "with the advantage of appetising flavours, healthful nourishment, purity, and economy" (Adventist Archives 2017). A larger illustration of two chefs, one below each can of the products, are shown holding trays with the products on them while a smaller illustration of a family of six seated at a table is included at the bottom of the page.

"A Welcome Change from Meat" is the headline of another advertisement for Protose (Quora 2022). To the right of the headline is an illustration of a dinnerplate with the product and a smaller image in a square of a can of Protose. The five paragraphs of text underneath the headline begin with "Now you can serve delicious health menus that satisfy the palate, while building and maintaining good health" continuing on to note that for "Friday menus and lighter, tastier meals in hot weather Protose is the most welcome change" (Quora 2022). The second paragraph notes that the product looks, tastes, and smells like meat but is made from vegetables while the third one notes that Protose can be served "any way meat" is—"roasted, broiled, stewed, fried or cold from the can" and also in sandwiches and salads (Quora 2022). The remaining two paragraphs call Protose "one of the greatest contributions" from Battle Creek and encourage consumers to find the product at their local health food store (Quora 2022). Underneath the image of the dinner plate is a smaller headline with the words "Free Diet Service," which mentions the Battle Creek "staff of graduate dieticians" who will help consumers with "any diet problem" and send personal suggestions as well as a copy of the book *Healthful Living*, which is written by "a leading nutrition expert," if readers would write their address in the margin of the advertisement (Quora 2022).

It's worth noting that those who choose to abstain from meat, known as vegetarians, and those who abstain from all animal products, identified as vegans, pursue this lifestyle for many different reasons, including health improvement, animal protection, social justice, environmental protection, and religious beliefs, none of which are criticized in this study. The purpose of this chapter is to create awareness about the Identity Health Halo used in ultra-processed foods in order to make them appear healthier. There is no intention to promote or condemn lifestyle choices but, instead, as is the foundation of this study, to create awareness of marketing techniques used in advertisements and on product labels. Furthermore, this particular theme is unique in that it not only serves as a halo for unhealthy ultra-processed foods, but it is also a designated food group as well. Like the gluten-free theme, foods are categorized in grocery stores as vegetarian or vegan. However, consistent with the focus of this study, the vegetarian theme is mainly used in ultra-processed food advertising and on product labels. It is rare that fresh fruits or vegetables contain labels and if they do, health halos are not used since the food is already accepted as healthy. In almost all cases, health halos are used to make unhealthy, ultra-processed foods appear to provide health benefits to consumers while the Health Belief Model constructs are employed to motivate purchase of these products. This being the case, products studied in this chapter, as throughout this study, are ultra-processed and, by definition, unhealthy and thus employing a health halo to distract from their unhealthiness and using constructs to motivate purchase of these products.

"Good Eating"

In the 1940s, another company would become a major producer of vegetarian meat substitutes. Among their products was Choplets, a canned product made of wheat and vegetables, which is still available today and lists ingredients including textured vegetable protein (wheat gluten, soy protein concentrate, water, for hydration), caramel color, broth: water, hydrolyzed soy, corn and wheat protein, autolyzed yeast extract, salt, dextrose, corn oil, caramel color, disodium inosinate, disodium guanylate, soybean oil. The first newspaper advertisement for Choplets appeared in the April 10, 1947, issue of the Indiana *Terra Haute Tribune* and featured a large headline with the name of the product with a line of "m-m-m"s beginning at the letter "C" and then looping around in a reverse S-form growing larger until they connected with an illustration of a man holding a fork near his mouth with the product on it (Worthington Libraries 2019). Underneath the illustration are the words "Americas *[sic]* Favorite Meat-like Treat!" and below that are nineteen lines of text that begin by asking consumers whether they have "discovered the tender, juicy goodness of Choplets," which is described as an "amazing new kind of food" tasting "more like meat cutlets than anything else" (Worthington Libraries 2019).

The text goes on to say that the product is made from "wholesome wheat grains with other tasty vegetable nutrients added" through "a special scientific process" that "takes the starchy, fattening elements *out* of the wheat and leaves the right protein *in*" (Worthington Libraries 2019; emphases in the original). Consumers are told that they will like the "meat-like treat" and the "low, low price" of the product which can be breaded, baked, or fried "in a jiffy" and doesn't need refrigeration (Worthington Libraries 2019). To the left of the text is an illustrated image of a can of Choplets with a slightly larger text in a rectangular box to the left of that. The text in the box tells consumers there are "10 to 12 Meat-like Cutlets, Tender, Tasty, Nourishing, Rich in Wheat Proteins" that are "All Food" without waste, fat, or starch with broth that "Makes Tasty Gravy!" (Worthington Libraries 2019). The final three lines in the box tell consumers that they can "Bake, Bread, Boil or Fry!" Choplets for "Only a Few Pennies for Each Large Serving!" (Worthington Libraries 2019). Large text centered across the bottom of the page says, "Ask Your Grocer for Choplets!" (Worthington Libraries 2019).

A little over a year later, the first color advertisement for the product would be published in the July 1948 issue of *Health and Life* magazine. At the top of the advertisement, bright yellow rays of sun surround the word "Choplets" in large red font centered on the page. Below this are the words "Family Favorite—Any Time-Anywhere" in blue font (Worthington Libraries 2017). A paragraph of text to the left of the page tells consumers that "with Choplets on hand" they are "ready for 'good eating' any time" since they are "high favorites" when "youngsters bring 'the gang' in for a snack" or when friends are over for a picnic or at a "full-course dinner" (Worthington Libraries 2019). Continuing, the text describes the product as "tender, juicy, slices of protein-rich, meat like nourishment-packed in wholesome broth that makes wonderful gravy" (Worthington Libraries 2017). To the right of the text is an illustration of two young couples cooking on a barbeque grill. They are dressed in brightly colored clothes with the women in pink and yellow sweaters and the men in yellow and light blue shirts.

Below that image is a plate filled with two Choplets, carrot sticks, peas, cauliflower, a tomato slice, and parsley. The plate is yellow against a light green background. Above the plate is a bun with the product and lettuce, to the left of which is an illustration of three rows of seven young people: a male and a female in the back row, two females and a male in the middle row with the female in the middle holding a tray filled with Choplets, and a male and a female in the front staring longingly at the tray. They are young and dressed in brightly colored clothes. Beneath this image is a recipe card with a can of Choplets to the left. The "Recipe of the Month" is for "MOCK CHICKEN A LA KING" and includes using a can of Choplets, sliced, celery, bell pepper, onion, and thyme with a white sauce made from butter, flour, milk, and salt (Worthington Libraries 2017). To the right of the recipe is an illustration of a mother serving her family a tray filled with Choplets as the husband, seated at the head of the table, smiles along with two young girls and a boy.

It's worth noting that Choplets, now produced under the Loma Linda brand, is available nationwide and online. The grass-green colored label on the thirteen-ounce can of the product includes the company's logo with a dark green background at the top of the can, the product name in white text below that, and above a partial image of two breaded Choplets with a white border and a banner appears the word "Vegetarian" in green text with a white background placed slightly over the left side of the product image. The company also manufactures other vegetarian products all of which use the vegetarian theme and the perceived benefits construct. Included in this product line is the popular "Vegetable Skallops," which contains a similar layout on its fifteen-ounce can except for an image of the product showing three skewers with vegetables and the words "Low Fat" underneath the vegetarian one.

Meat Monotony

A product called Mock Turkey would be introduced several years later by Nu Vita Foods. A 1954 advertisement for the product features a large headline with the words "Lange's Tasty Mock Turkey Is Loaded with Protein!" with an illustration of the product to the left of the page, an illustration of a turkey with a dialogue box saying, "Real Golden Brown Turkey-Like Flavor!" to the right and text in the middle that begins with the words "Healthful! Nutritious! Delicious! Different!" (r/vintagereads 2024). The text continues to call the product "a delightful food treat your family will love!" and encourages serving the "truly tasty meat substitute full of healthful high-protein foods" with a "delectable turkey-like flavor" (r/vintagereads 2024). In the illustration of the turkey, he is holding a box of text that proclaims the product to be "100% Vegetarian Made from 100% Whole Wheat Gluten" (r/vintagereads 2024). Three quarters of the way down the advertisement is information about the company's vegetarian breakfast links and other "energy-giving protein foods" from the company including "Lange Chops, Lange Steaks, Langeburgers, Lange Meatballs and Spaghetti, Lange Mulligan Meat" under which consumers are told that if the products aren't carried in their area, they can send $1.00 for a sample of breakfast links and Mock Turkey (r/vintagereads 2024).

The 1970s would bring an advertisement for Sanitarium Soyameat. Large text on the left side of the advertisement says, "Break the monotony of meat, meat, meat, meat, meat, meat, meat," with portions of the word behind a large photo of a plate with four vegelink cabbage rolls covered with a strip of tomato sauce down the middle (Scrapbook Layouts by Lisa 2024). Smaller text to the right of the large headline encourages consumers to "Put some variety into your high protein diet" before noting that now their bodies can "get all the protein that can come only from meat with Sanitarium high protein meat substitutes," including vegetarian sausages, "Vegelinks," and Nutmeal and Nutolene (Scrapbook Layouts by Lisa 2024). Readers are promised that "Once the family's tasted Sanitarium high protein foods," the company thinks "you'll buy them more often" positioned above an image of Soyameat Pastries below which are recipes for that and the Vegelink Cabbage Rolls followed by photos of cans of both products (Scrapbook Layouts by Lisa 2024).

Plant-based meat sales have continued to garner a large portion of the total sales of vegetarian foods, which reached a high of $7.4 billion for total industry sales in 2021 (Reynolds 2024). However, "dollar sales of plant-based meat and seafood in the US fell by 13 percent over the past two years" due, in part, to a rise in sales during the pandemic when slaughterhouses were shut down as well as a rise in the cost of plant-based meat products (Reynolds 2024). Despite this, "plant-based creamers, protein powders and liquids, and baked goods and other desserts saw both unit and dollar sales increase in 2023" with "six in 10 U.S. households purchased plant-based foods in 2023" (Good Food Institute 2023, 35). In addition to this, "Rising concerns about so-called ultraprocessed *[sic]* food have also buffeted the plant-based meat industry, given the high amount of processing usually needed to make its products" (Reynolds 2024). Though it's difficult to predict where sales will be in the future due to some of these reports being published during the growth period, there is a great variation in sales numbers for 2035, which "range from ambitious estimates of $88 billion to $368 billion for the plant-based meat market alone . . . [with the] combined alternative protein (plant-based, fermentation, and cultivated) market forecasts for the same year rang[ing] from $87 billion to $594 billion" (Good Food Institute 2023, 84).

Veggie Burger War

Two of the best-selling vegetarian meat burgers come from the Impossible Burger, which is believed to be the "first producer to really nail that beef burger taste and texture and . . . still [the] best option for a plant-based burger that mimics the real thing," and the Beyond Burger, "touted as 'the world's first plant-based burger patty that looks, cooks and satisfies like fresh ground beef' " (Watsky 2023). Both are ultra-processed foods and use the vegetarian theme and perceived benefits construct in their advertisements and on package labels. In an effort to compete with each other in a recently declining market, both brands have launched advertising campaigns designed to garner attention. Impossible Foods recently introduced a campaign based on the slogan "We're solving the meat problem with more meat," which presents its product as the solution to the environmental and health issues caused by eating meat (Business Wire 2024). In a press release issued by the company, Leslie Sims, chief marketing and creative officer of Impossible Foods said, "Meat eaters have historically shrugged at meat from plants as something that's not for them . . . We see this campaign as a way to let meat eaters know Impossible meat is the best way to keep eating meat you love, just without a lot of the problems associated with animal meat" (Business Wire 2024).

Many of the commercials in this campaign directly target men. An example of this is a thirty-second advertisement that begins with a muscular man who is in a fair setting. He is walking fast and determined in his speech when he says,

"Listen up, America. Meat has problems" at which point he knocks a hamburger out of a male teenager's hand in a karate chop motion and then replaces it with a bun that contains a flag with the word "Impossible" on it before continuing "and it's going to take us meat eaters to solve them. So, when the world says too much meat is bad and we should eat less of it, we say no world, we should eat more" at which time he walks by a bunch of balloons, a stack of hay, and a hot-dog eating contest where he pulls the tablecloth off the table used to hold the hot dogs just before the camera focuses on a stack of vegetarian hot dogs as he says the word "more" (THALIHITA 2024). The next shot is of him entering a kitchen saying, "Because now we can turn plants into burgers and hot dogs, even meatballs" as he moves through the house pushing meat off the counter, then putting a bag of Impossible Italian Meatballs on a table in front of a bowl of spaghetti topped with the product and a flag with the company's name on it (THALIHITA 2024). He is next shown at the doorway with several other younger men in the shot before he moves into a bar-like establishment walking on top of a table saying, "Now plants can be meat. Come on people, let's punch cholesterol in the face!" as the camera focuses on another man who makes a cheer-like sound (THALIHITA 2024). He is next shown on a dirt bike bursting through a wall as he says, "We're solving the meat problem with more meat," then yelling the product name as he rides outside where the word "Impossible" is shown in white text over the blue sky before a red band with the words "Meat from Plants" appears beneath the product name (THALIHITA 2024).

The aggressive actions of the actor slapping meat out of a teenager's hand, pulling a tablecloth off a table with hot dogs on it, walking on a table, and bursting through a wall on a dirt bike in addition to his hostile words about punching cholesterol in the face are clearly designed to appeal to a male audience. Taking this a step further, the props used in this advertisement and confrontational manner of the main actor resemble a war-like energy that may be interpreted as strength and commitment by some. Despite these things, the commercial is an example of the many ways in which the vegetarian theme and the Health Belief Model constructs can be used in advertising. The idea of "punching cholesterol in the face" represents the use of the perceived susceptibility Health Belief Model construct while the notion of the world saying "too much meat is bad" evidences the perceived severity construct with the call to eat more meat made from plants to solve the problem illustrating the perceived benefits construct. The visual of a strong, confrontational man eating in a way sometimes believed to be feminine uses the perceived barriers construct to motivate viewers to purchase the product.

For its part, Beyond Meat used reality-television star Kim Kardashian to promote its products. In a commercial as part of this campaign, Kardashian is shown in close up wearing a black sleeveless turtleneck sweater dress with white kitchen cabinets behind her saying, "I believe so much in the mission of Beyond Meat that I've stepped in to help with my greatest asset, my taste" as the camera pulls out to show a man and a woman dressed in white. The woman has a lab-like coat on and the man is dressed in chef-like attire. The man puts a covered plate on the counter in front of all three of them, which he uncovers to reveal a burger with a side of fried food underneath it before a close up of Kardashian with the words "Chief Taste Consultant" are shown as she continues, "This plant-based meat is not only amazingly delicious but it's also better for you and better for the planet. It's a simple change that makes a really big difference," during which time upbeat music is played softly in the background as Kardashian is shown eating various Beyond Meat products with the man and woman looking on, and bumping her fist with the man after tasting one of them (Beyond Meat 2022). She then says, "So fun. And now that I'm Beyond Meat's Chief Taste Consultant, there's never been a better time to go Beyond" as a shot of her stopping the man from taking the dish away while she is still eating is shown before we come to a final shot of a close up of her with the company's logo over it (Beyond Meat 2022).

It's worth noting that the Beyond Meat brand is known for using celebrities to promote its products. Some of these include Kevin Hart, Snoop Dogg, Chris Paul, Nikki Bella, Octavia Spencer, and Liza Koshy, even aligning with football quarterback Colin Kaeperknick's "Know Your Rights" campaign at one point (Stanley 2022). The company recently introduced its fourth version of its burger with a "new recipe . . . made with avocado oil . . . reduced saturated fat, reduced sodium and increased protein, with new nutrient dense plant based ingredients like red lentil and faba beans" taking into consideration a report issued by Whole Foods Market noting that "an increasing amount of shoppers are looking for recognizable ingredients in the items they buy" (Flood 2024).

Additional ultra-processed vegan/vegetarian meat products using the vegetarian theme and the perceived benefits and perceived susceptibility constructs on their packaging include, but is not limited to, the following: Gardein Plant Based Frozen Ground Beef, Gardein Plant Based Classic Vegan Meatballs, Gardein Plant Based Vegan Be'f Tips, Gardein Ultimate Plant Based Saus'ge Links Vegan Bratwurst, Gardein Vegan Plant-Based Frozen Seven Grain Crispy Tenders, Gardein Ultimate Plant Based Vegan Buffalo Chick'n Wings, Gardein Plant Based Vegan Chick'n Strips, Gardein Plant Based Vegan Golden

Fishless Filets, Quorn Meatless Grounds, Quorn Naked Meatless Chik'n Cutlets, Quorn Meatless Turk'y Roast, Daring Original Plant Based Frozen Gluten Free Chicken, Loma Linda Plant-Based Meats Vegetarian Burger, Loma Linda Plant Based Meats Swiss Stake with Gravy, Plant Basics Hearty Plant Protein Unflavored Crumbles, Tofurky Plant Based Hickory Smoked Deli Slices, Tofurky Italian Plant Based Sausage, Everything Legendary Plant Based Burger Patties, Everything Legendary Plant Based Ground Abbot's Plant Based Vegan Ground Beef, Rollingreens Plant Based Ground Taco Me'eat, Morning Star Farms Frozen Plant Based Sauced Sweet Riblets, Morning Star Farms Sweet BBQ Vegan Sauced Riblets, Morning Star Farms Grillers Original Veggie Burger, Field Roast Frozen Plant Based Sweet Chile BBQ Bites, Boca Original Veggie Crumbles, Boca Original Chik'n Veggie Patties, Originale Plant Based Meat.

Urban Accents Smokin' Chipotle Plant Based Street Taco, eat meati Mushroom Root Classic Steaks, Just Like Chicken Textured Vegetable Protein, Boca All American Veggie Burgers, Wholesome Provisions Meatless Crumbles, Hy-Vee Actual Veggies Black Bean Veggie Burger, Verisoy Vegan Meat, Yves Veggie Cuisine Ham, Yves Veggie Cuisine Veggie Bologna, Feed Your Head Ham, Feed Your Head Vegan Gyro Meat, May Wah Vegetarian Beef Chunks, Omni Foods Plant Based Meat Style Luncheon, Open Nature Plant Based Ground Meat, Field Roast Plant Based Field Burger, unMEAT Plant Based Meat, No Evil Foods Classic No Chicken, Bubba Burger Veggie Burger, Cooked Perfect Plant Based Veggie Grain Meatballs, V Soy Meatless Textured Beef Slices, Hilary's Super Cauliflower Veggie Burgers, Rainy Day Foods Imitation Meat Textured Vegetable Protein, Unreal Deli Corn'd Beef Plant Based Deli Slices, Be Lean Spicy Vegan Jerky, My Patriot Supply Vegetarian Taco Meat, Franklin Farms Beefless Seitan, Lightlife Plant Based Ground Meat, Lightlife Plant Based Hardwood Smoked Deli Slices, Lightlife Plant Based Korean BBQ Deli Slices, Hungry Planet Plant Based Ground Pork, Vezlay Vegan Veg Meat, Ozo Plant Based Burgers, Thrive Market Plant Based Shepherd's Pie, Open Nature Plant Based Patties, and Meet the Mushroom Shroomacon Plant Based Bacon.

The vegetarian theme is one of the more popular health halo themes due, in part, to the fact that it provides an even greater appearance than some previously mentioned ones of the healthiness of the products. Like the real fruit theme in the Natural and Real Health Halo, the vegetarian theme in the Identity Health Halo is used to provide a link to an already healthy natural food—vegetables—while simultaneously promoting unhealthy ultra-processed foods.

Motion, Movement, Masquerades

A happy cherub-looking young male child is shown ice skating while holding a can of Campbell's Vegetable Soup. He is wearing a sweater with 1916 on it and a cap with a "C" in the center of the band. He is known as a "Campbell Kid," one of several illustrated characters, who have been described as fresh-faced" and "roly-poly" (The Historical Marker Database 2024), created to promote the soup. Behind him is a female Campbell Kid wearing a sweater with a "C" on it and holding a 1915 flag. Behind the female is a snow-covered house and to the left, forming a white circle around most of the soup can is a full moon. To the right of the male skater is a short verse about saying goodbye to the old year and keeping on with what's best "Like this good Campbell 'kind' " under which are the words in large print "A good start—" (VTG Collectibles 2024). Text underneath this asks consumers whether they can "beat it" and "do better for the New Year" than " 'hold fast that which is good' " with the "high-efficiency food product" of Campbell's Vegetable Soup with the name of the product in large font across the middle of the page (VTG Collectibles 2024). The text underneath the product name discusses the "rich condensed stock—made from selected beef" of the soup as well as the "substantial ingredients," including "carrots, white potatoes, sweet potatoes, small peas, 'baby' lima beans, tender corn, green okra, tomatoes, celery, 'alphabet' macaroni and parsley" that make a "delicious and satisfying" soup (VTG Collectibles 2024). Underneath this, in larger print though not as large as the product name, are the words "21 kinds" on the left side and "10¢ a can" on the right side below which is the company's logo and the words "Look for the Red-and-White Label" (VTG Collectibles 2024).

This advertisement is an early example of an ultra-processed food's use of the movement theme in the Identity Health Halo as well as the perceived benefits and perceived susceptibility of the Health Belief Model constructs. It's worth noting that the manner in which the 1916 Campbell Kid is carrying the soup is athletic and loosely mimics an Olympic athlete carrying the Olympic torch, a clear illustration of the two constructs through motivation of illness prevention with images of an athlete (perceived susceptibility) and the promise of exceptionally good health (perceived benefits). Though scheduled for the summer of 1916, the Olympics were canceled due to the First World War as was the plan to include a week of winter activities that featured speed and figure skating among other sports. Though the soup was introduced in the late 1800s, the Campbell Kids didn't make their debut until 1904 when an artist created them for streetcar advertisements. A year later, they would be featured in the company's first national advertising campaign and become "an immediate hit . . . quickly moving from streetcar placards to all of the company's advertising, as well as souvenir postcards, place cards, lapel buttons, and even dolls, all of which are now highly popular collectible items" (The Historical Marker Database 2024). Though not included in all advertising, they currently remain in use in many of the company's advertisements, always representing "the Campbell Soup brand with an air of buoyant health, happiness and vitality" (The Historical Marker Database 2024).

Health through Play

A similar advertisement from the same period features a male Campbell Kid vaulting over a can of vegetable soup. The illustrated image, which is to the left of the page, includes a verse to the right of it which discusses Spring as being a time when "the young man's fancy lightly turns to thoughts of sport" with the product being the solution to making him "spry and prancey" (eBay Image 2024). Large text adjacent to the illustrated soup can says "A Spring Favorite—" and then goes on to discuss it being time to "modify the heavy winter diet" to " 'thaw out'—just as all nature is doing" to benefit digestion, nerves, and "your whole constitution" (eBay Image 2024). Below this in large text is the name of the product—"Campbell's Vegetable Soup" with text below about the "strengthening qualities of good meat" and the "tonic" of vegetables (eBay Image 2024). Once again, the connection to the Olympics is apparent in both the image and the text as is the use of the movement theme and the perceived benefits and perceived susceptibility constructs.

An advertisement from the 1930s focuses on play rather than professional sports. The illustrated color advertisement appeared in a 1932 issue of *The Saturday Evening Post* and featured a large image of children involved in a snowball fight. The four children in the foreground are sheltered by a large snowman and the four in the background by a snow fort. A large headline below the image says, "Play is just health out for a good time!" with an illustration of a can of vegetable soup underneath in between three paragraphs of text and a Campbell Kid dressed as a grocer with the words "Every grocer prides himself upon the Campbell's on his shelf!" (Old Fangled Finds 2024). In the three paragraphs of text, mothers are told that they want their children "in the thick of it, mingling with the rest of the children in normal, wholesome, healthful fun" so they can become "natural leaders in their little world" (Old Fangled Finds 2024). Mothers are encouraged to "let soup by your ally" to "keep the appetite healthy and digestion good" to "supply just the nutrients [that] growing bodies need [the] most" (Old Fangled Finds 2024). The last paragraph tells mothers that even if "rebellion lifts its obstinate head" and "children sulk about eating their vegetables," the soup will "change all this and give the children vegetables in a form they really love" (Old Fangled Finds 2024). Below the text is an illustration of a bowl filled with steaming soup next to a list of the "21 kinds to choose from" and the words "11 cents a can" at the bottom of the list. At the bottom of the page readers are reminded that planning meals is easier due to the number of choices from the company.

The company has expanded its vegetable soup offerings to include creamy versions, a few of which are Cream of Broccoli soup, Cream of Asparagus soup, Cream of Celery soup, as well as introducing both Heart Healthy and Healthy Request products. The ingredients in the Vegetable Soup in the Healthy Request line are listed as beef stock (water, dried beef stock), potatoes, carrots, tomato puree (water, tomato paste), green beans, corn, enriched pasta (wheat flour, egg whites, niacin, ferrous sulfate, thiamine mononitrate, riboflavin, folic acid), peas, celery, contains less than 2 percent of: potato starch, sugar, salt, potassium salt, dried onions, natural flavoring, white pepper, yeast extract, paprika extract for color at the manufacturer's website, classifying this as an ultra-processed food product and indicating the use of the movement theme and the perceived benefits and perceived susceptibility constructs in the advertisements described above.

A more recent advertisement focusing on play continues the snow theme but with the transport of a snowman. The animated commercial using only music as sound opens with a shot of the top of a snowman and the word "Campbell's" next to it with snow-covered houses in the background. The snowman is shown moving at which point the camera pulls out to review that he is being pulled on a sled by a young girl who is struggling to move him. She brings him to the window of a house and then throws a snowball. Inside the house, there is a young boy sitting on a couch with his leg in a cast and elevated. He smiles when he looks out the window as the girl motions that she is cold. He invites her in, and they are shown sitting at a table eating soup as her glasses fog up and they laugh. The words "Warm up inside and out." appear to the left of the screen as the two continue to laugh before there is an image of the company's logo in the final shot ("Campbell's Soup TV Spot, 'Snowbuddy'" 2020). Though the act of building the snowman is never shown, the struggle of the young girl pulling it on a sled is made clear in the advertisement, which indicates physical activity and, thus, the movement theme, while the joy her friend experiences from the good taste of the soup uses the perceived barriers construct to motivate consumers to purchase the product. Additionally, the inferred promise of friendship (perceived benefits) and the avoidance of undesirable health outcomes by eating warm food, which is promoted as healthy (perceived susceptibility), result in further use of the Health Belief Model constructs.

Soup for Men

In 1970, the Campbell Soup Company introduced Chunky soup, which is described at the manufacturer's website as the "first product geared specifically toward men." Seven years later, Chunky soup would become the Official Soup Sponsor of the National Football League (NFL) and would begin to feature star players in its advertisements. A 1988 commercial highlighting this partnership featured Oakland/Los Angeles Raiders Defensive Lineman Howie Long. The commercial opens with a close up shot of Long's hand wearing a Super Bowl ring. He is wringing his hands together and saying, "I've been waiting for this. I've been waiting all day. When I'm through with you . . ." as the camera shows a shot of him hitting a wooden post as he continues ". . . you're gonna be history man. I'm gonna eat you up and you know what. I'm gonna enjoy it," at which point a microwave beeps and the camera shows a shot of a bowl of soup with a spoon in it just as a male announcer says, "Nothing takes care of a mean appetite . . ." while the camera focuses on Long eating the soup before the announcer continues, ". . . like the tender chunks of chicken and rich egg noodles in Campbell's Chunky Chicken Nugget Soup" (Sports Odyssey 2020). The camera then focuses on a can of the soup before showing a shot of a young boy who says, "I'm gonna eat you up" as he looks at Long who is sitting at a table across from the child at which point Long looks into the camera before a final shot of the company's logo with the words, "It takes care of the meanest appetites" which the announcer reads, appear (Sports Odyssey 2020).

A print advertisement in this campaign from 1993 featured NFL Quarterback Donovan McNabb wearing his team jersey and looking through his locker filled with cans of Chunky soup. Words underneath say, "17 Weeks. 39 Varieties. Load

Up." (T3 Tonya's This and That 2024). A white banner at the bottom of the page has the NFL logo to the right with the words "The Official Soup Sponsor for the NFL" next to it, the company's logo with the words "It Fills You up Right" underneath, and an image of an illustrated football player carrying a football with the words "Players Inc." to the right (T3 Tonya's This and That 2024). In a similar move, the company would partner with the National Hockey League (NHL) and in 1996 feature Rangers NHL player Wayne Gretzky on its Chunky soup label. On the label was an illustrated picture of Gretzky in action with the words "Take a Check from the Great One" referencing his NHL nickname. A 1996 commercial in the campaign began with actor Steve Harris from *The Practice* saying, "When you're rushing, in a hurry . . ." before the camera cuts to another man saying "what's for dinner? Not to worry" then to director John DiMaggio saying, "When a pizza just won't cut it. More Chinese, you're sick of it" before the camera shows a shot of a bowl of soup as Harris continues, "For a warm and hearty supper, grab some Chunky from the cupboard" as the camera focuses on the bowl of soup (Mike's VHS Treasures 2020). Another man continues saying, "Peas and carrots and potatoes. Of course we've got tomatoes" as the camera shows each before Gretzky is shown saying, "Hey, it's all the beef that gets me" as one of the men says, "Hey, wasn't that Wayne Gretzky?" as another says, "Take a tip from you know who" before one of the men is shown with Gretzky saying, "Chunky soups and the Great One, too" as Gretzky laughs and continues to eat his soup before an announcer says, "Campbell's Chunky, soup that eats like a meal" as the words appear on the screen next to a fork and a spoon (Mike's VHS Treasures 2020). The use of professional athletes, who are deemed to be in superior physical shape, clearly indicates the movement theme as well as the perceived benefits construct through the promise of using the product resulting in superior athletic skills as well as avoidance of unfavorable health outcomes that athletes experience (perceived susceptibility).

Sports and Cereal

Gretzky also had another partnership with an ultra-processed food manufacturer—Post cereals. His image appeared on several boxes of the product including Honey-Toasted Spoon Size Shredded Wheat in Canada, which included a banner at the top with a light green background and Gretzky's name on the left side of the logo and "99 in (en) '99" (millerhousedotca2 2024).

Included on the back of the boxes and advertised to the left of Gretzky's image were "cut 'n collect" free 1998–99 Upper Deck NHL Hockey Player Cards as well as a "Meet Wayne Gretzky" section and information about how to win "99 Autographed Gretzky Replica Jerseys" and "99 Autographed Gretzky Pucks" (millerhousedotca2 2024). In addition to this, the company made a set of cards honoring the hockey star when he retired in 1999. Sports cards on Post cereal boxes are not a new invention.

In 1960, Post made Cereal Sports Stars, a nine-card set that took up the entire back of Grape-Nuts Flakes boxes, and included such players as Mickey Mantle, Bob Cousy, and Johnny Unitas. "This series marked the beginning of a four-year cycle where sport stars were used to promote Post cereal" during which time, "Post also included football and basketball—subsequent years featured baseball and football separately while dropping basketball altogether" after which "the next three years each cereal box had a sheet of several more regular sized cards on it" while before "1960, Post [had] other Baseball premiums such as Dizzy Dean pins and buttons, Joe DiMaggio baseball gloves, Ted Williams Baseball caps and . . . in 1930 a Christy Mathewson card that was part of a small series of famous Americans" (Post Cereal Baseball Card Museum 2024).

The tradition of using the movement theme and the perceived benefits and perceived susceptibility constructs by featuring athletes on cereal boxes goes back to 1934 when Yankees' player Lou Gehrig was first shown on the back of a box of Wheaties cereal. Prior to this, the cereal, which was introduced to consumers in 1924 under the name Gold Medal Whole Wheat Flakes and soon changed to Wheaties, began its association with athletes in the form of a fictional character named Jack Armstrong who appeared on the back of the cereal boxes, which included a large illustration of him dressed in shorts and a sleeveless t-shirt holding a basketball. In large text at the top to the left of this image in quotes, Jack "says" that Wheaties contain twice as much protein as corn or rice cereals since they are made from wheat and will help develop muscles. Three paragraphs of text appear below this that have the title that reads, "Wheaties also Take the Place of Hot Cereal" with the text underneath touting the cereal as offering "'pep,' energy, bigger, stronger muscles" as a "breakfast of champions," who include among others Babe Ruth and Lefty Grove and goes on to discuss the "wonderful crisp toasted whole wheat flakes" that give consumers "the same heat-producing elements as hot cereal" (Kindy 2021). Also noted in the text is the fact that the cereal was accepted by the Committee on Foods of the American Medical Association. Armstrong would also be featured on radio programs and eventually television.

Through the years, Wheaties has featured many athletes on its boxes. The same year Gehrig debuted on boxes, Elinor Smith, an airplane pilot was also featured. Other famous people include Babe Didrickson Zaharias, first Olympian in 1935; Brooklyn Dodgers catcher Roy Campanella, "first Black athlete in 1952;" gold medal gymnast Mary Lou Retton, the first female athlete on the front of the box in 1984; football legend Walter Payton, the first Black athlete on the front in 1986; female football player Sam Gordon, nine, the youngest athlete on a regional box in 2012; gold medalist Evan Strong, the first paralympic athlete in 2014; and gold medalist Jennifer Finzel, the "first Special Olympian in 1997" (Kindy 2021). Basketball player Michael Jordan appeared on eighteen different boxes while golf player Tiger Woods garnered fourteen appearances.

"Energy Builder" and "Good Shape"

Sports celebrities are not the only means that cereal companies have used to create a health halo or use constructs. A 1944 advertisement for Nabisco Shredded Wheat features a large illustration of a young, smiling boy holding two apples in one hand and a bushel full in the other. He has a hat on, and his skin is glowing, and his teeth are white. A headline below in large text says, "Energy Builder Breakfast Helps You Feel Tip-Top!" below which a sub-headline reads, "Build It Around a Star Course of Tasty Nabisco Shredded Wheat" under which are two paragraphs of text discussing a "recipe for smiling mornings" as being the cereal with "milk, sugar and a tangy baked apple or applesauce" and "plenty of energy" due to the fact that the cereal is made from "one of the Basic 7 Foods our Government advises us to help us keep strong" (VTG Collectibles 2024). To the left of the text is a rectangle with the headline telling how the cereal "contributes these essential food elements" that include "proteins for strength," "carbohydrates for energy," "vitamin B1 to aid in assimilation," "iron for blood-building," and "phosphorus for strong bones" (VTG Collectibles 2024). Though the association to healthy activity is somewhat more subtle, the idea of building energy and the image of a healthy boy who appears to have just picked a large basket of apples results in the use of the movement theme and the perceived benefits construct for an ultra-processed food product. The healthy boy also symbolizes avoidance of unhealthy outcomes, which is a clear illustration of the perceived susceptibility construct.

Another more subtle use of this theme and constructs can be seen in a 1960s commercial for Grape-Nuts cereal that begins with images of Dick Wilson and his six children from Rolling Hills, California, jumping on several trampolines at which point Wilson corrects the announcer by telling him that he only has five children, and that the sixth one is his wife. The announcer then asks how she keeps as "slim as her teenage daughter" to which the answer is by exercising and eating "the right kind of foods like a Post Grape-Nuts breakfast" that "fills you up, not out" and "gives you important protein and other nutrients" and helps to "keep your shape in good shape" (Duke University Libraries 2024). Viewers are then encouraged to "take a tip from the Wilson family" and "get plenty of exercise and be sure to start your day with a Post Grape-Nuts breakfast" (Duke University Libraries 2024). As with the previous advertisement, linking activity and exercise, both of which are healthy, creates a halo that leads consumers to believe that the products associated with these things are also healthy while images of lack of unfavorable health outcomes (perceived susceptibility) and the benefit of looking youthful (perceived benefits) employ constructs to motivate purchase of the products.

The Tiger and His Halos

One particular cereal mascot has been subtly, and sometimes not so subtly, using the movement theme and the perceived benefits and perceived susceptibility constructs almost since its creation. Tony the Tiger first appeared as the Kellogg's Frosted Flakes mascot after winning a contest against another mascot created by the company, Katie the Kangaroo in 1952. In early advertising, Tony was shown alongside Superman, played by George Reeves in the original series, since Kellogg's was a sponsor of the show. This association with one of the strongest television characters of the time, created a firm foundation for many Identity Health Halos to come. When the cereal was first introduced it was known as Kellogg's Sugar Frosted Flakes. The word "Sugar" was dropped in the early 1980s around the same time a more muscular and larger image of Tony appeared due to backlash about refined sugar products as well as recognition of the need for exercise. Early commercials for Sugar Frosted Flakes promoted the benefits of sugar, frosting, and "Super Energy" that consumers would gain from eating the cereal, with "Super Energy Stories" showing ways in which Sugar Frosted Flakes could benefit those who ate the cereal. One of these ads, which were all animated, opened with an announcer saying, "Tony and the Indians. Another super energy story" and then cuts to Tony standing by a tree eating a bowl of Sugar Frosted Flakes addressing viewers as if telling them a story (Cerealmad 2022). "There I was eating my Kellogg's Sugar Frosted Flakes. Delicious. Full of super energy. Sugar toasted. Tiger to tiger, I can tell you that for super energy, I wouldn't miss my Kellogg's Sugar Frosted Flakes" (Cerealmad 2022). While Tony is saying this, he is first shown being attacked by a group of Indians, then overcoming them all while continuing to hold his bowl of cereal. The commercial ends with an image of the box and Tony telling viewers that they are "Delicious. Sugar toasted for super energy" (Cerealmad 2022). The dialogue and format in the series of commercials are the same while the "attackers" changed.

By the early 1960s, the animation was replaced with real children in the commercials alongside Tony, many of which took place in active settings or involved team sports. Throughout the 1960s and 1970s, the slogan "Put a tiger on your team" would be used in a variety of ways and continue to be associated with many sports including skiing, gymnastics, boxing, sky diving, bull riding, and baseball, to name a few. In most of these commercials, Tony gives a child a bowl of Sugar Frosted Flakes and then either competes against or participates with the child in the activity. In one advertisement that takes place on a soccer field, Tony tells the child that he trains on Kellogg's Sugar Frosted Flakes creating a direct association between success, health, and sports as well as the use of the movement theme and the perceived benefits and perceived susceptibility constructs. The "Put a tiger on your team" slogan morphed into the more personal 1980s and 1990s slogan, "Brings out the tiger in you." During this time, a common theme seemed to be children who were unable to excel in sports, which was remedied by help from Tony the Tiger in the form of eating Frosted Flakes Cereal. One 1987 ad, in particular, stands out for the exaggerated physical benefits of eating the cereal. The commercial opens with a group of teenagers water skiing and a girl watching them with Tony. After seeing how successful they are, she tells Tony that they should forget about water skiing. Tony tells her that she'll feel ready to water ski after eating Frosted Flakes, which will "Bring out the tiger in you" (Retropond 2021). The girl is revitalized and starts to water ski alongside Tony as background music says, "Show them you're a tiger. Show them what you can do" as the girl, looking determined, says, "Great" and makes a very high jump after which Tony congratulates her (Retropond 2021). It's worth noting that the professionalism of the jump from a young girl who was initially unsure of herself results in a health halo that greatly exaggerates the benefits of eating the cereal (perceived benefits) as well as the avoidance of undesirable health outcomes (perceived susceptibility), all of which are designed to motivate consumers to purchase the product.

As the year 2000 dawned, Tony the Tiger's popularity grew and he became an acclaimed celebrity in Frosted Flakes commercials; yet, he was still primarily shown surrounded by children who were participating in sports or activities. Advertisements during this time featured groups of children doing various activities with Tony. A commercial aired in 2010 proclaimed Kellogg's Corn Flakes as being "everywhere we go" and featured a montage of children in different sporting events eating the cereal (Canipe 2016). In this particular commercial, the majority of children are dressed in team uniforms and at the end are encouraged to "earn their stripes" giving a team-like association with the product. Also, the phrase "We are tigers" is used, which lays the foundation for future advertisements as well as the creation of "The Mission Tiger" initiative, which as outlined on the website of the same name, was launched in 2019 and is part of a team effort with Donors Choose, a nonprofit organization focused on helping public school educators nationwide. When a receipt for the purchase of a box of Kellogg's Frosted Flakes is uploaded to the website, the company makes a $2 donation to help middle-school students "have better access to play sports" (Mission Tiger Website 2024). On the website, it is noted that if an athletic program has been cut or a team needs new uniforms, visitors can fill out a donation request form or view past efforts. A counter on the homepage at the website notes that, to date, 1,790,819 students have been helped. Visitors are urged to participate in the three-step process, which includes the following: (1) Eat like a tiger (buy a box of Frosted Flakes). (2) Help kids play (upload a receipt). (3) See the impact (get involved). Also, on the website are quotes from thank you notes about how much the program has helped schools, with photos of various sports teams and Tony. On the "Why Sports Matter" tab of the webpage, it's noted that "Sports Give Kids Skills That Help Them Succeed" below which is a promise from Tony that reads, "I, Tony the Tiger, want to make sure every kid has the chance to unleash their inner tiger. Join me on my mission, because I can't do it alone" (Mission Tiger Website 2024).

A 2019 commercial for the Mission Tiger project opens with a baseball player sitting on a bench in an empty field chanting, "In our schools today . . ." as the camera cuts to another child in an empty basketball court who chants ". . . sports have gone away . . ." before the lights are turned off and he is left in darkness as the camera cuts to two young girls in a locker room who are packing up their things as one chants ". . . kids just wanna play" before the camera cuts to a shot of Tony who firmly says, "So, this is what we say," and then to a group shot of athletes who say the same thing and are then shown playing various sports ("Frosted Flakes TV Spot, 'Help All Kids Be Tigers'" 2019). This is followed by various shots of young athletes playing sports and chanting "Bring back the tigers. The mighty, mighty tigers" before Tony goes on to describe how "schools across the country are having to cut sports" and that he is "Tony the Tiger" and is "on a mission to fix that" before the words "Buy a Box. Support the Mission" appear in white font above the website address and to the left of Tony as young athletes are shown playing volleyball in the background as Tony encourages viewers to "Buy a box and help all kids be tigers" ("Frosted Flakes TV Spot, 'Help All Kids Be Tigers'" 2019). In addition to the advertisements, "joined by a roster of top college athletes, Tony the Tiger began visiting communities at retailers across the country . . . to spread the fun of middle school sports" and provide "more opportunities for kids to play sports via Mission Tiger donations to local middle schools . . . across the country" which has created "almost 2 million sports and play experiences for kids" (Kellogg Company 2025).

A more recent social media commercial for the cereal opens with a young boy eating a bowl of cereal with a box of Frosted Flakes next to him while he is standing in a gym that is filled with balls. One of the balls hits him in the head as a male vocalist sings, "Making your way in the world today takes everything you've got," after which he eats a spoonful of cereal, then smiles before the camera cuts to a shot of two older hockey players, one of whom is smiling as he holds a spoonful of cereal which he then puts into his mouth as two other hockey players from the opposing team slam into him as the song continues "You wanna be where you can see troubles are all the same" as the camera cuts to a shot of a pilot who looks scared before Tony appears behind him and gives him a bowl of cereal as the pilot smiles and the song continues "You wanna go where everyone knows your name" before a final shot of the cereal box with the words "they're gr-r-reat!" appear above Tony's arm holding a bowl of cereal ("Frosted Flakes TV Spot, 'Help All Kids Be Tigers'" 2023). The impact of this particular health halo is widespread considering that Frosted Flakes is the second best-selling cereal by boxes sold in the United States with 132.3 million boxes sold every year, second only to Cheerios with 139.1 million sold each year (Cereal Secrets 2024). Additionally, "Of the more than 314 million people in the U.S., 49 per cent start their day with a bowl of cereal" and "there are 2.7 billion boxes—enough to wrap around the Earth thirteen times—of cereal sold every year" as well as a special day, called National Cereal Day that takes place on March 7th each year, to celebrate the product (nationalcerealday.com 2024).

All these commercials make use of the movement theme and the perceived benefits and perceived susceptibility constructs to promote an unhealthy, ultra-processed food product in an attempt to garner young consumers. Researchers who conducted a 2019 study, which examined the effect of advertising on the intake of 624 preschoolers, concluded that "child-directed advertising influences begin earlier and last longer than previously demonstrated, highlighting limitations of current industry guidelines regarding the marketing of high-sugar foods to children under age 6 years" (Emond et al. 2019). The lead research noted that "Our models accounted for several child, parent and household characteristics, and whether the child ate each cereal before the study started" meaning that the researchers "were able to isolate the effect of cereal advertisement exposure on kids' intake of cereals, independent of all of those other factors" (Dartmouth-Hitchcock Medical Center 2019). This is "the first naturalistic study to show a direct and concerning link between kids' exposure to TV ads for high-sugar cereal and their subsequent intake of that cereal" (Dartmouth-Hitchcock Medical Center 2019). In a study conducted a few years before of older children, researchers concluded that "Our results with children from 6 to 14 years old indicate that overweight cartoon character primes can activate the overweight stereotype, leading to relatively high levels of food intake" (Campbell 2016, 257).

Taking the results from both studies into consideration as well as those from studies about the effectiveness of health halos discussed in Chapter 1, it's not difficult to understand how the combination of healthy children participating in sports and the images of successful professional sports figures has the potential to increase the potency of the movement theme in the Identity Health Halo and thus create the mistaken belief that ultra-processed foods, specifically cereal in this case, have health benefits that they do not.

The International Movement

Though there are many other cereal brands that employ this particular heath halo, this section would not be complete without mentioning two of them. The first is a Canadian cereal, Vector, manufactured by Kellogg's and mentioned in

Chapter 3 for its use of the fortification theme in the Nutrition Health Halo. In addition to promoting the vitamins and minerals in Vector, Kellogg's also focuses on fitness in some of the commercials for this product, thus employing the movement theme and the perceived benefits and perceived susceptibility constructs as well. A six-second commercial opens with a box of the cereal in the background and a closeup of a hand holding a spoonful of cereal taken from the white bowl filled with the product. A male announcer says, "Get high protein and delicious Maple flavour . . ." as the words appear in white font next to the image before the camera cuts to a shot of the cereal on a countertop with a bowl filled with cereal and a spoon, as the announcer says, ". . . with Vector Maple Crunch Cereal" as a baseball rolls across the counter and stops next to the cereal box (Kellogg's Vector 2022). Though subtle, the baseball represents playing sports with the motion of the ball not only drawing attention to it but also mimicking the movement of the game and thus using the movement theme and the perceived benefit of being physically fit enough to participate in the sport while simultaneously avoiding illness or disease (perceived susceptibility).

The second cereal worth mentioning is an international one from Nestle, in which the very name of the product uses the movement theme and the perceived benefits and perceived susceptibility constructs. Nestle Fitness cereal is advertised in the manufacturer's website as a way to "Find Your Fitness!" in a section that continues by saying, "There's more to sports than performance. At Fitness, we believe that pleasure is the best fuel for sport. That's why we want you to enjoy sports like breakfast. A happy start to the day, like having a nutritious and delicious bowl of Fitness cereal, will lead to an equally enjoyable time at play," which is positioned to the left of images of women playing sports including boxing and soccer (Nestle Cereals Global 2024). In addition to this, a fifteen-second commercial on the website features Olympic Triple Jump champion Patricia Mamona and the Fitness logo, with Mamona getting ready to jump as the logo disappears and a female announcer says, "Behind every jump, every race . . ." as the camera cuts to Mamona running before the camera and then near a basketball court as the announcer continues ". . . every exciting move, there's the step that starts it all fueled by a tasty, crunchy, nutritious breakfast with Fitness cereal," as Mamona is shown running backward and into a house and then eating a bowl of cereal after a closeup of the product is shown (Nestle Cereals Global 2024). The final shot is of Mamona finishing breakfast and getting out of the chair where she ate as the female announcer says, "Take your first step and find your fitness" as the hashtag "#TakeYourFirstStep" is shown above the words “FIND YOUR FITNESS” (Nestle Cereals Global 2024). The images of an Olympic athlete training and being “fueled” by an ultra-processed food are a clear deployment of the movement theme and the perceived benefits and perceived susceptibility constructs.

Fruit Snacks, Weights, and Baseball

A 2017 commercial for Fruit by the Foot portrays the ultra-processed food as a helper in the weight room. The commercial begins with an opening shot of a box of Fruit by the Foot on a workbench surrounded by tools in a garage setting. Song lyrics talking about how long Fruit by the Foot is saying that “if you were maxing out on a bench press and got stuck, it can unroll itself and spot you” as images of the product unrolling itself over various things in the garage are shown before it reaches a young man struggling to lift weights (“Fruit by the Foot TV Spot, ‘Weights’” 2017). The product wraps itself around the middle of the weight bar as the boy lifts the bar aided by the Fruit by the Foot. “He’s so amped that he holds the box aloft and shouts, ‘FOOT!!!’ shattering the mirror behind him (“Fruit by the Foot TV Spot, ‘Weights’” 2017). The idea that an ultra-processed food can “make” a young man so strong as to shatter a mirror is a clear use of the movement theme and the perceived benefits and perceived susceptibility constructs.

In another fruit snack commercial, the opening shot is of a young man dressed in a baseball outfit with a hat holding a bag of Welch’s Fruit Snacks and then catching a baseball as a female announcer says, “Snack funfully. Snack homerunfully” as the product is shown inside a baseball glove that the young man used to catch it. There are two young women and one young man in the background cheering after the ball is caught before the next shot of the baseball player eating the snack is shown (Welch’s Fruit Snacks 2021b). The announcer continues saying, “Welch’s Fruit Snacks. Snack fruitfully” as a final shot of the product surrounded by fruit with the words “Snack Fruitfully” are shown above and the words “Fruit is our 1st ingredient” below (Welch’s Fruit Snacks 2021b). Though this commercial is only six seconds long, there is a clear association not only with the sport of baseball but also with superior sports performance and avoidance of illness. Through these images as well as use of the made-up word “homerunfully,” the movement theme and the perceived benefits and perceived susceptibility constructs are in full view in this commercial for the ultra-processed fruit snack.

A more recent example of the use of the movement theme and the perceived benefits and perceived susceptibility constructs for a fruit snack product comes from a 2024 commercial for Haribo Goldbears previously mentioned in Chapter 2 for use of the real fruit theme in the Natural and Real Health Halo. In the commercial, two professional football players, Donald Driver and Marquez Valdes-Scantling, are shown wearing football jerseys with the names "Robinson" and "Hayward" and sitting on a bench as a football is kicked. After the ball is kicked, Robinson slides closer to Hayward who is eating Goldbears. He tilts the bag toward Robinson who says in a child's voice, "Would you like some Haribo Goldbears?" as the camera shows a closeup of the product ("Haribo Gold-Bears TV Spot, 'Football Chat'" 2024). Johnson replies, also in a child's voice, "Ooh, I love these" as Hayward pours some into his hand as Hayward says, again in a child's voice, "The longer I chew it, the fruitier and fruiter it gets" to which Johnson replies, also in a child's voice, "These are the most bestest bears ever" ("Haribo Gold-Bears TV Spot, 'Football Chat'" 2024). Hayward then holds up a goldbear and says, still in a child's voice, "It would not . . . It would not be hard to tackle a goldbear 'cuz they're tiny," and they both laugh and are then interrupted by a whistle blowing, after which Johnson says, "Utto, I'm gonna sit this one out. It tastes too good" as both giggle before the bottom half of a coach who clears his throat is shown as both players looked chagrinned yet continue to eat before a final shot of three bags of the product in front of two football helmets is shown ("Haribo Gold-Bears TV Spot, 'Football Chat'" 2024). While this product does use the real fruit theme in the Natural and Real Health Halo, it also illustrates the movement theme in the Identity Health Halo through the use of professional sports players in the promotion of an ultra-processed food product as well as the perceived benefits Health Belief Model construct by portraying the consequence of using this product as professional level athleticism. The perceived susceptibility construct is also illustrated by leading consumers to believe that this product can be used to avoid undesirable health outcomes since two professional athletes are eating it.

"Pleasure Is the Path to Joy"

A discussion of the movement theme would not be complete without mentioning a 2022 Häagen-Dazs commercial that incorporates exercise in a paradoxical way to make fun of new age culture and was shown to contribute "to addictive eating as well as food addiction denial" (Danowski 2023, 96).

The commercial begins with Mr. Proctor, who is described as a Food Psychologist, asking his audience whether they wish they could be happier and tells them that "Sensual Eating" can make that happen before the camera cuts to a book of the same title and two containers of ice cream placed next to it (Rough 2020). In the background, a group of people dressed in exercise clothes are holding spoons with one hand and ice cream with the other as they lift their spoons in unison chanting, "Pleasure is the path to joy" before a woman named Martha May, who is identified as a "Sensologist," tells viewers to "Harness the intense pleasure of Häagen-Dazs through simple eating exercises carefully designed to deepen your appreciation. Sensual eating can open your inner cage" (Rough 2020). As she is speaking, images of people exercising with spoons and ice-cream containers are shown. First is a man on the ground with his face next to an ice-cream container lifting the spoon. He appears to be exerting himself. The camera zooms out to a shot of him with two other people on inclined benches with their feet raised with the ice cream nearby and spoons in their hands. The next "exercise" is of four people, two each with one of the pair wrapping arms around the seated ones as the ones seated attempt to reach a container of ice cream. The commercial ends with a shot of the ice cream floating in a pool and the group chanting, "Pleasure is the path to joy" (Rough 2020).

Even though the focus of this commercial appears to be making fun of new age authors and their followers, there is a clear use of the movement theme and the perceived benefits and perceived susceptibility constructs in this advertisement albeit one designed to be humorous, which is what makes it subtle yet still an attempt to associate an ultra-processed food with health benefits. Eating this product and experiencing pleasure (perceived benefits) are promoted as the "path to joy" while also joined with images of exercise thus creating an association of avoiding illness (perceived susceptibility).

Cracker Jill and Female Athletes

Though it is nearly impossible to track all the ultra-processed food products using the movement theme and the perceived benefits and perceived susceptibility constructs on their packaging and labels, there is one recent addition that some are calling inspirational (Hoeffner 2024). For the first time in over 100 years, five female athletes were featured on bags of Cracker Jill snacks, an initiative launched in 2022 to create a female mascot based on the long-standing Cracker

Jack mascot well known as baseball's most famous snack. "Each selected athlete excels in a different sport, including water polo champion Ashleigh Johnson, boxer Jennifer Lozano, wrestler Kennedy Blades, wheelchair basketball star Lindsey Zurbrugg, and Para Track & Field record holder Noelle Lambert" (Hoeffner 2024). The initiative is driven by a survey of seven hundred American teenagers conducted by the company, in which "only 12% of participants could name a single women's professional athlete competing on the global stage this summer, and 45% of teens couldn't name a single women's professional athlete" (Hoeffner 2024).

While the company's initiative is noteworthy as is its donation to the Women's Sports Foundation, the use of professional athletes, which creates an association between an ultra-processed food and health, is at the core of the movement theme and the perceived benefits and perceived susceptibility constructs through its association with sports and physical fitness.

Conclusion

This study encompassed the analysis of 1,176 food advertisements and product labels with the focus of determining various types of health halos and the Health Belief Model constructs used in the promotion of ultra-processed food products. Each of the advertisements mentioned throughout contained a minimum of one health halo and one Health Belief Model construct. In many cases, multiple halos and constructs were used. Each product label listed within included at least one health halo and one Health Belief Model construct.

Study Significance

Given that research suggests that health claims "influenced purchasing behavior for some" (Benson et al. 2019, 11) and "health-related claims have a substantial effect on dietary choices" (Kaur, Scarborough, and Rayner 2017), the significance of this study in highlighting misleading advertising and marketing techniques should not be underestimated nor should the influence of either industry. Evidence of this exists in a 2016 study in which elementary school students from ten schools were offered various scenarios to determine whether advertising healthy food would affect food choices. During a six-week period, some students were presented with a banner showing vegetable characters, some others were shown short television health education spots that included vegetable characters, and a third group was shown a combination of both. Researchers collected over 22,000 observations while tallying the number of vegetables taken from the salad bar. They found that "90.5% more students took vegetables from the salad bar when exposed to the vinyl banner only, and 239.2% more students visited the salad bar when exposed to both the television segments and vinyl banners," noting in their conclusion the "positive impact of branded media on children's vegetable selection" and the "potential opportunities for using branded media to encourage healthier choices for children" (Hanks, Just, Brumberg 2016).

Taking into consideration the fact that "35 million children under the age of 5 were overweight" in 2024 while more than "390 million children and adolescents aged 5–19 years were overweight in 2022, including 160 million who were living with obesity" (World Health Organization 2025), the significance of this study is apparent not only in the effectiveness of educating both children and adults about the misleading marketing techniques involving health halos and the Health Belief Model constructs but also in the power of positive change made possible with marketing food that truly is healthy. Furthermore, the misleading techniques described in this study can aid in increasing nutrition literacy in both children and adults.

Study Implications

Lack of effective regulation and enforcement in ultra-processed food advertising and on product labels is all but nonexistent in the United States. While much of this is due to the increasingly growing revenue earned by ultra-processed food manufacturers allowing them to create and utilize powerful promotional techniques, another part is due to lack of funding and clear guidelines from governmental agencies. The Federal Trade Commission (FTC) lists a policy created in 1994 regarding food advertising on its website, Section IV of which specifically addresses health claims by establishing general use standards, a portion of which includes allowing health claims to only be used

> for which there is "significant scientific agreement" that the relevant diet-disease relationship is supported by the scientific evidence; establishing disqualifying levels for total fat, saturated fat, cholesterol, and sodium, above which foods are disqualified from bearing any health claims; setting a threshold level for the amount of such substance in the food, that is either sufficiently low or sufficiently high to support the health claim; requiring that foods bearing health claims have some minimal nutritional value; [and] that health claims identify those factors, other than dietary intake of the substance, that affect the diet-disease relationship. (Federal Trade Commission 1994)

Even though the spirit of the policy may be designed to protect consumers, its wording allows for many loopholes through the use of nebulous terms such as foods having "minimal nutritional value," which can easily be satisfied through vitamin and mineral fortification of ultra-processed foods or the addition of ultra-processed fruits and vegetables. It's likely that a policy created in 1994 could not have imagined the highly sophisticated food production and marketing techniques used in today's marketplace. Though looking to governmental regulations is one way to lessen the use of health halos and the Health Belief Model constructs in the advertising of ultra-processed food products, the single most effective means that consumers have of not succumbing to these deceptive practices is by determining the healthiness of food products through education about the marketing tricks used to make unhealthy food appear healthier, as is the purpose of this study. The basis of this begins with health literacy education teaching consumers to read product labels carefully to understand the exact ingredients present in the foods they eat. Ingredients that aren't readily available in kitchens across the country or are unfamiliar almost always indicate the presence of ultra-processed foods, which have been shown to cause rampant health problems. By refusing to purchase or eat these food items, consumers have the power to force large food manufacturers to offer much-needed healthier options.

Limitations

This study does not profess to present an exhaustive list of every health halo or Health Belief Model construct used in the promotion of ultra-processed foods but rather offers a starting point through identification and classification of three different health halos used both historically and currently in food advertising and on food product labels as well as an outline of the four constructs used. With the current increased focus by consumers on health, it's more than likely that ultra-processed food manufacturers will be forced to create new health halos to make their products appear healthier. As shown throughout this study, some of the health halos discussed within these pages have been in existence for over a century. It's difficult to tell whether they will continue to be effective as society undergoes growth and change though the need for identification and classification will become ever more important.

Future Research

Future research in the areas of health halos and the Health Belief Model constructs can expand to include additional ultra-processed food and application of these concepts. Further classification of health halo types can be undertaken as advertising and marketing techniques change and grow.

Final Thoughts

The classification of health halos and their relationship to the Health Belief Model constructs used in ultra-processed food advertising and on product labels is a vital step in creating consumer awareness and encouragement of healthy eating which, when combined with education, has the potential to reduce the ever-growing rate of obesity. Though the most obvious method of reducing misleading advertising techniques would seem to be effective and stringent governmental regulations, current and past political climates appear to make this impossible. This being the case, the onus must be placed upon consumers and health professionals to educate themselves. This book is a step in that direction.

References

Unless otherwise stated, the websites listed here were last accessed prior to November 2025.

Adventist Archives. 2017. Facebook, December 5, 2017. https://www.facebook.com/GC.SDA.Archives/posts/many-people-have-christmas-traditions-from-attending-church-services-to-visiting/1648443308548668/?paipv=0&eav=AfY3hkCb1B3GXfye3tPhxbob78PS0SLwEW9aWx6olMNK1KGoiSCLy-u9FsUBefiyTCk&_rdr.

"Agency Standouts." 2024. *AdAge*, March 11, 2024. https://mag.adage.com/pugpig_enhanced_pdf/agency-standouts-8/content.html.

Agnihotri, Arpita, and Saurabh Bhattacharya. 2019. "The Relative Effectiveness of Endorsers: The Identity Badge of CEOs and Founders Versus the Attractiveness of Celebrities." *Journal of Advertising Research*, September 1. https://research-ebsco-com.sacredheart.idm.oclc.org/linkprocessor/plink?id=a8c5d4b7-da35-3bb4-8f84-30daf120bdcf.

aikyastore.life. 2024. "Vintage Fat Shaming Ads from Ry Krisp (So Bad)." https://www.aikyastore.life/index.php?main_page=product_info&products_id=8619820.

Algebramclain. 2021. "Kellogg's Pop-Tarts, 1964." Reddit. https://www.reddit.com/r/vintageads/comments/nbyfoy/kelloggs_poptarts_1964/.ALittleBitOfIrish. 2015. "TV Spot—Danimals Squeezables Low Fat Yogurt—Fridge on Mom's Back at School—Squeeze More Fun." YouTube, January 15, 2015. https://www.youtube.com/watch?v=0u3ppoUCDCI.

Alyafei, Anees, and Raul Easton-Carr. 2024. "The Health Belief Model of Behavior Change." StatPearls [Internet]. Treasure Island (FL): StatPearls. Accessed January 2025. https://www.ncbi.nlm.nih.gov/books/NBK606120/.

American Century Shop. 2024a. "Vintage 1940s Borden's Hemo Drink Advertisement Retro Gift Décor." eBay. https://www.etsy.com/listing/783306486/vintage-1940s-bordens-hemo-drink.

American Century Shop. 2024b. "Vintage 1940s Nabisco Shredded Wheat Cereal Ad, WW2 Era." eBay. https://www.ebay.com/itm/115880389000?_trkparms=amclksrc%3DITM%26aid%3D1110006%26algo%3DHOMESPLICE.SIM%26ao%3D1%26asc%3D266917%2C267607%2C267275%26meid%3D951c1a74566d47508af6a1b23b809913%26pid%3D101875%26rk%3D1%26rkt%3D8%26sd%3D305525581019%26itm%3D115880389000%26pmt%3D1%26noa%3D0%26pg%3D2332490%26algv%3DSimplAMLv11WebTrimmedV3MskuWithLambda85KnnRecallV1V2V4ItemNrtInQueryAndCassiniVisualRanker

AndBertRecallWithVMEV3CPCAutoWithCassiniEmbRecall&_trksid=p2332490.c101875. m1851&itmprp=cksum%3A1 15880389000951c1a74566d47508af6 a1b23b809913%7Cenc%3AAQAJAAABYLC2%252Ba5TgOFYgIvLQSBIYkURSzHvc7cCccVTU14STgixqt2LHVH3DQgpuMCV11vSwIPgiyFOwqAlvyaCYV%252F3KC%252BV%252Bw2hITE7xTLMc%252FUAdPVM74mBrClyfys6h0qSntiKTtamp%252FwRG%252FuVgTYA%252FQ9W3Ox1vA0GraSb4JMRxeVcTuw%252FbvfsO7mDS6tzWet1HTCrTXMDMEGV3LI%252FZwmboK8tJeoU5s9wrzEkjayYtcjhJEtLnQsyioYJAijkMG4r38v8780RTdOkyENj6xWrjOYgfTeRM5zIwAjroV5vFyc8DO2ZPrmkA6BtsO6tZlq5zzcUCbn7e6HeWf0yotU6QRHcWIsp7G1z3A2yDqvEYLkeB35ig9KbOx6aYDlHT97HjIt4CxBgI6wMzmXRpvitwixTRQTqNBGDhWk13G3gJahB6BNHB6%252FVOEgA0wea%252FSl3xl6FqkbJi2J0pKmUbzEQiYYyW7s%253D%7Campid%3APL_CLK%7Cclp%3A2332490&itmmeta=01J0XMRE8TRA747CRFYYZWRFTY.

Amson, Ashely, Lauren Remedios, Adena Pinto, and Monique Potvin Kent. 2021. "Exploring the Extent of Digital Food and Beverage Related Content Associated with a Family-Friendly Event: A Case Study." *BMC Public Health*, 21, no. 1: 1–9. https://doi-org.sacredheart.idm.oclc.org/10.1186/s12889-021-10716-w.

Andreeva, Valentina A., Jara Perez-Jimenez, and Marie-Pierre St-Onge. 2023. "A Systematic Review of the Bidirectional Association between Consumption of Ultra-Processed Food and Sleep Parameters among Adults." *Current Obesity Reports*, 12, no. 4: 439–52. doi:10.1007/s13679-023-00512-5.

Andrews, Mark, Matthijs Van Leeuwen, and Rick Van Baaren. 2014. *Hidden Persuasion: 33 Psychological Influence Techniques in Advertising*. The Netherlands: BIS.

Arrona-Cardoza, Pablo, Katherine Labonte, Jose Miguel Cisneros-Franko, and Daiva E. Nielsen. 2023. "The Effects of Food Advertisements on Food Intake and Neural Activity: A Systematic Review and Meta-Analysis of Recent Experimental Studies." *Advances in Nutrition*, 14, no. 2: 339–51. https://www.sciencedirect.com/science/article/pii/S2161831322013187.

Arshad, Husnain, Jenny Head, Felice N. Jacka, Melissa M. Lane, Mika Kivimaki, and Tasnime Akbaraly. 2024. "Association between Ultra-Processed Foods and Recurrence of Depressive Symptoms: The Whitehall II Cohort Study." *Nutritional Neuroscience*, 27, no. 1: 42–54. doi:10.1080/1028415X.2022.2157927.

Ates, Aaron, Rodney Holcomb, and Parker Terrell. 2019. "To Be or Not to Be: That Is the Gluten-Free Marketing Question." OKSTATE.EDU EXTENSION, November 2019. https://extension.okstate.edu/fact-sheets/to-be-or-not-to-be-that-is-the-gluten-free-marketing-question.html#:~:text=Food%20companies%20and%20retailers%20have,of%20the%20gluten%2Dfree%20diet.

Austin, Daryl. 2023. "Is Vitamin Water Actually Good for You? It's Complicated, Experts Say." *USA Today*, March 14, 2023. https://www.usatoday.com/story/life/health-wellness/2023/03/14/vitamin-water-good-you-pros-and-cons-explained-experts/11468717002/.

Bailey, Christopher, Ivanka Prichard, Claire Drummond, and Murray Drummond. 2024. "Australian Adolescents' Views About Healthy Eating and the Effects of Food Advertising on Dietary Behaviour: Perspectives of Athletes and Non-Athletes." *Health Education Journal*, 83, no. 1: 40–51. https://research-ebsco-com.sacredheart.idm.oclc.org/linkprocessor/plink?id=6ea9201d-b6e7-34a5-9e03-2512f972d2dd.

Baker, Ryan. 2023. "How Wonder Bread Has Survived Competition and the Fall of White Bread." CNBC, October 3, 2023. https://www.cnbc.com/2023/10/03/how-wonder-bread-has-survived-the-fall-of-white-bread.html#:~:text=With%20an%20increasingly%20health%2Dconscious,Wonder%20Bread%20is%20still%20around.

Beetham, Margaret. 1996. *A Magazine of Her Own: Domesticity and Desire in the Woman's Magazine, 1800–1914*. New York: Routledge.

Ben-Avraham, Sivan, Elkana Kohn, Sigal Tepper, Ronit Lubetzky, Dror Mandel, Matitiahu Berkovitch, and Danit R. Shahar. 2023. "Ultra-Processed Food (UPF) Intake in Pregnancy and Maternal and Neonatal Outcomes." *European Journal of Nutrition*, 62, no. 3: 1403–13. doi:10.1007/s00394-022-03072-x.

Benson, Tony, Fiona Lavelle, Amanda McCloat, Elaine Mooney, Tamara Bucher, Bernadette Egan, and Moira Dean. 2019. "Are the Claims to Blame? A Qualitative Study to Understand the Effects of Nutrition and Health Claims on Perceptions and Consumption of Food." *Nutrients*, 11, 2058. doi:10.3390/nu11092058.

Best Commercials. 2024. "NERDS Big Game Commercial ft. Addison Rae:30 | Super Bowl Commercial 2024 | Best Commercials." YouTube, February 8, 2024. https://www.youtube.com/watch?v=mi2BKw0cJas.

Beyond Meat. 2022. "Kim Kardashian Is Beyond Meat's Chief Taste Consultant." YouTube, May 24, 2020. https://www.youtube.com/watch?v=C4Z112ID7O8.

Bionic Disco. 2020. "Roman Meal Bread Commercial (1974)." YouTube, May 8, 2020. https://www.youtube.com/watch?v=TfoINjNAVVo.

Bits & Bobs. 2014. "TV Spot—Nature Valley Granola Bar—Energy from Whole Grains—Crunchy Oats & Caramel." YouTube, September 13, 2014. https://www.youtube.com/watch?v=2WEKzEeBOEw.

Blomquist, Kerstin K., Dorothy L. Schmalz, Sarah P. Pate, and Alissa Willmerdinger. 2020. "What Happens When You Compare Yourself to a Model Eating a Cheeseburger? An Experiment Testing the Impact of Models Promoting Calorie-Dense Foods on Beliefs About Weight Maintenance, Body Satisfaction, and Purchase Intent." *Journal of Eating Disorders*, 8, no. 1. Accessed September 4, 2025. http://dx.doi.org.sacredheart.idm.oclc.org/10.1186/s40337-020-00335-y.

bobobill21. 2024. “Vintage Bordens Hemo Malted Drink Mix Glass Jar.” eBay. https://www.ebay.com/itm/275554281771.

Boyland, Emma J., and Jason C. G. Halford. 2013. “Television Advertising and Branding. Effects on Eating Behaviour and Food Preferences in Children.” *Appetite*, no. 62 (March): 236–41. doi:10.1016/j.appet.2012.01.032.

Boyland, Emma, Lauren McGale, Michelle Maden, Juliet Hounsome, Angela Boland, Kathryn Angus, and Andrew Jones. 2022. “Association of Food and Nonalcoholic Beverage Marketing with Children and Adolescents’ Eating Behaviors and Health: A Systematic Review and Meta-Analysis.” *JAMA Pediatrics*, 176, no. 7: e221037. doi:10.1001/jamapediatrics.2022.1037.

Brown, Stephanie. 2021. “Are Strawberry Pop-Tarts Pretending to Be a Health Food?” *Verywell Health*, November 2, 2021. https://www.verywellhealth.com/strawberry-pop-tarts-misleading-label-5208032.

“Brownberry TV Spot, ‘This Is How It Starts.’ ” 2021. iSpot.tv, January 11, 2021. https://www.ispot.tv/ad/tsFV/arnold-this-is-how-it-starts.

“Brownberry Whole Grains TV Spot, ‘Nutritious’ Featuring John Stamos.” 2022. iSpot.tv, January 19, 2022. https://www.ispot.tv/ad/q3zh/brownberry-whole-grains-nutritious-featuring-john-stamos.

Buchanan Advertising. 2015. “Brand Power Nice & Natural Nut Bars.” YouTube, October 15, 2015. https://www.youtube.com/watch?v=VBGMANiIQlI.

Buckley, Nick. 2019. “Fake Meat Is Baked into Battle Creek’s History.” *Battle Creek Enquirer*, October 7, 2019. https://www.battlecreekenquirer.com/story/life/2019/10/04/fake-meat-battle-creek-kellogg-vegetarianism-seventh-day-adventist-protose/2301425001/.

Bui, My (Myla), Andrea Heintz Tangari, and Kelly L. Haws. 2017. “Can Health ‘Halos’ Extend to Food Packaging? An Investigation into Food Healthfulness Perceptions and Serving Sizes on Consumption Decisions.” *Journal of Business Research*, 75: 221–8. https://doi.org/10.1016/j.jbusres.2016.08.032.

Buiten, Denise. 2020. “It’s ‘Vile’ but Is It Violence? A Case Study Analysis of News Media Representations of Non-Consensual Sexual Image-Sharing.” *Feminist Media Studies*, 20, no. 8: 1177–94. doi:10.1080/14680777.2019.1708773.

Burns Group. 2014. “Great Grains ‘Whole, Whole Grain’ Commercial w/ Curtis Stone.” YouTube, February 13, 2014. https://www.youtube.com/watch?v=_9HFTtLjUBA.

Business Wire. 2024. “Impossible Foods Kicks Off First Major Marketing Campaign Featuring New Brand Identity.” May 6, 2024. https://www.businesswire.com/news/home/20240506181779/en/Impossible-Foods-Kicks-Off-First-Major-Marketing-Campaign-Featuring-New-Brand-Identity.

Butler, Julianna M., and Christian A. Vossler. 2018. “What Is an Unregulated and Potentially Misleading Label Worth? The Case of ‘Natural’-Labelled Groceries.” *Environmental and Resource Economics*, 70, no. 2: 545–64. doi:10.1007/s10640-017-0132-9.

buy sites. 2021. "1943 Baby Ruth Candy Bar Ad Today's Meals Make Tomorrow's Men." https://kombestar.live/product_details/42352123.html.

Campbell, Margaret C., Kenneth C. Manning, Bridget Leonard, and Hannah M. Manning. 2016. "Kids, Cartoons, and Cookies: Stereotype Priming Effects on Children's Food Consumption." *Journal of Consumer Psychology*, 26, no. 2: 257–64. https://doi.org/10.1016/j.jcps.2015.06.003; https://www.sciencedirect.com/science/article/pii/S1057740815000637.

"Campbell's Soup TV Spot, 'Snowbuddy.'" 2020. iSpot.tv, December 3, 2020. https://www.ispot.tv/ad/tSCE/campbells-soup-snowbuddy.

Canipe, Ricco. 2016. "Kellogg's Frosted Flakes (Everywhere We Go) (2010) Commercial." YouTube. https://www.youtube.com/watch?v=2wRjCflAJIU.

Castonguay, Jessica. 2015. "Portraying Physical Activity in Food Advertising Targeting Children." *Health Education*, 115, no. 6 (October 5): 10.1108/HE-07-2014-0080.

Castonguay, Jessica, Aysen Bakir, and Jeffrey G. Blodgett. 2019. "Adolescents' Responses to Cereal Ads: An Assessment of Weight and Gender." *Journal of Food Products Marketing*, 25 no. 8: 785–804. https://doi-org.sacredheart.idm.oclc.org/10.1080/10454446.2019.1678208.

Castro, Alex D. R. 2020. "267. Borden's HEMO Chocolate Drink, Print Ads 1951–61." *isa munang Patalastas!*, February 23, 2020. http://isamunangpatalastas.blogspot.com/2020/02/.

Cereal Secrets. 2024. "10 Most Popular Cereals Based on Revenue & Boxes Sold." https://cerealsecrets.com/most-popular-cereals/.

Cerealmad. 2022. "1950s–2010s Frosties Tony Tiger Adverts—Compilation 80+ Amazing Ads." YouTube. https://www.youtube.com/watch?v=tlZCJnrTPG8.

Cheerios. 2015. "Our Gluten Free Story: Why Gluten-Free?" YouTube, September 17, 2015. https://www.youtube.com/watch?v=_3c72M6t1-c.

Cheerios. 2016. "Honey Nut Cheerios, Gluten-Free just Got More Delicious." YouTube, June 28, 2016. https://www.youtube.com/watch?v=VirPD7BoVm0.

Cheerios. 2021. "Cheerios Commercial | Buzz's Big News Flavors (:15)." YouTube, January 25, 2021. https://www.youtube.com/watch?v=k3PWRRCe8nw.

Cheerios. 2024. "For the Ones You 💖." Pinterest. https://www.pinterest.com/pin/for-the-ones-you-video-in-2024--131800726591084445/.

"Cheerios TV Spot, 'Rappel.'" 2016. iSpot.tv, January 4, 2016. https://www.ispot.tv/ad/AnA_/cheerios-rappel.

Cheerios UK. 2024. "Cheerios Multigrain Made Tasty TV Advert 2024." YouTube, March 26, 2024. https://www.youtube.com/watch?v=IcuKPkwQwGM.

Chicago Tribune. 2021. "History, and Future, of Fortification." *Chicago Tribune*, August 20, 2021. https://www.chicagotribune.com/2001/05/02/history-and-future-of-fortification/.

Children's Hospital of Philadelphia. 2021. "Life with Celiac Disease: Anna's Story." June 14, 2021. https://www.chop.edu/stories/life-celiac-disease-anna-s-story.

Choi, Hojoon, and Jeffery K. Springston. 2014. "How to Use Health and Nutrition-Related Claims Correctly on Food Advertising: Comparison of Benefit-Seeking, Risk-Avoidance, and Taste Appeals on Different Food Categories." *Journal of Health Communication*, 19: 1047–63. 10.1080/10810730.2013.872723.

Chuan, Byron, Lanping Guo, Bryce Cooper, Sagar Rawal, Teresa Gallego-Martin, Yingze Zhang, Bryan McVerry, Christopher O'Donnell, and Faraaz Shah. 2020. "Physiologic Effects of Exogenous Dextrose in Murine *Klebsiella pneumoniae* Sepsis Vary by Route of Provision." *Nutrients*, 12, no. 10: 2901. https://doi.org/10.3390/nu12102901.

Classic90sFan. 2019. "Baskin Robbins Ad—Fat Free & Sugar Free (1991)." YouTube, February 11, 2019. https://www.youtube.com/watch?v=FmtDFIC6fd0.

Cleveland Clinic. 2020. "Is Yogurt Good for You?" https://health.clevelandclinic.org/is-yogurt-good-for-you.

Click Americana. 2021. "These 1980s Fruit Snacks Came in a Ton of Shapes, Flavors & Colors." Click Americana, March 27, 2021. https://clickamericana.com/topics/food-drink/vintage-1980s-fruit-snacks.

CNBC Digital Video. 2023. "The Journal Herald, Dayton, Ohio • Wed, Dec 30, 1964, Page 12." Newspapers.com, November 22, 2023. https://www.newspapers.com/article/the-journal-herald-oops-we-goofed/135597244/.

"Coca-Cola Zero Sugar TV Spot, 'Taste the Transformation' Song by Maggie Rogers." 2023. iSpot.tv, April 4, 2023. https://www.ispot.tv/ad/12UU/coca-cola-zero-sugar-taste-the-transformation-song-by-maggie-rogers.

Colamosca, Anne. 1974. "Health Foods Prosper Despite High Prices." *The New York Times*, November 17, 1974: 205. https://timesmachine.nytimes.com/timesmachine/1974/11/17/91082127.html?pageNumber=205.

Comedian Evan Wecksell + Breckett Sage. 2009. "Pizza Hut—The Natural." YouTube, February 28, 2009. https://www.youtube.com/watch?v=2ZVvOv4eA-g.

Comicstrips. 2024. "Sunshine Krispy Crackers Ad: Flaky Thin Crackers! 1940's." eBay. https://www.ebay.com/itm/175898564590.

Commercial Archiver. 2023. "Little Caesars Hot N Ready Pretzel Crust 3." YouTube, May 7, 2023. https://www.youtube.com/watch?v=lG_Tp9qmT20.

Commercial Break. 2023. "Little Caesars Corncob Crust | Pretzel Crust Ad Campaign—Eric Wareheim Commercials (2023)." YouTube, July 9, 2023. https://www.youtube.com/watch?v=E6eemdGh4NQ.

Commercials Funny. 2017. "Subway Commercial 2017 Steak & Cheese Footlong." YouTube, January 2, 2017. https://www.youtube.com/watch?v=HKTFOiYcK0c.

Commercials Funny. 2020. "Oreo Thins Commercial 2020 Bedtime." YouTube, September 19, 2020. https://www.youtube.com/watch?v=_hFKJWqfJWo.

Cross, Catherine. 2013. "Gluten-Free Industry Is Healthy, but Is the Food?" *CMAJ: Canadian Medical Association Journal (Journal De l'Association Medicale Canadienne)*, 185, no. 13: E610. doi:10.1503/cmaj.109-4555.

Cross, Ruth, Sam Davis, and Ivy O'Neil. 2017. *Health Communication: Theoretical and Critical Perspectives*. Malden, MA: Polity Press.

CRT Afterglow. 2022. "1990 Dannon Light Yogurt Fat Shaming Commercial." YouTube, January 31, 2020. https://www.youtube.com/watch?app=desktop&v=iuzYXTXIx-k.

da Cruz, Gabriela Lopes, Maria Laura da Costa Louzada, Jacqueline Tereza da Silva, Josefa Maria Fellegger Garzillo, Fernanda Rauber, Ximena Schmidt Rivera, Christian Reynolds, and Renata Bertazzi Levy. 2024. "The Environmental Impact of Beef and Ultra-Processed Food Consumption in Brazil." *Public Health Nutrition*, 27, no. 1: e34. doi:10.1017/S1368980023002975.

Dailymotion. 1983. "Wheat Thins with Sandy Duncan." https://www.dailymotion.com/video/xldreh.

Danowski, Debbie. 2024. *"Happy Eating" and Food Addiction in American Advertising*. New York: Lexington Books.

Dartmouth-Hitchcock Medical Center. 2019. "Exposure to Sugary Breakfast Cereal Advertising Directly Influences Children's Diets." https://www.sciencedaily.com/releases/2019/01/190107153410.htm.

Dave's Archives. 2020. "Retro Commercials—Iconic '80s Breakfast Cereal." YouTube, April 26, 2020. https://www.youtube.com/watch?v=7tDaML84m6k.

Davis William. 2019. *Wheat Belly: Lose the Wheat, Lose the Weight, and Find Your Path Back to Health*. New York: Harmony/Rodale.

Davis, William. 2022. *Super Gut: A Four-Week Plan to Reprogram Your Microbiome, Restore Health, and Lose Weight*. Boston: Hachette Go.

Di Market. 2024. "North America Yogurt Market Analysis Report 2024: Market to Grow by a CAGR of 5.11 to 2032, Driven by Government Incentives, Popularity of Virtual Assistants, and Strategic Partnerships." https://www.datainsightsmarket.com/reports/north-america-yogurt-market-5049#.

Dixon, Helen, Maree Scully, Melanie Wakefield, Bridget Kelly, Simone Pettigrew, Kathy Chapman, and Jeff Niederdeppe. 2018. The Impact of Unhealthy Food Sponsorship vs. Pro-Health Sponsorship Models on Young Adults' Food Preferences: A Randomised Controlled Trial. *BMC Public Health*, 18. https://doi.org/10.1186/s12889-018-6298-4.

Dong, Dong, Hao-chieh Chang, and Tianjiao Wang. 2017. "The CSR Green Halo Effect on the Corporate–Public Communication: An Experimental Study." *Asian Journal of Communication*, 27, no. 2: 213–30. doi:10.1080/01292986.2016.1257034.

Duke University Libraries. 2024. "Post: Grape-Nuts Cereal, 1960s." *Repository Collections and Archives*. https://repository.duke.edu/dc/adviews/dmbb34517.

dustystuffsantabarbara. 2024. "Kellogg's Pep Cereal 'Takes PEP to Make Graceful Dive' Ad Print 1926!" eBay. https://www.ebay.ph/itm/265711301351.

eBay Image. 2024. Google Search Thumbnail. https://i.ebayimg.com/thumbs/images/g/fSYAAOSwAPplJrtz/s-l1200.jpg.

Ede, Georgia. 2024. *Change Your Diet, Change Your Mind: A Powerful Plan to Improve Mood, Overcome Anxiety, and Protect Memory for a Lifetime of Optimal Mental Health.* New York: Balance.

Edelstein, Sally. 2015. "Metrecal for Lunch Bunch." *Envisioning the American Dream*, June 1, 2015. https://envisioningtheamericandream.com/2015/06/01/metre cal-for-lunch-bunch/.

Ellithorpe, Morgan E., Fashina Aladé, Robyn B. Adams, and Glen J. Nowak. 2022. "Looking Ahead: Caregivers' COVID-19 Vaccination Intention for Children 5 Years Old and Younger Using the Health Belief Model." *Vaccine*, 40, no. 10: 1404–12. doi:10.1016/j.vaccine.2022.01.052.

Emond, Jennifer A., Meghan R. Longacre, Keith M. Drake, Linda J. Titus, Kristy Hendricks, Todd MacKenzie, Jennifer L. Harris, et al. 2019. "Exposure to Child-Directed TV Advertising and Preschoolers' Intake of Advertised Cereals." *American Journal of Preventive Medicine*, 56, no. 2: e35–43. doi:10.1016/j.amepre.2018.09.015.

Evans, Sydney, and Ketura Persellin. 2022. Fruit Leather: A Snack Sometimes Chock Full of Pesticides and Sugar." *EWG*, September 15, 2022. https://www.ewg.org/resea rch/fruit-leather-snack-sometimes-chock-full-pesticides-and-sugar.

ewjxn. 2018a. "1990 *New* Simple Pleasures Ice Cream 'Fat Free' TV Commercial." YouTube, September 21, 2018. https://www.youtube.com/watch?v=3ko2OsYAzbo.

ewjxn. 2018b. "1995 Oreo Cookie 'Reduced Fat' TV Commercial." YouTube, August 10, 2018. https://www.youtube.com/watch?v=HSlQ4jRLQWg.

ewjxn. 2022. "1990 Total Cereal 'Can You Mix a Bowl? 100% of 12 Vitamins and Minerals' TV Commercial." YouTube, December 5, 2022. https://www.youtube.com/watch?v=iEggoWQ22ps.

ewjxn. 2023. "1981 Butternut Super White Bread 'Five Extra Vitamins and Minerals' TV Commercial." YouTube, October 5, 2023. https://www.youtube.com/watch?v=Zu7z PPGLq7o.

ewjxn. October 22, 2024, "1994 Nabisco Reduced Fat Ritz Crackers 'Terrific with cheese' TV Commercial." https://www.youtube.com/watch?v=RG4w3c-ybNY.

Fargo's Treasures. 2024. "2016 Magazine Advertisement Page Kraft Macaroni & Cheese Food Print Ad." eBay. https://www.ebay.com/itm/384914185660.

Farris, April L. 2010. "The 'Natural' Aversion: The FDA's Reluctance to Define a Leading Food-Industry Marketing Claim, and the Pressing Need for a Workable Rule." *Food and Drug Law Journal*, 65, no. 2: 403. https://research-ebsco-com.sacredheart.idm.oclc.org/linkprocessor/plink?id=5ae1a751-b265-3143-9bd9-d5c4b8919f55.

Federal Trade Commission. 1994. "Enforcement Policy Statement on Food Advertising." https://www.ftc.gov/legal-library/browse/enforcement-policy-statem ent-food-advertising#67.

Fera, Rae Ann. 2014. "The False Advertising Industry Is Here to Tell You 'Natural' Foods Are a Total Sham." *Fast Company*, February 25, 2014. https://www.fastcompany.com/3026901/the-false-advertising-industry-is-here-to-tell-you-natural-foods-are-a-total-sham.

Flaviano, Ron. 2011. "Vintage—Metrical Diet Shake Commercial." YouTube, October 18, 2011. https://www.youtube.com/watch?v=A89MjNeeo24.

Flood, Elizabeth. 2024. "Beyond Meat Unveils Its 'Most Significant Renovation to Date.'" *Food Dive*, February 21, 2024. https://www.fooddive.com/news/beyond-meat-unveils-most-significant-renovation-date/707985/.

Follett, Gillian. 2023. "How the Fruit Roll-Ups Ice Cream Tiktok Trend Influenced the Brand's Social Strategy." *Ad Age*, April 14, 2023. https://adage.com/article/digital-marketing-ad-tech-news/fruit-roll-ups-ice-cream-tiktok-trend-and-brand-social-strategy/2487156.

Fox 4 Now. 2020. "Oreo Goes Gluten Free." YouTube, November 17, 2020. https://www.youtube.com/watch?v=ikX9qjpUwt0.

Free Carpet Store. 2021. "1911 Ad Malt Nutrine Anheuser Busch Barley Health Drink ORIGINAL PM2." https://freecarpet.best/product_details/51076774.html.

Freedhoff, Yoni. 2006. "Kids, Remember to Drink Your Diet Coke Multivitamin!" *Weighty Matters*, December 19, 2006. https://www.weightymatters.ca/2006/12/kids-remember-to-drink-your-diet-coke.hitml.

Freedonia Group. 2023. "Gluten-Free Foods: US Market Trends and Opportunities, 7th Edition Report Overview." https://www.freedoniagroup.com/packaged-facts/gluten free foods in the us.

"Freschetta TV Spot, 'Real Taste for Real Life.'" 2016. iSpot.tv, January 4, 2016. https://www.ispot.tv/ad/AnZN/freschetta-real-taste-for-real-life.

Friedman, Daniela B., Sarah B. Laditka, James N. Laditka, and Anna E. Price. 2011. "A Content Analysis of Cognitive Health Promotion in Popular Magazines."https://research-ebsco-com.sacredheart.idm.oclc.org/linkprocessor/plink?id=45b49072-3776-39f7-bb27-2b7bd495c8d4.

Friedman, Laura F. 2014. "8 Insane Vintage Ads That Make Sugar Seem Like a Health Food." *Business Insider*, October 29, 2014. https://www.businessinsider.com/vintage sugar as diet-aid-ads-2014-10.

"Frosted Flakes TV Spot, 'Forget Your Problems: Hockey.'" 2023. iSpot.tv, August 10, 2023. https://www.ispot.tv/ad/5VS9/frosted-flakes-get-your-problems-hockey.

"Frosted Flakes TV Spot, 'Help All Kids Be Tigers.'" 2019. iSpot.tv, August 5, 2019. https://www.ispot.tv/ad/olWd/frosted-flakes-help-all-kids-be-tigers.

"Fruit by the Foot TV Spot, 'Weights.'" 2017. iSpot.tv, July 31, 2017. https://www.ispot.tv/ad/w1El/fruit-by-the-foot-weights.

"Fruttare Strawberry and Milk TV Spot." 2013. iSpot.tv, April 22, 2013. https://www.ispot.tv/ad/7Zkd/fruttare-strawberry-and-milk.

Gearhardt, Ashley N., Sonja Yokum, Jennifer L. Harris, Leonard H. Epstein, and Julie C. Lumeng. 2020. "Neural Response to Fast Food Commercials in Adolescents Predicts Intake." *American Journal of Clinical Nutrition*, 111, no. 3: 493–502. https://doi.org/10.1093/ajcn/nqz305.

"General Mills TV Spot, 'For More Whole Grain.'" 2012. iSpot.tv, June 27, 2012. https://www.ispot.tv/ad/7Vwx/general-mills-more-whole-grain.

"General Mills TV Spot, 'Again.'" 2016. iSpot.tv, January 11, 2016. https://www.ispot.tv/ad/An_w/general-mills-again.

"General Mills TV Spot, 'The Cereals You Love, Now with Twice the Vitamin D.'" 2023. iSpot.tv, September 18, 2023. https://www.ispot.tv/ad/5OM_/general-mills-the-cereals-you-love-now-with-twice-the-vitamin-d.

Glick, A. A., D. M. Winham, M. M. Heer, M. C. Shelley, and A. M. Hutchins. 2024. "Health Belief Model Predicts Likelihood of Eating Nutrient-Rich Foods Among U.S. Adults." *Nutrients*, 16, no. 14. doi:10.3390/nu16142335.

Global Health Advocacy Incubator. 2022. "GHAI Industry Alert No. 1 | Industry Alerts 2022 Series." https://assets.advocacyincubator.org/uploads/2022/08/2022_08_alert.pdf.

GlutenFreeville. 2011. "Gluten Free Commercial.mov." YouTube, January 28, 2011. https://www.youtube.com/watch?v=D_BwF0R2S7g.

Good Food Institute. 2023. "2023 Annual State of the Industry Report—Plant Based: Meat, Seafood, Eggs, Dairy." https://gfi.org/wp-content/uploads/2024/04/2023_State-of-the-Industry-Report-Plant-based-meat-seafood-eggs-and-dairy.pdf.

Goodrum, Michael. 2008. "'His Greatest Enemy? Intolerance!' The Superman Radio Show in 1946—First Part." *Scan Journal*, 5 no. 2 (September).

Grand View Research. 2023. "Gluten-Free Products Market Size, Share & Trend Analysis Report Overview." https://www.grandviewresearch.com/industry-analysis/gluten-free-productsmarket#:~:text=The%20global%20gluten%2Dfree%20products%20Market%20market%20size%20was%20estimated,USD%207.07%20billion%20in%202023.

Greer, Anna E., Sara J. Corwin, and Daniela B. Friedman. 2011. "Physical Activity and Cognitive-Health Content in Top-Circulating Magazines, 2006–2008." https://research-ebsco-com.sacredheart.idm.oclc.org/linkprocessor/plink?id=484e287a-1eae-369a-b4da-cafc48845de1.

Güner, Demet, and Hakkı Çilginoğlu. 2023. "The Health Belief Model and the Gluten-Free Diet: Are Gluten-Free Products Really Beneficial in Athlete Diets?" *Journal of Sports Sciences Research/Spor Bilimleri Araştırmaları Dergisi*, 8, no. 2: 371–85. doi:10.25307/jssr.1258771.

"Häagen-Dazs New York Strawberry Cheesecake TV Spot, 'True Comfort.'" 2024. iSpot.tv, May 9, 2024. https://www.ispot.tv/ad/6uUD/hagen-dazs-new-york-strawberry-cheesecake-true-comfort.

"Häagen-Dazs Strawberry TV Spot, 'Simple Strawberry.'" 2017. iSpot.tv, April 17, 2017. https://www.ispot.tv/ad/wYw0/haagen-dazs-strawberry-simple-strawberry.

Hall, Kevin, D., Alexis Ayuketah, Robert Brychta, Peter J. Walter, Shanna Yang, Shanna, and Megan Zhou. 2019. "Ultra-Processed Diets Cause Excess Calorie Intake and Weight Gain: An Inpatient Randomized Controlled Trial of Ad Libitum Food Intake." *Cell Metabolism*, 30, no. 1 (July): 67–77.

Hanks, Andrew S., David R. Just, and Adam Brumberg. (2016). "Marketing Vegetables in Elementary School Cafeterias to Increase Uptake." *Pediatrics*, 138, no. 2 (August): e20151720. 10.1542/peds.2015-1720.

"Haribo Gold-Bears TV Spot, 'Football Chat.'" 2024. iSpot.tv, February 5, 2024. https://www.ispot.tv/ad/67AG/haribo-gold-bears-football-chat.

Harriman, Cynthia. 2017. "Pulling Ancel Keys Out from Under the Bus." Oldways Cultural Food Traditions, August 1, 2017. https://oldwayspt.org/blog/pulling-ancel-keys-out-under-bus.

Harris, Jennifer L., John A. Bargh, and Kelly D. Brownell. 2009. "Priming Effects of Television Food Advertising on Eating Behavior." *Health Psychology*, 28, no. 4: 404–13. doi:10.1037/a0014399.

Harris, J. L., K. S. Haraghey, M. Lodolce, and N. L. Semenza. 2018. "Teaching Children about Good Health? Halo Effects in Child-Directed Advertisements for Unhealthy Food." *Pediatric Obesity*, 13 (April): 256–64. doi:10.1111/ijpo.12257.

"Healthy Choice Power Bowls TV Spot, 'Adobo Chicken: Wholesome Ingredients.'" 2019. iSpot.tv. https://www.ispot.tv/ad/Znlj/healthy-choice-power-bowls-adobo-chicken-wholesome-ingredients

"Hebrew National TV Commercial for Girl at Carnival." 2012. iSpot.tv, August 1, 2012. https://www.ispot.tv/ad/7VUW/hebrew-national-girl-at-carnival.

Heller, Rebecca, Jennifer Martin-Biggers, Amanda Berhaupt-Glickstein, Virginia Quick, and Carol Byrd-Bredbenner. 2015. "Fruit-Related Terms and Images on Food Packages and Advertisements Affect Children's Perceptions of Foods' Fruit Content." *Public Health Nutrition* 18, no. 15: 2722–8. https://doi.org/10.1017/S1368980015000701.

Henney, Alex E., Conor S. Gillespie, Uazman Alam, Theresa J. Hydes, and Daniel J. Cuthbertson. 2023. "Ultra-Processed Food Intake Is Associated with Non-Alcoholic Fatty Liver Disease in Adults: A Systematic Review and Meta-Analysis." *Nutrients*, 15, no. 10: 2266. doi:10.3390/nu15102266.

Hester, Jessica Leigh. 2016. "Save the Fleet, Eat Less Wheat: The Patriotic History of Ditching Bread." NPR, February 23, 2016. https://www.npr.org/sections/thesalt/2016/02/23/466956650/save-the-fleet-eat-less-wheat-the-patriotic-history-of-ditching-bread.

Hoeffner, Melissa Kravitz. 2024. "Here's How Cracker Jack Is Supporting Female Athletes This Summer." *Food and Wine*, June 11, 2024. https://www.foodandwine.com/cracker-jack-cracker-jill-spotlight-squad-campaign-8661189.

Horovitz, Bruce. 2007. "Food Marketers Go on a Berry Fruity-Licious Kick. *USA Today*, July 9, 2007. http://usatoday30.usatoday.com/money/industries/food/2007-07-08-fruit-products_N.htm.

Houseofblair. 2024. "Muffets Whole Wheat Cereal Print Ad—*Good Housekeeping Magazine* January 1928." eBay. https://www.ebay.com/itm/235442386304.

HRTVFan2. 2017. "1996 Hershey's Chocolate Syrup Commercial." YouTube, October 10, 2017. https://www.youtube.com/watch?v=NPDJNvv1b-A.

I Heart Publix. 2024. "Against the Grain Gourmet Gluten-Free & Grain-Free Bread." Facebook, March 11, 2024. https://www.facebook.com/iheartpublix/videos/916306536815827/.

Iles, Irina A., Jennifer L. Pearson, Eric Lindblom, and Meghan Bridgid Moran. 2021. " 'Tobacco and Water': Testing the Health Halo Effect of Natural American Spirit Cigarette Ads and Its Relationship with Perceived Absolute Harm and Use Intentions." *Health Communication*, 36, no. 7: 804–15. doi:10.1080/10410236.2020.1712526.

Ingredion. 2023. "Maximize Brand Value by Formulating to 2023 Consumer Food Preferences." https://www.ingredion.com/na/en-us/be-whats-next/2023-consumer-food-preference-trends.html#claims.

Institute of Medicine (US) Committee on Use of Dietary Reference Intakes in Nutrition Labeling. 2003. "Overview of Food Fortification in the United States and Canada." *Dietary Reference Intakes: Guiding Principles for Nutrition Labeling and Fortification*. Washington, DC: National Academies Press (US). https://www.ncbi.nlm.nih.gov/books/NBK208880/.

International Food Information Council Foundation. 2016. "2016 Food and Health Survey." https://foodinsight.org/wp-content/uploads/2016/05/2016-Food-and-Health-Survey-Report_-FINAL_0.pdf.

Internet Lurker. 2008. "Wheat Thins Commercial with Sandy Duncan." YouTube, October 22, 2008. https://www.youtube.com/watch?v=Q-cR87NQtIA.

Itzler, Jesse. 2024. "Fake Friday." LinkedIn, February 2024. https://www.linkedin.com/feed/update/urn:li:activity:7159252665267339264/.

Jeff Morgan 07. 2024. "Original 1920s Advertisement Advertising MELLIN'S FOOD for Babies, Consumer Magazine Advert Circa 1924." Almay. https://www.alamy.com/original-1920s-advertisement-advertising-mellins-food-for-babies-consumer-image61044968.html.

Johnseller. 2023. "1920 Print Ad—Charms: The Pure Fruit Tablets Hard Candy, The Charms Co. Newark, NJ." eBay. https://www.ebay.com/itm/355042101399?.

Johnson, Sarah Wassberg. 2021. "World War Wednesday: Save a Loaf a Week." Food History Blog, October 27, 2021. https://www.thefoodhistorian.com/blog/world-war-wednesday-save-a-loaf-a-week.

Johnson, Sarah Wassberg. 2023. "World War Wednesday: Mr. Peanut Goes to War." Food History Blog, May 17, 2023. https://www.thefoodhistorian.com/blog/world-war-wednesday-mr-peanut-goes-to-war.

Juber, Mahammad. 2022. "Is Maltitol Better or Worse Than Sugar? Are There Side Effects?" Medicine Net, September 22, 2022. https://www.medicinenet.com/is_maltitol_better_worse_than_sugar_side_effects/article.htm.

Kapadia, Jess. 2023. "A History of Gluten-Free Bread." The Spruce Eats, January 25, 2023. https://www.thespruceeats.com/a-history-of-gluten-free-bread-4796997.

Karlis, Nicole. 2023. "Celiac Disease Numbers Keep Going Up—Yet Due to Lack of Funding, Researchers Still Aren't Sure Why." *Salon*, April 23, 2023. https://www.salon.com/2023/04/23/celiac-disease-numbers-keep-going-up--yet-due-to-lack-of-funding-researchers-still-arent-sure-why/.

Kaur, A., P. Scarborough, and M. Rayner. 2017. "A Systematic Review, and Meta-Analyses, of the Impact of Health-Related Claims on Dietary Choices." *International Journal of Behavioral Nutrition and Physical Activity*, 14, no. 93. https://www.researchgate.net/publication/318377307_A_systematic_review_and_meta-analyses_of_the_impact_of_health-related_claims_on_dietary_choices.

Kébé, Saliou Diombo, Adama Diouf, Papa Mamadou Dit Doudou Sylla, Kalidou Kane, Caroline dos Santos Costa, Fernanda Helena Marrocos Leite, Giovanna Calixto Andrade, et al. 2024. "Assessment of Ultra Processed Foods Consumption in Senegal: Validation of the Nova-UPF Screener." *Archives of Public Health*, 82, no. 1: 1–12. doi:10.1186/s13690-024-01239-y.

Kellogg Company. 2023. "Tony the Tiger Recruits 5-Star Roster of College Athletes to Bring the Fun Back to Youth Sports with Kellogg's Frosted Flakes Mission Tiger." PR Newswire, June 1, 2023. https://www.prnewswire.com/news-releases/tony-the-tiger-recruits-5-star-roster-of-college-athletes-to-bring-the-fun-back-to-youth-sports-with-kelloggs-frosted-flakes-mission-tiger-301840447.html.

Kellogg's Vector. 2025. "Mission Tiger™ Celebrates Major Milestone: Now Making an Impact in All 50 States." https://newsroom.wkkellogg.com/2024-08-21-Mission-Tiger-TM-Celebrates-Major-Milestone-Now-Making-an-Impact-in-All-50-States.

Kellogg's Vector. 2022. "Vector® Maple Crunch Cereal Maple Meets Protein." YouTube, November 15, 2022. https://www.youtube.com/watch?v=9QxhAcEXQ5k.

Kellogg's Vector. 2023. "Be Ready with 22 Vitamins and Minerals." YouTube, April 3, 2023. https://www.youtube.com/watch?app=desktop&v=COA9H1YUUUk.

Kelly, Deirdre M., and Dawn H. Currie. 2021. "Beyond Stereotype Analysis in Critical Media Literacy: Case Study of Reading and Writing Gender in Pop Music Videos." *Gender and Education*, 33, no. 6: 676–91. doi:10.1080/09540253.2020.1831443.

Keyser, Catherine. 2017. "Ingestion/The White Rabbit and His Colorful Tricks." *Cabinet*, Fall 2017/Winter 2018. https://www.cabinetmagazine.org/issues/65/keyser.php.

Kidd, Chloe, and Natalie J. Loxton. 2018. "Junk Food Advertising Moderates the Indirect Effect of Reward Sensitivity and Food Consumption via the Urge to Eat." *Physiology and Behavior*, 188 (May): 276–82. doi:10.1016/j.physbeh.2018.02.030.

Kim, Yeo Jung, and Hye Jin Yoon. 2017. "Predicting Green Advertising Attitude and Behavioral Intention in South Korea." *Social Behavior and Personality: An International Journal*, 45, no. 8: 1345–64. doi:10.2224/sbp.5675.

Kindy, David. 2021. "How Wheaties Became the 'Breakfast of Champions.'" *Smithsonian Magazine*, July 26, 2021. https://www.smithsonianmag.com/innovation/how-wheaties-became-breakfast-champions-180978246/.

Kiner, Deb. 2023. "This New Jell-O Not Only Jiggles but It Also Can Sparkle." PENN Live Patriot-News, May 11, 2023. https://www.pennlive.com/food/2023/05/this-new-jell-o-not-only-jiggles-but-it-also-can-sparkle.html.

Klaus-Tapes. 2024. "Pillsbury Reduced Fat Chocolate Chip Cookies 1995 Commercial." YouTube, May 6, 2024. https://www.youtube.com/watch?v=Y02wEadMd74.

Knox, Dave. 2023. "How Magic Spoon Brought Innovation to the Breakfast Table." *Forbes*, May 10, 2023. https://www.forbes.com/sites/daveknox/2023/05/10/how-magic-spoon-brought-innovation-to-the-breakfast-table/?sh=7e9648ca4dc9.

Kraft Mac & Cheese. 2020. "Gluten Free Kraft Mac & Cheese." Facebook, November 20, 2020. https://www.facebook.com/watch/?v=657663164910983.

Kristen's Vintage Paper. 2024. "1943 BORDEN'S HEMO Vitamins Milk Drink Elsie Elmer Cow Boat World War 2 Vintage Print Ad." eBay. https://www.etsy.com/listing/1102365750/1943-bordens-hemo-vitamins-milk-drink.

Kroker-Lobos, Maria F., Monica Mazariegos, Monica Guamuch, and Manuel Ramirez-Zea. 2022. "Ultraprocessed Products as Food Fortification Alternatives: A Critical Appraisal from Latin America. Nutrients." *Nutrients*, 14, no. 7 (March): 1413. https://doi.org/10.3390/nu14071413.

KTAR Newsroom. 2012. "Want Some Taste with That Ice Cream?" KTAR News 92.3 FM, September 27, 2012. https://ktar.com/story/109617/want-some-taste-with-that-ice-cream/.

Kuchler, F., M. Bowman, M. Sweitzer, and C. Greene. 2020. "Evidence from Retail Food Markets That Consumers Are Confused by Natural and Organic Food Labels." *Journal of Consumer Policy*, 43, no. 2: 379–96. https://research-ebsco-com.sacredheart.idm.oclc.org/linkprocessor/plink?id=8f1510ce-18fb-3744-87d7-1771b0dd447b.

Laudanno, Oscar M. 2023. "Changes in the Microbiota Due to Ultra-Processed Foods: Obesity, Cancer and Premature Death." *Medicina*, 83, no. 2: 278–82. https://research-ebsco-com.sacredheart.idm.oclc.org/linkprocessor/plink?id=30ba8807-7940-3a6e-adf8-7292e58c8fef.

Laurent, Michelle. 2016. "Dannon Oikos Greek Yogurt Plane Kiss with John Stamos." YouTube, May 8, 2016. https://www.youtube.com/watch?v=gUqq2PIDjbo.

Lay's. 2022. "Baked Lay's—The Perfect Snack." YouTube, November 21, 2022. https://www.youtube.com/watch?v=PYQKZmUduTc.

Lee, Sang Hyeon, Doo Bong Han, and Rodolfo M. Nayga, Jr. 2014. "Cultural Inflow Effects on Japanese Import Demand for Consumer Products: Importance of Halo Effects." *Journal of the Asia Pacific Economy*, 19, no. 3: 506–21. https://research-ebsco-com.sacredheart.idm.oclc.org/linkprocessor/plink?id=81e4e53c-2de0-3745-9e7b-d75f2bdd7fbe.

Leonie, Elizabeth, Priscila Machado, Marit Zinöcker, Phillip Baker, and Mark Lawrence. 2020. "Ultra-Processed Foods and Health Outcomes: A Narrative Review." *Nutrients*, 12, no. 7: 1955. doi:10.3390/nu12071955.

Leuthesser, Lance, Chiranjeev S. Kohli, and Katrin R. Harich. 1995. "Brand Equity: The Halo Effect Measure." *European Journal of Marketing*, 29, no. 4: 57. DOI:10.1108/03090569510086657.

Levy, AnneMarie, Avi Salamon, Mark Tucci, Cheryl L. Limebeer, Linda A. Parker, and Francesco Leri. 2013. "Co-Sensitivity to the Incentive Properties of Palatable Food and Cocaine in Rats; Implications for Co-Morbid Addictions." *Addiction Biology*, 18, no. 5: 763–73. doi:10.1111/j.1369-1600.2011.00433.x.

Li, Huiping, Shu Li, Hongxi Yang, Yuan Zhang, Shunming Zhang, Yue Ma, Yabing Hou, Xinyu Zhang, Kaijun Niu, Yan Borné, and Yaogang Wang. 2022. "Association of Ultraprocessed Food Consumption with Risk of Dementia: A Prospective Cohort Study." *Neurology*, 99, no. 10 (September): 1056–66. DOI:10.1212/WNL.0000000000200871.

Lil Nas X Media. 2023. "Lil Nas X | Vitamin Water AD #1. YouTube, June 27, 2023. https://www.youtube.com/watch?v=Qgy0mNHNcOw.

Liu, R., N. H. Hooker, E. Parasidis, and C. T. Simons. 2017. "A Natural Experiment: Using Immersive Technologies to Study the Impact of 'All-Natural' Labeling on Perceived Food Quality, Nutritional Content, and Liking." *Journal of Food Science*, 82, no. 3: 825–33. doi:10.1111/1750-3841.13639.

Liyanapathirana, Navoda Nirmani, Amanda Grech, Mengyu Li, Arunima Malik, Rosilene Ribeiro, Timur Burykin, Manfred Lenzen, and David Raubenheimer. 2023. "Nutritional, Environmental and Economic Impacts of Ultra-Processed Food Consumption in Australia." *Public Health Nutrition*, 26 (December): 3359–69. doi:10.1017/S136898002300232X.

Loft Life Ads. 2024. "1943 Shredded Ralston Cereal Breakfast Food Vintage Old Print Ad Wartime Dessert." eBay. https://www.ebay.com.au/itm/305045142658.

Lost in Time Vintage Ads. 2024. "1951 Vintage Ad Kellogg's PEP Whole Wheat Cereal/Mother/Daughter (071213)." eBay. https://www.ebay.com/itm/401748805695.

Loukachouk, Juliana. 2024. "Corn: The Food of the Nation." *American History Virtual Museum*. https://blogs.shu.edu/americanhistory/project/corn-the-food-of-the-nation/.

Luma Research. 2020. "Oreo—Stay Home, Stay Playful." YouTube, May 19, 2020. https://www.youtube.com/watch?v=OcFSiBJ-bdA.

Lustig, Robert H. 2021. *Metabolical: The Lure and the Lies of Processed Food, Nutrition, and Modern Medicine*. New York: Harper Wave.

Ma, Lingyan, Yuan Wang, and Jiyoun Kim. 2023. "How Health Organizations Communicate about COVID-19 on Social Media: A Comparative Content Analysis." *Journal of Communication in Healthcare*, 16, no. 1: 83–92. doi:10.1080/17538068.2022.2103334.

MacDonald, Cecelia. 2018. "Not 'All Natural': Modernizing Privity to Allow Breach of Contract Claims for Mislabeled Food Products." *Iowa Law Review*, January 1. https://research-ebsco-com.sacredheart.idm.oclc.org/linkprocessor/plink?id=b475b72d-9447-3052-997e-daa6897e2609.

Machado, Fernando. 2020. "5 Lessons Burger King Learned by Unleashing the Moldy Whopper." Ad Week, March 10, 2020. https://www.adweek.com/brand-marketing/5-lessons-burger-king-learned-by-unleashing-the-moldy-whopper/.

Madden, T. J., M. S. Roth, and W. R. Dillon. 2012. Global Product Quality and Corporate Social Responsibility Perceptions: A Cross-National Study of Halo Effects. *Journal of International Marketing*, 20, no. 1: 42–57.

Maehara, Andrea. 2019. "100% All Natural Ambiguity: A Comparative Approach to Food Labeling Requirements for the Term Natural by the Food and Drug Administration and the European Union." *Washington University Global Studies Law Review*, 18, no. 1: 263–92. https://research-ebsco-com.sacredheart.idm.oclc.org/linkprocessor/plink?id=6f92c9e7-991e-33ba-86de-908d85e920dc.

"Magic Spoon TV Spot, 'Our Own Cereal.'" 2022. iSpot.tv, July 5, 2022. https://www.ispot.tv/ad/bXaL/magic-spoon-our-own-cereal.

Martin, Douglas. 2010. "C. Joseph Genster, Marketer of Metrecal, Dies at 92." *The New York Times*, August 26, 2010. https://www.nytimes.com/2010/08/27/business/27genster.html.

Maunder Larah. 2021. "Motivating People to Stay at Home: Using the Health Belief Model to Improve the Effectiveness of Public Health Messaging during the COVID-19 Pandemic." *Translational Behavioral Medicine*, 11, no. 10: 1957–62. doi:10.1093/tbm/ibab080.

Mayo Clinic Staff. 2024. "Whole Grains: Hearty Options for a Healthy Diet." Mayo Clinic. https://www.mayoclinic.org/healthy-lifestyle/nutrition-and-healthy-eating/in-depth/whole-grains/art-20047826#:~:text=Whole%2Dgrain%20foods%20are%20good,heart%20disease%20and%20other%20conditions.

Mazloomi, Seyadeh Narges, Sepide Talebi, Sanaz Mehrabani, Reza Bagheri, Abed Ghavami, Mahsa Zarpoosh, Hamed Mohammadi, et al. 2023. "The Association of Ultra-Processed Food Consumption with Adult Mental Health Disorders: A

Systematic Review and Dose-Response Meta-Analysis of 260,385 Participants." *Nutritional Neuroscience*, 26, no. 10: 913–31. doi:10.1080/1028415X.2022.2110188.

McRae, Marc P. 2017. "Health Benefits of Dietary Whole Grains: An Umbrella Review of Meta-Analyses." *Journal of Chiropractic Medicine*, 16, no. 1 (March):10–18. https://www.ncbi.nlm.nih.gov/pmc/articles/PMC5310957/.

Meach, Rachel. 2018. "From John Yudkin to Jamie Oliver: A Short but Sweet History on the War against Sugar." In *Proteins, Pathologies and Politics: Dietary Innovation and Disease from the Nineteenth Century*, edited by David Gentilcore and Matthew Smith, chapter 7. London: Bloomsbury Academic. https://www.ncbi.nlm.nih.gov/books/NBK542158/.

Meier, Brian P., Amanda J. Dillard, and Courtney M. Lappas. 2019. "Naturally Better? A Review of the Natural-Is-Better Bias." *Social and Personality Psychology Compass*, 13, no. 8. doi:10.1111/spc3.12494.

Mellin's Food Company. 1913. "1913 Ad Mellins Food Company Baby Boy Infant Formula." Period Paper. https://www.periodpaper.com/products/1913-ad-mellins-food-company-baby-boy-infant-formula-original-advertising-066216-em1-014.

Member Berries. 2017. "Home Pride—Butter Top—Wheat White Bread Commercial (1987)." YouTube, April 3, 2017. https://www.youtube.com/watch?v=IQ32cLZTW98.

Midnight Munchies. 2018. "Iron Kids Bread 90's Ad." YouTube, April 3, 2018. https://www.youtube.com/watch?v=bQ0g2Aso_40.

Mike's VHS Treasures. 2020. "Wayne Gretzky (W/ Steve Harris & John Dimaggio) Commercial—Chunky's Soup (1996)." YouTube, August 28, 2020. https://www.youtube.com/watch?v=0CA5 bUH2 E.

millerhousedotca2. 2024. "1998 Post Honey Toasted Shredded Wheat Cereal W/Wayne Gretzky 620g Full Box Sealed." eBay. https://www.ebay.com/itm/234323471491?_trkparms=amclksrc%3DITM%26aid%3D1110006%26algo%3DHOMESPLICE.SIM%26ao%3D1%26asc%3D267276%2C270395%26meid%3Dad392859d4d34b36816b520d15a5b033%26pid%3D101506%26rk%3D5%26rkt%3D10%26sd%3D355771419466%26itm%3D234323471491%26pmt%3D0%26noa%3D1%26pg%3D4481478%26algv%3DDefaultOrganicWebWithV11WebTrimmedV3VisualRankerWithKnnV3AndUltBRecall%26brand%3DPost&_trksid=p4481478.c101506.m1851.

Mindshare. 2024. "Nature Valley: Take in the Outdoors." https://www.mindshareworld.com/work/take-in-the-outdoors-nature-valley.

Mission Tiger Website. 2024. Kellogg's Frosted Flakes. https://www.missiontiger.com/en_US/home.html.

Mister Cola. 2024. "Vintage Magazine Ad SHOTWELLS from 1946 Shur Mac Big Yank Hi Mac Candy Bars Pictured." https://mistercola.com/products/vintage-magazine-ad-shotwells-from-1946-shur-mac-big-yank-hi-mac-candy-bars-pictured.

Montana Historical Society. 1898. "The Anaconda Standard, Morning," January 30, 1898, 7. https://chroniclingamerica.loc.gov/lccn/sn84036012/1898-01-30/ed-1/seq-7/#loclr=blogadm.

Monteiro, Carlos A., Geoffrey Cannon, Renata Levy, et al. 2016. "NOVA: The Star Shines Bright." *World Nutrition*, 7, nos. 1–3 (January–March): 28–38. https://archive.wphna.org/wp-content/uploads/2016/01/WN-2016-7-1-3-28-38-Monteiro-Cannon-Levy-et-al-NOVA.pdf.

Monteiro, Carlos A., Geoffrey Cannon, Renata B. Levy, Jean-Claude Moubarac, Maria L. C. Louzada, Fernanda Rauber, Neha Khandpur, et al. 2019. "Ultra-Processed Foods: What They Are and How to Identify Them." *Public Health Nutrition*, 22, no. 5 (2019): 936–41. https://doi.org/10.1017/S1368980018003762.

Montone, Christian. 2009. "Domino Sugar 1950s Vintage Advertisement Illustration Ad." Flickr, September 12, 2009. https://www.flickr.com/photos/christianmontone/3911746313/.

Morgan, Kat, and Mark Bittman. 2024. "How to Help Americans Eat Less Junk Food." *The New York Times*, June 30, 2024. https://www.nytimes.com/2024/06/30/opinion/food-warning-labels-ultra-processed-food.html.

Moss, Michael. 2021. *Hooked: Food, Free Will, and How the Food Giants Exploit Our Addictions*. New York: Random House.

Mr. Tayto. 2023. "Tayto Lentil Chips." YouTube, December 19, 2023. https://www.youtube.com/watch?v=Fj567ccMfuU.

MSU Libraries. 2024. https://lib.msu.edu/sliker/load_object/5971/pdf#:~:text=Pettijohn%20is%20whole%20wheat%2C%20each,of%20a%20strong%2C%20healthy%20constitution.

Museum of Hoaxes. 2014. "Vitamin Donuts." December 6, 2014. https://hoaxes.org/weblog/comments/vitamin_donuts#google_vignette.

Mustard. 2009. "Nutri-Grain Cereal Ad." MrBreakfast.com, July 30, 2009. https://www.mrbreakfast.com/cereal_ucp_slideshow.asp?id=723&picid=804.

Naidenko, Olga V., David Q. Andrews, Alexis M. Temkin, Tasha Stoiber, Uloma Igara Uche, Sydney Evans, and Sean Perrone-Gray. 2021. "Investigating Molecular Mechanisms of Immunotoxicity and the Utility of ToxCast for Immunotoxicity Screening of Chemicals Added to Food." *International Journal of Environmental Research and Public Health*, 18, no. 7: 3332. https://doi.org/10.3390/ijerph18073332.

Nardocci, Milena, Jane Y. Polsky, and Jean-Claude Moubarac. 2021. "Consumption of Ultra-Processed Foods Is Associated with Obesity, Diabetes and Hypertension in Canadian Adults." *Canadian Journal of Public Health = Revue Canadienne de Sante Publique*, 112, no. 3: 421–9. doi:10.17269/s41997-020-00429-9.

National Center for Complementary and Integrative Health. 2024. "Natural Doesn't Necessarily Mean Safer, or Better." https://www.nccih.nih.gov/health/know-science/natural-doesnt-mean-better#:~:text=Chlorine%20and%20isopropyl%20alcohol%20are,and%20ricin%20from%20castor%20beans.

National Institutes of Health. 2023. "Erythritol and Cardiovascular Events." *NIH Research Matters*, March 14, 2023. https://www.nih.gov/news-events/nih-research-matters/erythritol-cardiovascular-events.

nationalcerealday.com. 2024. "National Cereal Day—March 7, 2024." https://nationalcerealday.com/.

"Nature Valley Oats 'N Honey Crunchy Granola Bars TV Spot, 'You Could Miss It.'" 2024. iSpot.tv, June 3, 2024. https://www.ispot.tv/ad/6JUh/nature-valley-oats-n-honey-crunchy-granola-bars-you-could-miss-it.

Nature Valley UK. 2017. "Nature Valley TV Ad." YouTube, July 3, 2017. https://www.youtube.com/watch?v=rWrBn74ZGdU.

Nature's Own Bread. 2009. "Nature's Own Specialty Breads Commercial." YouTube, October 8, 2009. https://www.youtube.com/watch?v=k5mtwDMgotg.

Nestle Cereals Global. 2024. "Nestle Cereals/Fitness : Fitness, Find Your Fitness Cereals!" https://www.nestle-cereals.com/global/cereals/fitness.

Nilson, Eduardo, A. F., Gerson Ferrari, Maria Laura C. Louzada, Renata B. Levy, Carlos A. Monteiro, and Leandro F. M. Rezende. 2022. "Premature Deaths Attributable to the Consumption of Ultra-Processed Foods in Brazil." *American Journal of Preventative Medicine*. https://www.ajpmonline.org/article/S0749-3797(22)00429-9/fulltext#articleInformation.

Nisbett, Richard E., and Timothy DeCamp Wilson. 1977. "The Halo Effect: Evidence for Unconscious Alteration of Judgments." *Journal of Personality and Social Psychology*, 35, no. 4: 250–6.

Nymark, Hadassaha. 2009. "Watchdog Bans Ogilvy Formula Milk Ads." Campaign US. Haymarket Media Group. https://www.campaignlive.com/article/watchdog-bans-ogilvy-formula-milk-ads/921663.

Ocak, Altuğ. 2025. "The Role of Perceived Benefits, Barriers, and Susceptibility in Free-from Gastronomy: A Health Belief Model Perspective." *OPUS Journal of Society Research*, 22: 706–17. 10.26466/opusjsr.1697883.

oddzenenz254. 2024. "Print Ad 1940's Woman Soldier Saluting Nabisco Shredded Wheat Cereal." eBay. https://www.ebay.com/itm/305602846575?_trkparms=amclksrc%3DITM%26aid%3D1110006%26algo%3DHOMESPLICE.SIM%26ao%3D1%26asc%3D266917%2C267607%2C267275%26meid%3D33255a37e9294c50a09a9daef7e8ca6f%26pid%3D101224%26rk%3D2%26rkt%3D3%26sd%3D305525581019%26itm%3D305602846575%26pmt%3D0%26noa%3D1%26pg%3D2332490%26algv%3DDefaultOrganicWebV9BertRefreshRankerWithCassiniEmbRecall&_trksid=p2332490.c101224.m-1.

Official Johnsonville. 2021. "Johnsonville Rope Sausage: This and That." YouTube, July 23, 2021. https://www.youtube.com/watch?v=30dED_wU8_E.

Old Fangled Finds. 2024. "1932 Campbell's Tomato Soup Magazine Ad with Play Is Just Health Out for a Good Time." eBay. https://www.etsy.com/listing/847152802/1932-campbells-tomato-soup-magazine-ad.

Oliveira, Giovanna Angela Leonel, Vivian Siqueira Santos Gonçalves, Eduardo Yoshio Nakano, and Natacha Toral. 2024. "Consumption of Ultra-Processed Foods and Low Dietary Diversity Are Associated with Sedentary and Unhealthy Eating Behaviors: A Nationwide Study with Brazilian Schoolchildren." *PLoS ONE*, 19, no. 1: 1–17. doi:10.1371/journal.pone.0294871.

Pam. 2013. "Mmmmmmm . . . Metrecal!" Go Retro. https://www.goretro.com/2013/08/mmmmmmmmetrecal.html.

Pan, Po-Lin, Manu Bhandari, and Juan Meng. 2022. "Promoting Healthy Eating: The Intervening Role of Health and Nutrition-Related Claims in Food Advertisements." *Health Education Journal*, 81, no. 8: 993–1005. https://research-ebsco-com.sacredheart.idm.oclc.org/linkprocessor/plink?id=d5827221-f5ae-317b-8417-36a5114b544c.

Park, Sangchan, Daegyu Yang, Hyeonjin Cha, and Seobin Pyeon. 2020. "The Halo Effect and Social Evaluation: How Organizational Status Shapes Audience Perceptions on Corporate Environmental Reputation." *Organization and Environment*, 33, no. 3: 464–82. https://research-ebsco-com.sacredheart.idm.oclc.org/linkprocessor/plink?id=e4608954-9cf5-361a-9861-94e638505a54.

Peng, Yalan, Yantong Wang, Wenzhi Huang, Ji Lin, Qinghui Zeng, Yi Chen, and Fu Qiao. 2024. "Exploring Perceptions and Barriers: A Health Belief Model-Based Analysis of Seasonal Influenza Vaccination among High-Risk Healthcare Workers in China." *Vaccines*, 12, no. 7: 796. doi:10.3390/vaccines12070796.

"Pepsi: 'Great Acting or Great Taste (Ben Stiller)?'" 2023a. *Ad Age*, October 22, 2023. https://www.youtube.com/watch?v=yVT5Y-QRUrA.

"Pepsi: 'Great Acting or Great Taste (Steve Martin)?'" 2023b. *Ad Age*, October 22, 2023. https://www.youtube.com/watch?v=VCziVcMU60o.

Period Paper. 2016a. "1908 Ad Saazer Hop Barley Anheuser Busch Malt Nutrine Grain Liquid Extract." https://www.periodpaper.com/products/1908-ad-saazer-hop-barley-anheuser-busch-malt-nutrine-grain-liquid-extract-drink-104165-em2-444?pr_prod_strat=e5_desc&pr_rec_id=5570177b2&pr_rec_pid=9236656977&pr_ref_pid=9217432593&pr_seq=uniform.

Period Paper. 2016b. "1926 Ad Quaker Oats Chicago Illinois Bear Cereal Pettijohn Whole Wheat NGM3." https://www.periodpaper.com/products/1926-ad-quaker-oats-chicago-illinois-bear-cereal-pettijohn-whole-wheat-montana-142560-ngm3-039.

Period Paper. 2024. "1917 Ad Five Cent Breakfasts Quaker Oats Cereal Mills." https://www.periodpaper.com/products/1917-ad-five-cent-breakfasts-quaker-oats-cereal-mills-original-advertising-077050-tin2-479.

Perlmutter, David, and Kristin Loberg. 2018. *Grain Brain: The Surprising Truth about Wheat, Carbs, and Sugar—Your Brain's Silent Killers*. Boston: Little, Brown Spark.

Peterson, Dan. 2024. "Why Tony the Tiger Is Trying to Trick Us." TeamSnap. https://www.teamsnap.com/community/sports-science/sports-nutrition/why-tony-the-tiger-is-trying-to-trick-us.

Play Pause Video. 2018a. "Subway Low Fat Sandwiches Commercial (2003)." YouTube, May 7, 2018. https://www.youtube.com/watch?v=MYmTqS2eVAA.

Play Pause Video. 2018b. "Subway Low Fat Sub 'Cupid' Commercial #2 (2003)." YouTube, May 2018. https://www.youtube.com/watch?v=m7ajTgVmmZY.

Pop Culture Safari. 2015. "Vintage Ad: Superman for Pep Cereal." January 21, 2015. https://www.popculturesafari.com/2015/01/vintage-ad-superman-for-pep-cereal.html.

Pop-Tarts. 2023. "Pop-Tarts | Strawberry Goes Off-Script." YouTube, October 17, 2023. https://www.youtube.com/watch?v=_wWe3Ry4w8o.

"Pop-Tarts TV Spot, 'What Would Pop-Tarts Do?'" 2021. iSpot.tv, June 11, 2021. https://www.ispot.tv/ad/OCXJ/pop-tarts-what-would-pop-tarts-do.

Posavac, Steven S., Michal Herzenstein, Frank R. Kardes, and Suresh Sundaram. 2010. "Profits and Halos: The Role of Firm Profitability Information in Consumer Inference." *Journal of Consumer Psychology*, 20, no. 3: 327–37. doi:10.1016/j.jcps.2010.06.020.

Post Cereal Baseball Card Museum. 2024. "1960 Post Gallery." https://postcerealbaseballcardmuseum.weebly.com/1960-post.html.

Pu, Jian-Yuan, Wei Xu, Qian Zhu, Wei-Ping Sun, Jie-Jun Hu, Dong Cai, Jun-Yong Zhang, Jian-Ping Gong, Bin Xiong, and Guo-Chao Zhong. 2023. "Prediagnosis Ultra-Processed Food Consumption and Prognosis of Patients with Colorectal, Lung, Prostate, or Breast Cancer: A Large Prospective Multicenter Study." *Frontiers in Nutrition* 10 (October). doi:10.3389/fnut.2023.1258242.

Quaker Oats Rationing Ad [1943]. 2024. Newspapers.com. https://www.newspapers.com/article/the-spokesman-review-quaker-oats-rationi/47819257/.

Quora. 2022. "Was Hitler Following a Plant-Based Diet Ahead of His Time?" https://www.quora.com/Was-Hitler-following-a-plant-based-diet-ahead-of-his-time.

r/vintage reads. 2024. "1954 Nu Vita Foods Ad for Lange Mock Meat Vegetarian Canned Turkey and Breakfast Sausage Links." reddit. https://www.reddit.com/r/vintageads/comments/xtet56/1954_nu_vita_foods_ad_for_lange_mock_meat/.

Rajagopal, Selvi. 2024. "Gluten-Free Diet: Is It Right for Me?" *Johns Hopkins Medicine*. https://www.hopkinsmedicine.org/health/conditions-and-diseases/celiac-disease/what-is-a-glutenfree-diet.

Ramos, Arvelisse Bonilla. 2024. "Coke Zero Sugar Uses AI to Create Custom Font as Part of Global Campaign." *Ad Age*, February 14, 2024. https://adage.com/article/marketing-news-strategy/coke-zero-sugar-uses-ai-create-custom-font/2541616.

Ramstad, Evan. 2016. "General Mills Begins Marketing Cereals without Artificial Colors, Flavors." *Star Tribune*, January 22, 2016. https://www.startribune.com/general-mills-begins-marketing-cereals-without-artificial-colors-flavors/366129821.

Rare Historical Photos. 2024. "Vintage Fat-Shaming Weight Loss Ads from Ry-Krisp, 1930–1950." https://rarehistoricalphotos.com/ry-krisp-vintage-ads/.

Retro Rabbit Ears. 2018. "1984 Wayne Gretzky Pro Stars Cereal No Sugar Added General Mills." YouTube, January 12, 2018. https://www.youtube.com/watch?v=5RCC0gFYHGA.

Retropond. 2021. "FROSTED FLAKES—50s 60s 70s 80s 90s 00s Commercials Compilation." YouTube. https://www.youtube.com/watch?v=o6uO2d0tVu8.

Reynolds, Matt. 2024. "Plant-Based Meat Boomed. Here Comes the Bust." Wired, April 22, 2024. https://www.wired.com/story/plant-based-meat-sales-2023/.

Rice, Natalie. 2023. "Why Kellanova's Pop-Tarts Sales Are Going Strong 60 Years Later." CNBC, December 22, 2023. https://www.cnbc.com/2023/12/22/why-america-will-never-give-up-on-kelloggs-pop-tarts.html.

Riedl, Marcel, Michal Hrib, Vilém Jarský, and Martina Jarkovská. 2018. "Media Analysis in a Case Study of Šumava National Park: A Permanent Dispute among Interest Groups." *Forest Policy and Economics*, 89 (April): 71–9. doi:10.1016/j.forpol.2016.07.009.

Robare, Shawn. 2020. "The Great Fruit Snack Wars of 1985." *Branded in the 80s*. April 7, 2020. https://brandedinthe80s.com/18808/the-great-fruit-snack-wars-of-1985.

Roe, Brian, Alan S. Levy, and Brenda M. Derby. 1999. "The Impact of Health Claims on Consumer Search and Product Evaluation Outcomes: Results from FDA Experimental Data." *Journal of Public Policy and Marketing*, 18, no. 1 (Spring): 89–105.

Rose, Ivy. 2024. "1917 Kellogg's Toasted Corn Flakes—J. C. Leyendecker." Pinterest. https://in.pinterest.com/pin/cookbook--454722893640402364/.

Roseli, C. M. 2008. "14—Vitamin and Mineral Fortification of Bread." In *Food Science, Technology and Nutrition Technology of Functional Cereal Products*, edited by Bruce R. Hamaker, 336–61. Sawston, UK: Woodhead.

Rosenstock, Irwin M. 1974. "Historical Origins of the Health Belief Model." *Health Education and Behavior*, 2, no. 4: 328–35.

Rothburn, Nicole, Ruth Fairchild, and Maria Zeta Morgan. 2022. "Gluten-Free Foods: A 'Health Halo' too Far for Oral Health?" *British Dental Journal*, July 2022. DOI:10.1038/s41415-022-4424-2.

Rough, Mackenzie. 2020. "Haagen Dazs Ice Cream 'Eating Exercise' Commercial 2002." YouTube. https://www.youtube.com/watch?v=QdDd7vJ7YFA.

Salas, Emily. 2024. "Advertising Campaigns, Social Experiments and Other Related Executions Made by Creative Director Emily Salas." https://www.emilysalas.com/kraft-blind-taste-test.

Saleem, Diane. 2024. "Are Fruit Roll-Ups Bad for You?" IIBFY, January 26, 2024. https://www.isitbadforyou.com/questions/are-fruit-roll-ups-bad-for-you.

saltycotton. 2010. "Tiny Woman Loses Weight!" Flickr, March 3, 2010. https://www.flickr.com/photos/28153783@N08/4405290986.

Sampson, H. A., and S. Cooke. 1992. "The Antigenicity and Allergenicity of Microparticulated Proteins: Simplesse." *Clinical and Experimental Allergy: Journal of the British Society for Allergy and Clinical Immunology*, 22, no. 10: 963–9. doi:10.1111/j.1365-2222.1992.tb02071.x.

Samson, Emily. 2021. "The "Natural" Label on Food Products." UT Austin Blog, February 23, 2021. https://sites.utexas.edu/think-twice/2021/02/23/the-natural-label-on-food-products/#:~:text=However%2C%20neither%20the%20FDA%20nor,and%20should%20be%20minimally%20processed.

Santomier, James, Harald Dolles, and Reinhard Kunz. 2023. "The National Basketball Association's (NBA) Digital Transformation: An Explanatory Case Study," April. https://research-ebsco-com.sacredheart.idm.oclc.org/linkprocessor/plink?id=6c142947-382f-36f9-8e1b-53c5dd0406d5.

SarahZen Products. 2023. "Sad Fruit Life Savers Candy Vintage 1959 Ad Art Magazine Print Pineapple Cherry." eBay. https://www.ebay.com/itm/334840928660?.

Savard, J. 2024. "1980 Hershey's Got the Itch to Bake Chocolat (sic)." Pinterest. https://www.pinterest.com/pin/1980-hersheys-got-the-itch-to-bake-chocolat--79798224640875186/.

Schär. 2017. "Schär—Best in Gluten Free." YouTube, May 2, 2017. https://www.youtube.com/watch?v=r5onqmpfnDU.

Scheiber, Rebecca, Matthias Karmasin, and Sandra Diehl. 2023. "Exploring the Dunning-Kruger Effect in Health Communication: How Perceived Food and Media Literacy and Actual Knowledge Drift Apart When Evaluating Misleading Food Advertising." *Journal of Health Communication*, 28, no. 11: 707–27. doi:10.1080/10810730.2023.2258085.

Schultz, E. J. 2013. "How 'Skinny' Became the Hottest Phrase in Marketing." *Ad Age*, May 21, 2013. https://adage.com/article/news/skinny-hottest-phrase-marketing/241562.

Scrapbook Layouts by Lisa. 2024. "Vegan Vegetarian Canned Food Advertisement Ad March 1970 Vintage Retro." Pinterest. https://ru.pinterest.com/pin/521432463088890354/.

Sessions at Studio B. 2009. "1997 Starburst Fruit Twists Commercial." YouTube, June 12, 2009. https://www.youtube.com/watch?v=dgY1wx2YGUk.

Seven Countries Study. 2024. Google Scholar. sevencountriesstudy.com/.

Shakeri, Esmaeil, and Behrouz H. Far. 2020. "Exploring the Requirements of Pandemic Awareness Systems: A Case Study of COVID-19 Using Social Media Data." *2020 35th IEEE/ACM International Conference on Automated Software Engineering Workshops (ASEW)* (September): 33–40. doi:10.1145/3417113.3422151.

Shannon, Elaine, and Jose Aguayo. 2016. "The Real Deal behind Kraft's 'New' Mac & Cheese." EWG, March 30, 2016. https://www.ewg.org/news-insights/news/real-deal-behind-krafts-new-mac-cheese.

Shateri, Zainab, Sevda Eskandarzadeh, Mehran Nouri, Shahrokh Ezzatzadegan Jahromi, Fatemeh Mansouri, and Siavash Babajafari. 2024. "The Role of Ultra-Processed Food Consumption in Protein-Energy Wasting and Sarcopenia Development in Patients with Chronic Kidney Diseases." *BMC Nephrology*, 25, no. 1: 4. doi:10.1186/s12882-023-03409-6.

Sheryl. 2020. "1920 Puffed Grain Cereals Advertisement." A Hundred Years Ago, November 12, 2020. https://ahundredyearsago.com/2020/11/12/1920-puffed-grain-cereals-advertisement/.

Shivaram, Deepa. 2022. "A Federal Judge Dismisses a Lawsuit that Claimed Pop-Tarts Aren't Strawberry Enough." NPR, April 1, 2022. https://www.npr.org/2022/04/01/1090301198/pop-tarts-lawsuit-strawberry#:~:text=A%20federal%20judge%20in%20New,Pop%2DTarts%20box%20is%20misleading.

Singh, Shrish, Vijay Kumar Jain, Hemraj Verma, and Preeti Sharma. 2025. "Exploring Consumer Intentions to Purchase Organic Food with the Health Belief Model and Theory of Planned Behavior." *Discover Food*, 5, no. 1: 1–27. doi:10.1007/s44187-025-00559-4.

"Skinny Cow Divine Filled Chocolates TV Spot, 'Massage.'" 2013. iSpot.tv, March 11, 2013. https://www.ispot.tv/ad/7IWB/skinny-cow-divine-filled-chocolates-massage.

"SkinnyPop TV Spot, 'Hot Air Balloon.'" 2024. iSpot.tv, April 19, 2024. https://www.ispot.tv/ad/6R8J/skinnypop-hot-air-balloon.

"SkinnyPop TV Spot, 'Never Have to Stop.'" 2024. iSpot.tv, April 19, 2024. https://www.ispot.tv/ad/6RJU/skinnypop-never-have-to-stop.

Smith, Ernie. 2015. "The History of Fake Meat Starts with the Seventh-Day Adventist Church." Gastro Obscura, August 17, 2015. https://www.atlasobscura.com/articles/the-history-of-fake-meat-starts-with-the-seventh-day-adventist-church.

Smith, Rachel, Bridget Kelly, Heather Yeatman, Christopher Moore, Louise Baur, Leslie King, Emma Boyland, Kathy Chapman, Claire Hughes, and Adrian Bauman, A. 2020. "Advertising Placement in Digital Game Design Influences Children's Choices of Advertised Snacks: A Randomized Trial." *Journal of the Academy of Nutrition and Dietetics*, 120 no. 3: 404–13. https://doi-org.sacredheart.idm.oclc.org/10.1016/j.jand.2019.07.017.

Solve. 2018. "Real'Za All-Natural, Frozen Pizza | Swords." YouTube, October 1, 2018. https://www.youtube.com/watch?v=XjH38vzxgEs.

Sparling, Philip B. 2020. "Legacy of Nutritionist Ancel Keys." Mayo Clinic Proceedings, 95, no. 3 (March): 615–17. https://doi.org/10.1016/j.mayocp.2019.12.012.

Sports Odyssey. 2020. "(1988) Campbell's Soup Commercial (Howie Long)." YouTube, October 26, 2020. https://www.youtube.com/watch?v=pmC_y6ZvRiw.

spuzzlightyeartoo. 2012. "Good Measure Canned Diet Food Commercial (1960s?)." YouTube, June 8, 2012. https://www.youtube.com/watch?v=dG7NrtOhZ0I.

Stanley, T. L. 2022. "Beyond Meat Adds Kim Kardashian to Its Celeb Stable as 'Chief Taste Consultant.'" Ad Week, May 25, 2022. https://www.adweek.com/brand-market

ing/beyond-meat-adds-kim-kardashian-to-its-celeb-stable-as-chief-taste-con sultant/.

Stanley, T. L. 2022. "Not a World Class Athlete or Hollywood Action Star? Just Egg Says You Can Still Eat Like One." Ad Week, May 23, 2022. https://www.adweek.com/brand-marketing/not-a-world-class-athlete-or-hollywood-action-star-just-egg-say s-you-can-still-eat-like-one/.

Star Tribune. 2024. "Goodbye Wonder Bread." Pinterest. https://www.pinterest.com/pin/goodbye-wonder-bread--465138086414007291/.

Stewart, Kristin, and Rebeca Perren. 2023. "Under the Spell of Your Smartphone: How Dependence Evokes a Halo of Trust in Advertising." *Journal of Promotion Management*, 29, no. 1: 106–24. doi:10.1080/10496491.2022.2108188.

Stridsberg, Michael R. 2023. "The Illustrious History of the Klondike Bar." Daily Meal, March 1, 2023. https://www.thedailymeal.com/1214606/the-illustrious-hist ory-of-the-klondike-bar/.

Sütterlin, Bernadette, and Michael Siegrist. 2015. "Simply Adding the Word 'Fruit' Makes Sugar Healthier: The Misleading Effect of Symbolic Information on the Perceived Healthiness of Food." *Appetite*, 95 (December 1): 252–61. https://www.sciencedirect.com/science/article/abs/pii/S0195666315003281?via%3Dihub.

Sweet Loren's. 2021. "Sweet Loren's Let's Be Taste Buds (:30)." YouTube, November 9, 2021. https://www.youtube.com/watch?v=DWlZkITGtjQ.

T3 Tonya's This and That. 2024. "1993 Campbells Chunky Soup Print Ad Featuring Donovan McNabb NFL Quarterback." eBay. https://www.ebay.com/itm/31465 2758245.

Tate's Bake Shop. 2020. "Tate's Bake Shop Storybook (Full Version)." YouTube, July 10, 2020. https://www.youtube.com/watch?v=gzYqNT980GQ.

Terrell, Ellen. 2020. " 'The Battle Creek Diet System:' A Pamphlet and Birth of the Fake Meat Industry." Library of Congress Blogs, February 19, 2020. https://blogs.loc.gov/inside_adams/2020/02/battle-creek-diet-fake-meat/.

THALIHITA. 2024. "Impossible Foods—We Can Have Our Meat and Eat It, Too." YouTube, May 8, 2024. https://www.youtube.com/watch?v=uUqOkLdwcGc.

The Antique Advertising Expert. 2024. "Anheuser-Busch Malt-Nutrine Tin Sign 1905." https://antiqueadvertisingexpert.com/project/anheuser-busch-malt-nutr ine-tin-sign-1905/.

The Baby Historian. 2021. "Ruth Gordon: A Mellin's Food Baby." March 23, 2021. https://thebabyhistorian.com/2021/03/23/ruth-gordon a mellins-food-baby/.

The Historical Marker Database. 2024. "The Campbell Kid Beloved Icons of Campbell Soup Company." https://www.hmdb.org/m.asp?m=7427.

The Housewife. 1914. A.D. Porter, June 1914.

The Jumping Frog. 2024. "Eat Shotwell's Hi-Mac Candy Bar and Eat Right! Ad 1947 SEP." https://www.thejumpingfrog.com/product/2344000/Eat-Shotwells-Hi-Mac-candy-bar-and-eat-right-Ad-1947-SEP.

the*maxx. 2024. "Ovaltine 1946 Ad Original Vintage 1940s Food Art Print Retro Illustration Health." eBay. https://www.ebay.com/itm/384172311010.

The Museum of Classic Chicago Television. 2020. "'Tang—'Susie Needs Vitamin C' (Commercial, 1978)." YouTube, November 5, 2020. https://www.youtube.com/watch?v=ug5x18FB4wM.

The Museum of Classic Chicago Television. 2023. "Firm 'n Fruity Yogurt for Kids—'Kids Go for It!' (Commercial, 1977)." YouTube, May 25, 2023. https://www.youtube.com/watch?v=w6EAjYNSZ8g.

The One Club for Creativity. 2020. "'Moldy Whopper' by INGO, DAVID Miami & Publicis Bucharest for Burger King | The One Show 2020." YouTube, June 22, 2020. https://www.youtube.com/watch?v=f9B9HGQsx0k.

Thorndike, Edward L. 1920. "A Constant Error in Psychological Ratings." *Journal of Applied Psychology*, 4, no. 1 (March): 25–9.

TRAVSD, 2018a. "The Birth of Superman." Travalanche, April 18, 2018. https://travsd.wordpress.com/2018/04/18/superman-turns-80/.

TRAVSD. 2018b. "Of Superman and Kellogg's Pep." Travalanche, March 7, 2018. https://travsd.wordpress.com/2018/03/07/of-superman-and-kelloggs-pep/.

True Health Initiative. 2017. "Ancel Keys and the Seven Countries Study: An Evidence-Based Response to Revisionist Histories." White Paper, August 1, 2017. https://www.truehealthinitiative.org/wp-content/uploads/2017/07/SCS-White-Paper.THI_.8-1-17.pdf.

TV Toy Memories. 2010. "General Mills Cheerios with Bullwinkle Working Out in the Gym by Rowing." YouTube, November 30, 2010. https://www.youtube.com/watch?v=66HNG2Y-iyE.

TV Toy Memories. 2012. "Vintage 1952 Wonder Bread Commercial." YouTube, October 15, 2012. s.

UConn Rudd Center for Food Policy and Health. 2017. "Food Marketing." Accessed February 21, 2024. https://uconnruddcenter.org/research/food-marketing/#f(1).

Underwood, Robert L., and Julie L. Ozanne. 1998. "Is Your Package an Effective Communicator? A Normative Framework for Increasing the Communicative Competence of Packaging." *Journal of Marketing Communications* 4, no. 4: 207–20.

Underwood, Robert L., and Noreen M. Klein. 2002. "Packaging as Brand Communication: Effects of Product Pictures on Consumer Responses to the Package and Brand." *Journal of Marketing Theory and Practice*, 10, no. 4: 58–68.

United States Department of Agriculture. 2024. "Food Standards and Labeling Policy Book." https://www.fsis.usda.gov/sites/default/files/import/Labeling-Policy-Book.pdf.

United States Food and Drug Administration. 2023. "Code of Federal Regulations Title 21." https://www.accessdata.fda.gov/scripts/cdrh/cfdocs/cfcfr/cfrsearch.cfm?fr=101.22.

U.S. Food and Drug Administration. 2024a. " 'Gluten-Free' Means What It Says." https://www.fda.gov/consumers/consumer-updates/gluten-free-means-what-it-says.

U.S. Food and Drug Administration. 2024b. "CFR—Code of Federal Regulations Title 21." https://www.accessdata.fda.gov/scripts/cdrh/cfdocs/cfcfr/cfrsearch.cfm?fr=101.60.

Van Tulleken, Chris. 2023. *Ultra-Processed People: The Science behind Food That Isn't Food*. New York: W.W. Norton.

Vance, Lenny, Maria M. Raciti, and Meredith Lawley. 2016. "Beyond Brand Exposure: Measuring the Sponsorship Halo Effect." *Measuring Business Excellence*, 20, no. 3: 1–14. doi:10.1108/MBE-07-2015-0037.

Vegetarian History Blog. 2010. Protose Vegetable Meat Advertisement. http://vegetarianhistory.blogspot.com/2010/06/welcome.html.

Vintage Fanatic. 2013. "Vintage Old 1950's Edward Dalton Co. Good Measure Diets Dinners Commercial." YouTube, July 23, 2013. https://www.youtube.com/watch?v=cpREIZiW7CE&t=21s.

Vintage Paper Ads. 2024. "1933 Kellogg's Pep Cereal Ad—Keep Going with Pep." eBay. https://www.ebay.com/itm/225361760429.

Vintage Paper Ads 2. 2024. "1966 Wonder Bread Ad—Make the Most of Wonder Years." eBay. https://www.ebay.com.au/itm/283968292245.

Vintage Prints and Collectibles. 2024. "1923 Original Vintage Mellin's Food Print Ad—US Babies Photography." eBay. https://www.ebay.com/itm/325406414074?chn=ps&norover=1&mkevt=1&mkrid=711-117182-37290-0&mkcid=2&mkscid=101&itemid=325406414074&targetid=1529493989182&device=c&mktype=pla&googleloc=9008490&poi=&campaignid=19851828444&mkgroupid=145880009014&rlsatarget=pla-1529493989182&abcId=9307249&merchantid=114168253&gad_source=1&gclid=CjwKCAjw17qvBhBrEiwA1rU9wytNziQTGxLzg6ZCoGrcdifiY3pa7EN1KxLdTHL-h-yIlzQmGxPpsRoCYpgQAvD_BwE.

Visioli, Francesco, Franca Marangoni, Vincenzo Fogliano, Daniele Del Rio, J. Alfredo Martinez, Gunter Kuhnle, Judith Buttriss, Hugo Da Costa Ribeiro, Dennis Bier, and Andrea Poli. 2023. "The Ultra-Processed Foods Hypothesis: A Product Processed Well beyond the Basic Ingredients in the Package." *Nutrition Research Reviews*, 36, no. 2: 340–50. doi:10.1017/S0954422422000117.

VTG Collectibles. 2024. "1916 Campbell's Soup Kids Ice Skating New Years Vegetables Beef Okra Ad 136." eBay. https://www.ebay.com/itm/266678432185?itmmeta=01J3ZB4FABZDBSWMM1GA76VGWY&hash=item3e1745f1b9:g:P9cAAOSwrullz9mZ&amdata=enc%3AAQAJAAAA0FPOcK201D0ISLrexSoxJTpMbDtEhqbcjdpDvG1fQLZWIIy%2BYoVo%2Ftw7Wc%2FaPGQhyKh5p

Q0D%2FtMv0d1J%2FmvyGnGNrKuHcnycBy4LCa9B93tieKyRqC%2Bf
mQUR84plSH3XIAa%2B6Y7WQzQjIbD8E7fEbg4S8WIT%2BYLL1oq
k45%2F77wK3e0mn4Jyu8b8oLiXUjRfwVKQbXtfYJWSQe0WgpYD3kGolE50DoF
D4yla83EPvDWxs5ENQG%2FskuIyUbQWqFuKZZzMrvl3SZimsdbe1kMMN
gM8%3D%7Ctkp%3ABFBMnvWR659k.

Wakeman, Gregory. 2024. "The Contentious History of the Pop-Tart." *Smithsonian Magazine*, May 3, 2024. https://www.smithsonianmag.com/innovation/the-contentious-history-of-the-pop-tart-180984270/.

Warner, Melanie. 2010. "Pizza Hut Quietly Hops Off the All-Natural Bandwagon." CBS News Money Watch, April 23, 2010. https://www.cbsnews.com/news/pizza-hut-quietly-hops-off-the-all-natural-bandwagon/.

Watsky, David. 2023. "Best Veggie Burgers and Plant-Based Grillers for 2023." CNET, July 18, 2023. https://www.cnet.com/health/best-veggie-burgers-and-vegan-meats-for-the-grill/.

Welch's Fruit Snacks. 2021a. "Welch's® Fruit Snacks: Open Up Possibility!" YouTube, December 21, 2021. https://www.youtube.com/watch?v=kdlFVuUYJ0Q.

Welch's Fruit Snacks. 2021b. "Welch's® Fruit Snacks: Snack Teamfully, Snack Fruitfully." YouTube, December 21, 2021. https://www.youtube.com/watch?v=q6Llj1qrpcM.

Wen, Zheng. 2024. "Haribo Super Bowl Commercial (2024)." YouTube, February 10, 2024. https://www.youtube.com/watch?v=yHKClxWHXAE.

Whalen, Rosa, Joanne Harrold, Simon Child, Jason Halford, and Emma Boyland. 2018. "The Health Halo Trend in UK Television Food Advertising Viewed by Children: The Rise of Implicit and Explicit Health Messaging in the Promotion of Unhealthy Foods." *International Journal of Environmental Research and Public Health*, 15, doi:10.3390/ijerph15030560.

"Wheat Thins Popped TV Spot, 'Air Chase.'" 2014. iSpot.tv, March 31, 2014. https://www.ispot.tv/ad/7SCk/wheat-thins-popped-air-chase.

Wheless, Erika. 2023. "Jell-O Rebrands to Attract Younger Parents and Kids." *Ad Age*, July 27, 2023. https://adage.com/article/marketing-news-strategy/jell-o-rebrands-attract-younger-parents-and-kids/2506571.

Whole Foods Market. 2017. "We Believe in Real Food™ | Whole Foods Market." YouTube, January 1, 2017. https://www.youtube.com/watch?v=Asqdy71l0EE.

Wilson, N. L., and A. E. Blackhurst. 1999. "Food Advertising and Eating Disorders: Marketing Body Dissatisfaction, the Drive for Thinness, and Dieting in Women's Magazines." *Journal of Humanistic Counseling, Education and Development*, 38, no. 2: 111–22. https://doi-org.sacredheart.idm.oclc.org/10.1002/j.2164-490X.1999.tb00069.x.

Wonder. 2022. "Wonder Gluten Free Ad (15s)." YouTube, September 20, 2022. https://www.youtube.com/watch?v=Rw68QtUoHd0.

World Health Organization. 2022. "Follow-Up to the Political Declaration of the Third High-Level Meeting of the General Assembly on the Prevention and Control of Non-Communicable Diseases." *Seventy-Fifth World Health Assembly* (April 27, 2022). https://apps.who.int/gb/ebwha/pdf_files/WHA75/A75_10Add6-en.pdf.

World Health Organization. 2025. "Obesity and Overweight." https://www.who.int/news-room/fact-sheets/detail/obesity-and-overweight.

World Obesity Federation. 2022. "One Billion People Globally Estimated to Be Living with Obesity by 2030." World Obesity. https://www.worldobesity.org/news/one-billion-people-globally-estimated-to-be-living-with-obesity-by-2030.

Worthington Libraries. 2017. "Worthington Foods Advertisement." *Worthington Memory*. Accessed May 2024. http://www.worthingtonmemory.org/scrapbook/text/worthington-foods-advertisement-2.

Worthington Libraries. 2019. "Worthington Foods Advertisement." *Worthington Memory*. http://www.worthingtonmemory.org/scrapbook/text/worthington-foods-advertisement-0.

Yazdanpanah, Masoud, Masoumeh Forouzani, and Mohammad Hojjati. 2015. "Willingness of Iranian Young Adults to Eat Organic Foods: Application of the Health Belief Model." *Food Quality and Preference*, 41 (April): 75–83. doi:10.1016/j.foodqual.2014.11.012.

Ye Olde Commercials. 2018. "Low Fat Eggo Commercial (1998)." YouTube, January 25, 2018. https://www.youtube.com/watch?v=zkikOzmqWsw.

Young Ju Jin, Wonjung Min, and Jae-Woong Yoo. 2016. "The Impact of Tourism Advertising on Corporate Attitudes and Tourism Intentions: Country and Corporation Interactions in the Halo Effect and Public Diplomacy." *Tourism Culture and Communication*, 16, no. 3: 109–21. doi:10.3727/109830416X14750895902756.

Yu, Kun, Xiaoxiu Huang, Zehao Yu, Chunxu Chen, Peiyan Li, Di Wu, and Chuanlai Du. 2023. "Application of Steam Explosion Pretreatment for Accelerating the Phenolics Extraction from Pomegranate Peel: Mechanism and Modeling." *Journal of Food Engineering*, 357 (111629). https://doi.org/10.1016/j.jfoodeng.2023.111629.

Yuan, Lingyao, and Alan R. Dennis. 2019. "Acting Like Humans? Anthropomorphism and Consumer's Willingness to Pay in Electronic Commerce." *Journal of Management Information Systems*, 36, no. 2 (June): 450–77.

Yudkin, John. 1998. *Pure, White and Deadly: How Sugar Is Killing Us and What We Can Do to Stop It*. London: Penguin.

Zhang, Xueying, Kim Baker, Sarah Pember, and Kim Bissell. 2017. "Persuading Me to Eat Healthy: A Content Analysis of YouTube Public Service Announcements Grounded in the Health Belief Model." *Southern Communication Journal*, 82, no. 1: 38–51. doi:10.1080/1041794X.2016.1278259.

Zhang, ZengYi, BiaoWen Huang, and XiaoDan Li. 2017. "A Frame Analysis of Newspaper Reports about Cults in English: A Case Study of the New York

Times." *Alternative Spirituality and Religion Review*, 8, no. 2: 203–18. doi:10.5840/asrr20178248.

Zimmerman, Frederick J., and Sandhya V. Shimoga. 2014. "The Effects of Food Advertising and Cognitive Load on Food Choices." *BMC Public Health*, 14, no. 1: 1–18. https://doi-org.sacredheart.idm.oclc.org/10.1186/1471-2458-14-342.

Zyber9. 2011"Amazin' Fruit Gummy Bears (1993)." YouTube, May 21, 2011. https://www.youtube.com/watch?v=eLROt3RVXiw.

Index

About the Author

Debbie Danowski, Ph.D., is an associate professor of communication and media at Sacred Heart University where she teaches classes in Health Communication and Advertising, including Food Advertising, Studies in Self-Help Books, Magazines and Body Image, and Women and Advertising. Her research focuses on representations of health, eating, and addiction in food advertising. Her book, *"Happy Eating" and Food Addiction in American Advertising* is a groundbreaking analysis of the addictive behaviors in ultra-processed food advertisements. She has been published widely including in the *Popular Culture Studies Journal*, the *Iowa Journal of Communication*, and the *Journal of American College Health*. She is also the author of five popular books including the best-selling *Why Can't I Stop Eating?* and *The Emotional Eater's Book of Inspiration*.

www.ingramcontent.com/pod-product-compliance
Ingram Content Group UK Ltd.
Pitfield, Milton Keynes, MK11 3LW, UK
UKHW021906150926
475560UK00003B/207

9 781666 965032